designing galleries: the complete guide to developing and designing spaces and services for temporary exhibitions

a joint publication funded by the lottery departments of the **Arts Council of England,** the **Arts Council of Northern Ireland,** the **Arts Council of Wales** and the **Scottish Arts Council**

mike sixsmith

acknowledgements

Following convention, I have asserted my moral right to be identified as author of this book, since I was responsible for the overall structure and much of the detail. However, I do owe a huge debt of gratitude to a wide range of people from all over the UK, who supplied architect's briefs and other information, discussed their experiences of construction projects, showed me round their new buildings, commented on the text, and supplied photographs. Had any one contribution been missing, the book would have been different. Large or small, each input made the book what it is, and I take this opportunity to thank the following people:

Alasdair Alldridge, David Anderson, Patricia Andrew, Anne Baker, Jon Benington, Rosemary Bennett, Terry Bennett, Barry Bentley, Lewis Biggs, Valerie Bott, Andy Bramwell, Kate Brindley, Michaela Butter, Ian Cameron, Norah Campbell, May Cassar, Vivien Chapman, Ian Charlton, Marcus Cole, Alison Coles, Carol Cotterill, Carol-Anne Davies, Colin Dawes, Mark Dey, Laureen Dillon, Graham Dixon, Nicholas Dodd, Gail Durbin, Peter Dworok, Mark Failles, Benedict Farr, Ann Fletcher, Tony Fretton, Christine Galey, Nicholas Gilbert Scott, John Gillett, Elizabeth Goodall, Richard Gray, Hilary Gresty, Michael Harrison, Eleanor Hartley, Joanna Hayward, Robert Hopper, Peter Jenkinson, Vic Johnson, Helen Juffs, Christine Kapteijn, David Kay, Maria Kiffin, Sylvia King, Elizabeth Kwasnik, Catherine Lampert,

Barry Lane, Mary La Trobe Bateman, Alf Longhurst, Sasha Lubetkin, Bruce McAllister, Sarah McDonald, Aileen McEvoy, Elizabeth A. Macgregor, Paul McMullen, Jem Main, Sarah McDonald, Chris McIntyre, Alison Mcfarlane, Tony Makos, Stephen Mapp, Sandra Marwick, Sally Medlyn, Janet Mein, Janet Moore, John Moran, Gregor Muir, Graeme Murray, Sune Nordgren, Simon Olding, Peter Osborne, Julia Peyton-Jones, Richard Pharro, Catherine Pyke, Jacky Puzey, Tom Roberts, Clive Russell, Carole Sartain, David Scruton, Veronica Sekules, Wendy Shales, Kirsten Simister, Alan Smith, Stephen Snoddy, Mike Stubbs, Adam Sutherland, Virginia Tandy, Holly Tebbutt, David Thomas, Jane Thomas, Sue Todd, Mike Tooby, Kate Tregaskis, Alexandra Walker, Catherine Wallis, Lynne Wealleans, Sandy Wilderspin, Gillian Wilson, Heather Wilson, Ken Wilson, Peter Wilson and Joanne Wright.

It is always invidious to pick out people for special mention, but I really must single out Andrew Nairne because the excellent competition brief for Dundee Contemporary Arts formed the nucleus of much of Part Two. Last but not least, I would like to thank the members of the Steering Group - Ian Gilzean, Isabel Hitchman, James Kerr, Sue Pirnie, Bridget Sawyers, Jeremy Theophilus and Monica Tross - for their support and patience.

Mike Sixsmith

March 1999

previous page, page iv ◄

location:
Henry Moore Institute, Leeds.

architect:
Jeremy Dixon.Edward Jones BDP.

description:
'At One Remove' installation, showing the full-height translucent doors which also serve as service access.

photograph:
Jerry Hardman-Jones, reproduced courtesy of the Henry Moore Foundation.

foreword

The need for a comprehensive publication on the design of galleries for temporary exhibitions has been evident for many years. Opportunities offered by Lottery capital funding brought this sharply into focus when the Scottish Arts Council's Visual Arts Department, together with its new Lottery Department, commissioned research into the area.

The first priority identified by this research was for a widely-accessible, practical guide for developing and designing exhibition galleries. This would not only be a comprehensive technical guide, but - perhaps more importantly - it would provide a tool for navigating through the process of consultation and negotiation, from initial vision to finished building.

The Arts Council of England, the Arts Council of Wales and the Arts Council of Northern Ireland welcomed the opportunity to collaborate on the publication. A steering group worked with the author, Mike Sixsmith, and extended and widened the consultation which had led to the book in the first place.

Mike has succeeded with a publication that is informative without being prescriptive and inspiring while being practical. It is designed to offer advice to those approaching this area whatever their level of skill or scale of project - a challenging task. It is not a blueprint for the perfect gallery, but it will assist all those involved in the process to realise a gallery as unique as the art that will be shown in it and the people who will work in and visit it.

Sue Pirnie

Sue Pirnie
Visual Arts Officer - Scottish Arts Council
on behalf of the Steering Group

Composition of the Steering Group

Ian Gilzean
Lottery Department - Scottish Arts Council

Isabel Hitchman
Visual Arts Department - Arts Council of Wales

James Kerr
Visual Arts Department - Arts Council of Northern Ireland

Sue Pirnie
Visual Arts Department - Scottish Arts Council

Bridget Sawyers
Lottery Department - Arts Council of England

Jeremy Theophilus
Visual Arts Department - Arts Council of England

Monica Tross
Lottery Department - Arts Council of England

introduction

designing galleries is intended to help and guide you if you are intending to refurbish your exhibition spaces or build a gallery from scratch. At the same time, the book should also be useful to the people with whom you will be dealing during the project - with architects and other professionals on the Design Team, with local authorities, funding bodies and other people drawn into planning an exhibition gallery.

Although the availability of Lottery funding provided the stimulus, **designing galleries** will not tell you how to write a Lottery application for a gallery project. It should help you to arrive at a brief for your architect which will lead to an effective and successful building, and to plan for the capital project and beyond, all of which, by the by, might just help to to attract Lottery funding. Despite the occasional nod to Lottery requirements, the book should be just as useful to those who do not have access to this funding.

designing galleries is designed to be useful for very small projects as well as for large ones, for conversions as well as new buildings, and for exhibition spaces that are part of a library, theatre, arts centre or museum as well as stand-alone exhibition galleries.

With this breadth of scope the book could not be prescriptive, but the form of exhibition galleries must, in any case, be a reflection of the policies and personalities that govern them, as well as the buildings and resources available. It is up to you to define the programme envisaged and then to specify what facilities are required for this programme. The book should then help you to achieve a 'best fit' between your ambitions, facilities and resources.

PART ONE: THE DEFINITION PHASE

designing galleries is in two halves. Part One concentrates on the process of planning which is the earliest stage of a capital project. Before design and construction begin, there is a period when you will be setting out what you will contribute to the project and where you will need external assistance.

This period is sometimes called the pre-design, feasibility or planning stage, because it contains all of these activities to a greater or lesser extent. However, it is also the crucial period when you define most of what is required from the building, so this book uses "Definition Phase" for this period.

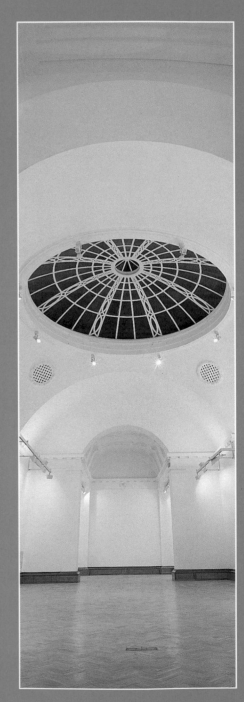

location:
National Museum & Gallery, Cardiff.

architect:
Smith and Brewer (1912),
Davis Langdon and Everest (1998).

description:
Art in Wales Gallery.

photograph:
Reproduced courtesy of the
National Museum & Gallery Cardiff.

CROSS-REFERENCES

As well as the division into two halves, the book is subdivided into a number of short sections which are linked by cross-references to other relevant sections.

The title of the section to which reference is being made is shown in colour in the text.

The Definition Phase begins with a Vision Statement, the first statement of what is required (►► clarifying the vision), and ends with three documents which provide agreed points of reference that everyone involved can consult subsequently to ensure that the project remains on course:

- a project plan which brings together all aspects relating to the management and financing of the building project;

- a business plan which sets out how the completed building will be managed and financed after hand-over;

- a technical brief which records what the building should be and do, and which constitutes a set of instructions to the design team

As well as being essential planning tools, these documents are normally required by the Lottery distributors as evidence that the project has been thought out well and is viable.

Although the Definition Phase has different stages with different outputs, Part One stresses the continuity of the planning process. There is broad guidance on possible formats and contents, but the emphasis is less on isolated documents and more on the relationships between them.

Although it discusses what goes into a Technical Brief, Part One is equally concerned with the consequences that decisions in the Technical Brief might have on the cost or timing in the Project Plan or on the revenue costs in the Business Plan.

PART TWO: THE TECHNICAL BRIEF

The Technical Brief lies at the centre of **designing galleries**. Approaches to preparations for a capital project in a Project Plan or to staffing issues in a Business Plan are common to all types of arts organisation, and there is an abundance of general guidance available for writing either document. By contrast, there is little specific guidance in one place for the design of exhibition galleries. Part Two aims to fill this gap, and is designed to help you to set out your intentions and the performance that you want from the building. The purpose of the Technical Brief is to provide the detailed information which will enable an architect to design a building which not only looks and feels good but also works well. The effectiveness and efficiency of the final building depends on this document, so Part Two is devoted to helping you to articulate and convey your requirements to your architect.

part one: your own planning will be
the earliest work in a capital project

◀

location:
art.tm, Inverness.

architect:
Sutherland Hussey.

description:
Examples of ceramic ware by
Richard Slee on one of the tables
by Mike Malig.

photograph:
David Churchill/Arcaid.

clarifying the vision

A vision statement should:

- be the primary description of what the project is intended to achieve;
- be clear, focused and shared by everyone involved;
- translate your mission into building terms;
- provide a series of benchmarks for the project.

REVIEWING THE MISSION

Your Board and staff must have a clear idea of their overall objectives, before beginning to define the sort of building they need. The project might be the first opportunity for some while to review an earlier statement, or you might even need to articulate for the first time what you want to do. This exercise in self-assessment evaluates past and present activities in order to plan for the future.

PURPOSE OF THE PROJECT

The vision statement should be:

- agreed and shared by everyone involved in the project;
- a definition of the ambience that you hope to achieve, both for artists and for visitors;
- the cornerstone for all subsequent planning;

- a reminder of the original concept during times of stress and doubt in the midst of deadlines, financial targets and construction difficulties;
- an aid to resolving differences of opinion, and to establishing priorities throughout the life of the project;
- the basis for evaluation at the end of the project, when the success of the completed building can be measured against what was envisaged at the outset.

The vision statement is a qualitative statement that should be eloquent and persuasive. It is concerned with your philosophy, the image that you wish to project and the ideas and values you wish to communicate. It is vital that the whole organisation is fully committed to a shared statement defining the building required. Such a commitment is important in the short term, e.g. for raising funds, but it is crucial in the long term, to avoid differences of opinion as time passes and difficulties appear.

Although dealing in intangible ideas, the vision statement is a definition of belief and purpose, which will be invaluable to the design team, consultants, funders and anyone else involved in the project, helping them to understand and believe in the project.

location:
New Art Gallery, Walsall.

architect:
Caruso St. John.

description:
East elevation of the building in the final stages of construction in early 1999, from the main shopping street in Walsall.

photograph:
Hélène Binet.

For the architect in particular, it will convey ideas and qualities that will eventually be expressed in the proportions, relationships and finishes of the final design.

CONTENT OF THE VISION STATEMENT

The vision statement will set out your ambitions in terms of what the project will allow you to do that you cannot already do. It should rank these ambitions in order of priority, so that everyone involved understands the relative importance of each objective. It is vital that there is no ambiguity, or that different people do not have differing sets of priorities, either of which can lead to confusion and conflict later.

The vision statement might define your gallery in some or all of the following ways:

- How the building will display exhibitions and accommodate other activities, possibly expressed in terms of creating spaces which are functional but stimulating, which complement and enhance the particular types of work you will show in future and which have appropriate levels of control. This might include a general statement on the content and scope of the exhibitions, e.g. the type of new exhibitions that you would like to show which you cannot show at present, as well as the policy to involve artists in the project.

- As a 'visitor facility', expressing the ambience you wish to provide for your visitors, potential as well as current, and defining the type of visitors you are aiming at, from the local community or beyond. Considerations might include how art might be seen and experienced, and what role a gallery should have in the community, as well as your policies to extend access intellectually and physically.

- The quality of the architectural experience. How a gallery looks and feels is an important part of the visitor's experience and can enhance a visit, so part of the vision may be to make a building of architectural significance and merit which is an attraction in its own right. This part might outline attitudes or expectations about design, the desired level of prestige, the location, size, proportions, character, presence and finishes (external and internal) of the building, its relationship with other buildings and any landscaping requirements.

- The development of the site and its contribution to the social fabric. Breadth of support may depend on the way that the project relates to community participation, education and training, urban renewal, tourist development and other social and economic considerations. Aims might include servicing educational requirements (e.g. contributing to the National Curriculum) as well as providing informal learning opportunities.

planning the project

RIBA PLAN OF WORK

The preparation of the Technical Brief corresponds to stages A to D of the 'Plan of Work' published by the Royal Institute of British Architects (RIBA). The RIBA Plan of Work is frequently used as a checklist for monitoring the preparations for a building project. It provides an architect in the UK with a standard framework for work to be done, beginning at Stage A (Inception) and ending at Stage M (Feedback). Only the two stages K (Operations on Site) and L (Completion) are directly concerned with the construction phase, so most of the checklist is devoted to the architect's responsibilities in terms of analysing the brief, working out the design and preparing for work on site.

As well as a framework for architects, the RIBA Plan of Work provides useful information for their clients. It indicates when decisions need to be taken. It also states when changes are no longer possible. For example, the architect's brief should not be modified after Stage D, and any change in location, size, shape or cost after Stage E will result in abortive work.

THE CLIENT'S PLAN OF WORK

Because they involve significant capital investment and because they are open to a wide range of risks, building projects need rigorous management. Effective planning is essential for their successful conclusion - and for the health and well-being of those leading them. Stress is impossible to avoid entirely, but can be alleviated if there is a clear plan of action and a realistic time-scale. It is crucial that you commit adequate time and resources to planning, not only to set out the requirements for the project, but also to provide the basis for subsequent control which will enable corrective action to be taken when necessary.

Some of your planning will run parallel to the RIBA Plan of Work. It will be particularly close during Stages B (Feasibility) and C (Outline Proposals), when the architect puts forward proposals for a building to answer your requirements, and when you will be examining how these proposals might work and be funded. Subsequently, your planning will run at a greater distance, as the architect concentrates on detailed design work and preparing for tendering and construction, whilst you might be more concerned with planning for the period of closure. However useful the RIBA Plan of Work, you need your own plan, both for the period before the architect is brought in and for maintaining the gallery's work during the construction period and after completion.

Much of the Definition Phase may precede RIBA Stage A. During this period, you might need to:

- secure agreement amongst the Board and staff;
- consult and gather support, especially financial assistance, from external bodies;
- examine the viability of different options;
- define the external expertise required, and commission it.

Your planning must also include the construction period and the period after completion, since your objective is not simply to complete a building successfully but also to manage the transition from old to new and to operate effectively within the new building. Planning might include:

- temporary accommodation for staff;
- funding and organising activities at other sites;
- the ongoing management of the gallery if one or more senior members of staff are diverted to the project;
- preparations for the initial period of occupancy and shakedown after hand-over; and
- developing procedures and undertaking training for staff to use the new building.

location:

Dundee Contemporary Arts.

architect:

Richard Murphy Architects.

description:

The principal exhibition gallery under construction (January 1999).

photograph:

Reproduced courtesy of Richard Murphy Architects.

A project can involve a wide range of variables, and there is no single correct way to plan a capital programme. The 'client's plan of work' (◄◄ inside front cover) therefore provides a framework in the form of a checklist of tasks in an approximate sequence.

SCHEDULING THE DEFINITION PHASE

If the 'client's plan of work' is a checklist in an approximate sequence, a schedule is instead a plan to which as many as possible of the known variables - people, funding and other resources and time, costs and other constraints - have been added.

A schedule sets out:

- a time-scale which is achievable within the available resources;

- a level of detail which is appropriate for planning and monitoring purposes;

- a sequence of activities which are arranged logically to make best use of available resources;

- a timetable which is flexible and can be updated easily.

During the Definition Phase, many different activities will take place, often at the same time, with a number of consultants producing reports and requiring payment. Any of these activities may throw the project off course, unless there is a firm timetable which determines when activities are due to begin and end and which prevents activities from going ahead before preliminary work is completed.

The project's time-scale must be realistic. Time is managed by reconciling the amount of time available and the time needed to complete a task. The time available between the present moment and a future deadline will almost certainly not be the same as the time actually needed to carry out the task, and several attempts may be necessary to balance the two sides. In many cases, the time actually available will be fragmented by a succession of external deadlines, for Board meetings, planning consents, funding applications, consultations, etc. External deadlines (and the expected dates of the announcement of

decisions) need to be identified first, because they will set the overall pace for the project.

Within the time-scale set by these deadlines, a schedule is usually drawn up by:

- identifying each of the individual activities into which the whole project can be divided, e.g. distinct areas of work or the responsibility of a particular consultancy;

- estimating the time that each activity will take;

- determining the sequence in which different activities should be carried out.

Sufficient time must be allowed, for the overall project and for the individual activities. Time-scales should not be shortened arbitrarily, nor reserves and contingencies removed, because time is short. Unrealistic expectations and impossible deadlines will lead to actual delays which may have major consequences further down the line, when more expense will be required to bring the project back on track. A common problem with building projects is the failure to start on time, because of inadequate planning in the early stages. Projects that do not start on time will not finish in time, since contractors cannot be expected to perform miracles because of poor planning earlier. Projects that do not start on time will usually exceed their budget as well, and shortage of time and funding means that corners will be cut.

Time can be reduced by increasing resources and/or by re-arranging the sequences of activities. Many activities will depend on the successful completion of a previous task, so the schedule should ensure that all activities are arranged in logical sequences, in order that any preliminary work is completed and checked before moving on to the next stage. Network analysis techniques are useful for brain-storming and initial planning, to represent sequences in which tasks must be done, where work can be done in parallel and when activities must come together again. By showing tasks in logical relationships and interdependencies, they allow priorities to be quantified and critical jobs to be highlighted. In the critical path method, sequences are defined and the longest sequence gives the shortest length of time needed for that group of tasks.

If the results are unacceptable, then the way that activities are placed in the network, the estimates for individual activities or the overall time-scale must be changed. Time may be gained by employing extra consultants to carry out work previously planned in-house. A deadline may be extended when there is clearly no way that a task can be completed in time. Both options will have cost implications which must be weighed against their benefits.

For the purposes of monitoring and control, it is important that you understand, first, where the project should be, and second, where it is at any moment. A bar-chart is often used to represent activities graphically. In a bar-chart, the horizontal axis represents the time-scale in units appropriate to the duration of the project, whilst the vertical scale lists tasks. A cursor indicates the current date, to the left of which are the activities that should have been completed, whilst to the right are the tasks that remain to be done.

Simple bar-charts do not represent interdependent or related tasks, although linked bars can show where tasks need to be completed in order to allow other work to progress.

SCHEDULING DESIGN AND CONSTRUCTION

Scheduling for the design and construction phases is a specialist task which should be delegated to the person managing this aspect of the project. The latter should be given sufficient time to draw up a schedule with realistic targets, and should agree with you a comprehensive timetable for managing the time available in a way which allows sufficient time for each stage in the architect's Plan of Work. Any schedule needs to be reviewed and updated, so that the consequences of ongoing decisions (and any delays) can be added to the picture, and so that corrective measures can be introduced if necessary.

For the **RIBA Plan of Work**, see: **The Architect's Job Book**, editors Stanley Cox and Alaine Hamilton, RIBA Publications, 6th edition, 1995. **ISBN 1 859 460 070**.

For an approach to planning museums and galleries based on the stages of the RIBA Plan of Work, see: Geoff Matthews, **Museums and Art Galleries: A Design and Development Guide**, Butterworth, 1991. **ISBN 0 7506 1227 4**.

Dennis Lock, **Project Management**, Gower, 1996 (sixth edition). **ISBN 0 566 07738 8**.

getting organised

The Definition Phase is vital in helping you to clarify what the project is designed to achieve, what the eventual building needs to provide, and for whom these facilities and activities are being provided. As well as articulating these requirements, you should consider what formal methods and procedures will be necessary, for making decisions and for supervising the project, which will allow the following people to make a direct input:

- Board or elected members;
- staff;
- representatives of the end-user.

CLIENT TEAM

Before embarking on a capital project, you will need an effective 'client team' to make the decisions and supervise the project. Depending on the size and type of your organisation, the client team may be a sub-committee or working party, a group of representatives of different departments or a group of users. It is important to clarify how much work will be required by staff and Board members. Anyone offering to take an active role should be able to show that they have the time, skills and experience to do so.

The client team should be allocated administrative support, and have access to legal and technical advice.

The client team's responsibilities are to:

- agree the aims and objectives of the project in a Vision statement (◄◄ clarifying the vision);
- direct the project, by initiating action, providing instructions and responding with decisions, maintaining an overview and exercising control;
- explore the demands and limits of the project, by evaluating any appraisal of need and by agreeing what is required (►► analysing need);
- evaluate an Options Analysis (►► considering the options), and select which options to pursue;
- explore funding opportunities, ensuring that funds are available and agreeing what can be afforded;
- agree what external assistance is required, and when consultants should be engaged;
- compile and update the technical brief, project plan and business plan, to ensure that they adequately represent the gallery's needs.

This committee would be managed by a "Project Leader" (►► managing the project).

BOARD

Board members must have the opportunity to make a direct input into the project, even if it is only to agree proposals prepared by staff and/or consultants. This stage should allow time to review the whole proposal and to make radical changes where necessary. Options will need time for appraisal and decision. Differences of opinion may need to be identified and resolved, and priorities agreed. Inevitably this process will involve subjective considerations as well as objective criteria, and will require clear decisions on what is appropriate and possible. Technical requirements can be quantified, but abstract criteria may be more controversial, and will need time for debate. Above all, it is crucial to get a proposal that the whole organisation can stand by.

A Board will often form a sub-committee to oversee the Definition Phase, in part to tap the expertise and commitment of its members, and in part to ensure continuing ownership. Ownership is not a trick but a necessity. It is vital that the whole Board signs up to a common vision and purpose at the outset. Problems will arise later if

individual members have different visions of the outcome. If committee or Board members are kept at a distance, then other people will take control of the project, which might be run by consultants rather than by the client organisation itself. Conversely, the Board must determine how far decision-making can be delegated and what approvals it will make itself and at what meetings these will be required. The Board needs to understand fully proposals from staff and consultants. It must absorb their implications in terms of future activities, staff and funding, but be prepared to adapt recommendations in the light of its internal priorities and external limitations.

STAFF

Ownership of the project extends beyond the Board to the staff who will be running the new operation overall. In setting out the reasons for the project and broadly what facilities are required, the Definition Phase gives the staff the opportunity to work out with colleagues what is required. Where staff are already in post, it is important that they are - and feel themselves to be - an integral part of the client team, and can contribute to or take part in formal discussions or brain-storming sessions, along with any sub-committee of Board members (➤➤ analysing need).

As likely as not, the building will be only one expression of a new shape for the organisation as a whole. The building

itself may be a response to proposed changes in activities, but in turn it will involve changes to staff numbers, structure and/or procedures. The human dimension can be the most difficult aspect of the Definition Phase, and can complicate internal staff relations. It is also time-consuming, and time must be set aside for debate and dialogue, to identify and solve problems and to define objectives, constraints, and resources. At the same time, engaging the staff in the planning process brings significant benefits not only in terms of defining the requirements for the building, but also in terms of helping the staff to live through the changes. It can give them the incentive to adapt to a new situation and - by bringing in experts from outside - introduce them to new standards and methods.

NEW PROJECTS

In some cases, initial planning is undertaken by an organisation which will not be the end-user. Staff to run the space will not yet be appointed because the organisation is afraid that capital funding may not be secured or because it wants to avoid the cost of extra staff, especially where they will not be able to run activities until the building is open. Notwithstanding, the proposed users of the building should be involved as early as possible in the Definition Phase, so that they can be consulted on priorities and can influence the design. It is essential that the two parties agree on how they will work together, and the

relationships between themselves - and with the design team, other consultants, funders, etc. - must be clarified at the outset. Even where representation on a client team is conceded as a privilege rather than as a right, representation will at least ensure that those eventually running the building have a say in its design.

---

location:
An Tuireann Art Centre, Portree.

architect:
Wittets Architects.

description:
Reception area (top),
Craft Gallery (bottom).

photographs:
Iain Smith, reproduced courtesy of Wittets Architects.

Although written from the point of view of museums, Patrick Greene, **"The role of the Museum Director, Staff and Trustees in a Capital Project"**, in Gail Dexter Lord & Barry Lord (Eds.), **The Manual of Museum Planning**, HMSO 1991, can be applied mutatis mutandis to exhibition galleries.

managing the project

You should consider:

- who should be the Project Champion;
- who should be the Project Leader, and how much time can be allocated for this work;
- whether there is a need for a project manager; and if so,
- at what stage this person should be appointed;
- what roles this person should have;
- what relationship this post should have to the Project Leader, the architect and other consultants;
- who should take the responsibility of planning supervisor.

PROJECT CHAMPION

It is normal practice to identify a "client patron" or "project champion". This would be the person - possibly the chair of the Board - who has a long-term interest in seeing the project is successful and who will be the public figurehead who gathers political and financial support.

PROJECT LEADER

At the same time, there should be a "Project Leader" to lead and co-ordinate the client team, especially where many people - members of staff, Board or committee members, users and external consultants - are involved. This person will need delegated authority, qualities of leadership and a belief in the project, in order to be able to resolve points of conflict and arrive at a consensus of the priorities for the future shape and image of the organisation. Personality conflicts and differences of opinion are likely amongst the staff and the Board, and patience, tolerance and compromise will be required to deal with disappointment, frustration and exhaustion. The stresses of leading a capital project should not be under-estimated.

As far as the design team is concerned, a Project Leader has a two-way responsibility. In one direction, he or she has to ensure that the Technical Brief fairly represents to the design team the requirements which reflect the conclusions and recommendations of consultants and which have been agreed by Board and colleagues. He or she must ensure that ancillary activities are given the same attention to detail as the core exhibition facilities. In the other direction, as the client's representative to whom the design team answers, the Project Leader has to ensure that design proposals reflect the organisation's priorities.

If the design team puts forward alternatives for the use of a space, the Project Leader must have both authority and appropriate knowledge to decide which option should be given priority. Colleagues should be encouraged to take part in evaluating the design team's proposals, but the Project Leader must be able to make the final decision. This person should retain editorial control over all documents written during the Definition Phase, especially the business plan, the project plan and the technical brief

Often, the responsibility of Project Leader is delegated to the director of the gallery or another senior member of staff, because tasks such as co-ordinating the contributions from staff and Board, raising funds and representing the organisation to external funders are extensions of this person's normal work. No matter how good their time-management skills are, this person must be allocated sufficient time for this work, by transferring much of the normal routine to a colleague or to a temporary post. You should not under-estimate the commitment required, especially for major projects taking place over a long time-scale. Balancing a full-time job with the pressures of a building project is neither viable nor recommended.

The Project Leader should ensure that he or she has been delegated sufficient authority and should be clear when approvals must be sought.

PROJECT MANAGER

In this context, the phrase "project manager" is used for the person who has overall responsibility for all or part of the project on your behalf. Unless the Project Leader has skills and direct experience of managing construction work, a project manager will be necessary sooner or later. The stage at which a project manager is appointed will depend on the size and complexity of the project, the skills and experience of the Project Leader and the amount of time the latter can afford.

A project manager will usually be needed because the skills required by the project are quite different from those that exist in-house. It is more cost-effective to employ a specialist with appropriate skills and experience than for you to train someone on the job and divert them from the work that they normally do, which must either be neglected or paid for through another post. It is also more efficient to delegate the management of a project to someone with the appropriate skills, than for you to risk delays and costs by

holding on to the project for as long as possible.

A project manager is different from a lead consultant in that the former's principal role and responsibility is to plan and co-ordinate the contributions of all the people involved in a project. By contrast, a lead consultant - for example the architect on the design team - has a dual responsibility. He or she must co-ordinate the contributions of other consultants, and make a contribution to the project on the basis of his or her training, skills and creativity.

DESIRABLE QUALITIES

The qualities required of a project manager might include some or all of the following:

- experience in design and contract work and in planning procedures;
- skill in problem-solving;
- enthusiasm, commitment and determination to persuade and motivate;
- skill in management: an ability to make clear decisions and to give precise and achievable instructions;
- a capacity to listen objectively to advice and recommendations, combined with sufficient familiarity

with the skills of the other professionals to assess how far information might be inaccurate or misleading;

- a personality, additional to any delegated authority and status, which commands respect from all parties;
- an ability to gather data, to co-ordinate scattered inputs, to standardise procedures, and to record and use information effectively.

RESPONSIBILITIES

The responsibilities of a project manager can vary from planning and co-ordinating the work of others - relying on persuasion and tact but calling on senior management in difficult situations - to a complete delegation of authority and overall responsibility for the successful completion of a project. The Project Leader should establish at the outset the balance of work and responsibility between him/herself and a project manager, and between this person and the architect (if they are not the same). A Project Leader will, for instance, need to work closely with a project manager, if the former has to organise the day-to-day running of the gallery around the construction work where a building

location:
University of Hertfordshire,
Hatfield.

architect:
Giuliano Todeschini of Quantic
Associates.

description:
Art and Design Gallery.

photography:
Chris Moyes, reproduced courtesy
of the University of Hertfordshire,
Faculty of Art and Design.

remains open during the construction period. A Project Leader should not interfere with the day-to-day running of the project, or with a project manager's exercise of delegated authority.

The role of a project manager is to schedule, initiate and supervise consultants and contractors, to ensure that their activities are carried out to time and budget and that the project is successfully completed. At whatever stage a project manager is brought in, this person should:

- represent the interests of the client, acting as the conduit between you and consultants and/or contractors, and presenting you with progress reports to an agreed level of detail;

- manage the project to the required standard: a broad technical understanding of all aspects of the project will ensure that all participants know their roles, that work is monitored and that unsatisfactory performance is corrected;

- ensure that the project is managed to the agreed cost, by putting in place appropriate monitoring and recording procedures to give early warning of difficulties;

- ensure that the project is managed within an acceptable time-scale, by devising a realistic schedule, ensuring that all activities are completed in time and in sequence, and taking action where necessary to keep the project on course.

This person should be given sufficient authority and access to your senior management, so that the latter can exert its authority if required (►► communication). He or she should have a status at least equivalent to the people whose work is being co-ordinated, and a suitable contract if appropriate. In addition, a project manager must have appropriate accommodation, facilities, equipment, administrative staff and finance.

MANAGING THE DEFINITION PHASE

A project manager might be brought in at the outset to plan and implement the Definition Phase. An early appointment can be important where a number of consultants - not only the people who will eventually form the design team but also marketing and business specialists - have to be selected, briefed and supervised, and where their contributions have to be brought together into the Technical Brief, Project Plan and Business Plan. In the early stages when the project is being put on track, an early appointment can avoid the lost or wasted time which can have major repercussions down the line in terms of further delays and increased costs.

At this stage, a project manager might be engaged on a limited assignment, and you will be under no commitment to extend the contract into subsequent phases, not least the construction phase when a different range of skills will probably be required. This approach gives maximum flexibility for deciding the procurement strategy, and does not commit you to paying fees for work into an undetermined future. On the other hand, engaging a project manager at the outset to manage all the stages can make the most of the initial investment in this person's experience and knowledge of the project, and ensures continuity.

One variation on this approach is for the Project Leader to retain responsibility for the business side, holding a watching brief for the project whilst looking beyond its completion at plans for operating the gallery again. In this case, a project manager would be principally concerned with co-ordinating the brief for the design. The danger with this divided responsibility is that there might be no single co-ordinator to ensure that everything is completed and in its proper sequence, so one or other must take overall responsibility for

scheduling of work on the Technical Brief, Project Plan and Business Plan.

Frequently, an architect is employed on a short-term consultancy to advise on particular aspects or to assist in writing the brief. Again, this person is usually appointed on a limited contract, with no commitment to make him or her eventually responsible for the design work. In this case, he or she might be responsible for some or all of the following:

- drafting the brief for the design, including the objectives of the project;

- considering its feasibility, including the appointment of consultants for options appraisals;

- setting a cost estimate, identifying sources and applying for funding;

- resolving legal issues and applying for outline approvals;

- setting out the scope of the appointments to the Design Team, arranging short-lists and interviews, confirming appointments, and agreeing procedures.

MANAGING THE DESIGN PHASE

Where quality is a prime consideration, the management of the design team will be the responsibility of the architect. The latter might also be in an

ideal position to act as project manager, especially on uncomplicated projects where the number of consultants is small. This would avoid another tier of management, with its consequences in terms of marginalising the architect and erecting a barrier between yourself and the Design Team. It would also help continuity between planning the building and planning for the new operation, since members of the design team could make a direct input into the Business Plan, e.g. on disabled access or facilities management where physical provision needs to be accompanied by appropriate procedures and staff training. If this option is pursued, this should be a separate form of appointment from the architect's responsibility for design.

On the other hand, it can be unreasonable and counter-productive to load the architect with detailed organisational issues at a time when design development should be the priority. Constraints of time and funding may also require a project manager who is able to balance conflicting demands, ensuring, for instance, that cost planning influences design proposals and that design is sufficiently detailed for accurate estimates. Traditional Procurement also makes it the client's duty to control design development and manage the design team, which implies the need for an independent consultant if you do not have the necessary expertise in-house.

MANAGING THE CONSTRUCTION PHASE

Traditionally, the management of a construction project is undertaken by the architect, and the RIBA Plan of Work includes the administration of the contract as an integral part of the architect's services for the client. However, the task has grown considerably, especially where a short time-scale, large number of consultants and/or complicated services require careful management. As a result, administering the contract is increasingly regarded as a separate service that attracts a separate fee, and on complex projects it is common to appoint an independent project manager as a consultant separate from the architect and design team, and directly responsible to the client. As well as architects, building surveyors or quantity surveyors are frequently appointed as project managers for this phase.

PLANNING SUPERVISOR

Under the CDM Regulations - the Health and Safety Construction (Design and Management) Regulations 1994 - you must ensure that there is a health and safety plan for everyone involved in the construction and subsequent maintenance of the building. You must formally appoint a 'planning supervisor' who is competent in health and safety matters, which might be an in-house responsibility or an additional role for either the architect or the project manager (if different).

The professional institution for project managers in the UK is the **Association for Project Management (APM)**. Its trading arm, the **Association for Project Management Group Ltd (APMG)**, publishes a register of consultants who are competent in the PRINCE method of project management, and will assist in selecting a project manager if required. **APMG** has also developed Standard Terms for the Appointment of a project manager, including a version for construction projects. Contact **APMG** at:
85 Oxford Road, High Wycombe, Buckinghamshire, HP11 2DX.
tel: 01494 452450, **fax:** 01494 459559
email: apmgroup@compuserve.com
web: www.apmgroup.co.uk

The **Health and Safety Executive (HSE)** has a series of information sheets on the CDM Regulations, outlining the roles of: the client **(no.39)**, the planning supervisor **(no. 40)**, and the designer **(no. 41)**; and describing the pre-tender stage health and safety plan **(no. 42)**, the health and safety plan during the construction phase **(no. 43)**, and the health and safety file **(no. 44)**. These information sheets are available from **HSE** area offices or from the Internet, at:
www.open.gov.uk/hse.html

consultants

REASONS FOR APPOINTING CONSULTANTS

Most capital projects involve a number of external consultants, who are specialists paid for their expert advice and considered proposals about a future operation, the services it should provide and the design of facilities to house these services. Some consultants are specifically concerned with the design of the building and make up the design team, whilst others are more concerned with the feasibility of the project and the long-term viability and management of the new operation. The following is principally concerned with the latter, although many of the considerations also apply to the appointment of members of the design team.

An organisation usually appoints consultants because:

- it does not have the capacity in-house to carry out a task;
- it needs access to technical expertise which may not be available within the organisation;
- it wants an objective view on how to achieve specific objectives.

Consultants can supply in-depth knowledge and practical experience where there is a need to improve display lighting or some other specialist services or to introduce catering or other new operations. They are also useful where very particular areas of skill and experience are needed at an early stage in the project to help to define requirements. In general, the more detailed the requirements at the outset, the more precise will be the plans and the more realistic the estimates of cost. A consultant may even be a prerequisite of financial support. For example, most Lottery distributors expect an access audit by an independent assessor. Several consultants may be appointed to advise on the feasibility of a project, each looking at the project from the point of view of his or her area of expertise. Their function is to stimulate and clarify - not replace - your own thinking.

IDENTIFYING REQUIREMENTS

The Definition Phase should define what work can be done in-house and where consultants need to be brought in. You should determine the advice needed from professional advisers for preliminary studies, and set out the skills and knowledge required from any consultants. Depending on the size and complexity of the project and the skills available in-house, you may require expert advice on a range of topics.

Some topics will be general, i.e. where a knowledge of the visual arts, though it might be helpful, is not essential, e.g. access, business management, catering, legal, library, marketing and retailing. Other topics will require experience and skills that are specific to the visual arts, e.g. commissioning, digital technology, education, environmental management, handling, security and storage. It might be sufficient to know how to use computers as part of management or communication systems, but it may also be important to understand artists' use of digital technology.

Where a team of consultants is to be appointed, the responsibility and experience of each consultant should be defined in relation to the others, and at the end of the selection process a final check should be made to ensure that the consultants together will give the complete service required for the project. Time wasted is irretrievably lost and can cost time and money later, so it is important not to delay appointments. If there is any doubt about the scope of the consultancies, it is preferable to make a preliminary agreement for limited services and to extend it subsequently when the need is clearer.

CONSULTANT'S BRIEF

The brief for a consultancy should be drafted with key staff. The RIBA (RIAS in Scotland), RICS and other professional institutions can supply model forms of agreement. These list the normal services offered by their members and can form the basis of a consultant's brief. The brief might include:

- the name, location and background of the project, including aims and objectives, using any existing project description as supporting information and/or referring to the consultant's part in the preparation of any new materials;

- the names and contact details of Project Leader, Project Manager, other consultants and their assignments and responsibilities;

- a description of the services to be provided by the consultant, setting out how the consultant's skills and experience will help to take the project further;

- the subject and type of any reports or drawings, number of copies required, when needed, and how they will be used;

- a timetable for the project, and the deadline(s) for the supply of the consultant's services;

- any delegation of authority;

- the frequency and location of any presentation, progress or site meetings, including the names of attendees;

- budget for the consultancy and how the consultant will be reimbursed.

SELECTION

The success of a project often depends on selecting the right consultants. The purpose of the selection process is to identify likely participants and to choose the most suitable person from this group. In smaller projects, word-of-mouth and personal recommendation from people who have administered similar projects might be sufficient to develop a shortlist of suitable practices. Many arts funding bodies and disability organisations maintain registers of consultants who offer services relating to their areas of interest. The **Museums Yearbook** lists consultants across a range of activities from business planning to marketing. The RIBA and other professional bodies also offer advice to potential clients.

The larger the project, the greater the pressure - not least from the Lottery distributors - for selection processes that are open and fair. Even for smaller projects, a more formal selection process can:

- throw the project open to high-quality solutions and fresh ideas;

- find consultants who identify most with the aims and vision of the project;

- locate professional knowledge, appropriate experience, access to specialist knowledge and organisational ability;

- help to ensure fruitful working relationships between consultants and with the client, and effective team-work where members are able to listen as well as to communicate;

- be cost-effective, by helping to avoid loss of time and waste of effort;

- comply with statutory requirements and EC or GATT rules.

You should agree a formal structure for managing the selection process. The rules and criteria for selection should be clearly defined at the outset, published with any announcement and followed throughout the competition itself. Contenders can be invited to respond to the brief, but it should be clear that a worked-up proposal is not a requirement. Payment should be made if they are asked to undertake any work as part of the selection process.

It is important that you retain ownership of the selection process, and that the staff, Board members and sponsors of the project make up the majority of the selection panel.

However, there should be at least one independent assessor whose background is similar to that of the contenders, to advise you and help to mediate between you and the shortlisted consultants.

The selected consultants can be invited to respond with an expression of interest, practice statements, details of similar work and initial comments on the brief. A shortlist can then be invited to present their more detailed responses in interview.

Consultants should be asked to include risk management when bidding for work, not only for the benefits that this discipline will bring but also to flag up your determination to reduce uncertainties.

CONTRACT

A formal agreement between you and the chosen consultant will normally take as its starting point the consultant's brief and supporting documentation on the project, expanding on any modifications agreed during the selection process. Consultants should be required to take full responsibility for the quality of their work, in terms of meeting the brief, the presentation of any financial or technical information and

recommendations, any supervisory function, etc. Model forms of agreement that are available from RIBA, CIBSE and other professional institutions can help to define responsibilities. Terms and conditions should be written to help the consultancy, and might include the following:

- the consultant's relationship to your organisation, specifying clear lines of reporting and accountability especially where the client appears to be multiple, and including any standard performance specifications and procedures manuals;

- the consultant's relationship to other consultants and/or users; procedures for communication, including circulating papers and arranging meetings;

- responsibilities for financial control, and for ensuring that sufficient information is given to the Project Leader or project manager to control budgets;

- any requirements in terms of documentation to be presented along with conclusions and recommendations.

FEES

Although some advice (e.g. from the Fire Officer or from the Museums Security Adviser) may not cost anything, consultants are generally engaged on the basis of a required result (e.g. a report) and an agreed method for calculating a fee. The basis of the

main photograph	▶

location:
art.tm, Inverness.

architect:
Sutherland Hussey.

description:
Main entrance: door furniture designed by Wendy Ramshaw.

top right	▲

description:
Detail of door handle designed by Wendy Ramshaw.

bottom right	▼

description:
Exterior of 20 Bank Street, Inverness.

photographs:
Reproduced courtesy of the Scottish Arts Council.

fee and the timing of stage payments should be agreed as part of the terms of appointment.

The different methods commonly in use share risk to different degrees between you and the consultant:

- a lump sum is useful where the extent of the work can be adequately defined at the start, but there should be provision for adjustment if the

temporary sign.fm

scope of the services changes or if you introduce changes;

- hourly or daily rates up to fixed ceiling are useful where it is impossible to estimate precisely the amount of work required, but the disadvantages are that the consultant has no incentive to finish and you may find it difficult to control cost;

- a percentage - fixed, on a sliding scale or up to ceiling - on part or all of the cost of a project gives the consultant no incentive to keep down the cost of the project;

- a retainer on a monthly, quarterly or annual basis is difficult to relate to any output.

Expenses should be included in the fee, but where this is not possible the nature of out-of-pocket expenses (cost of drawings, travel and subsistence, etc.) that might be claimed, and the ceiling for expenses, should be defined at the outset.

DEMANDS ON THE ORGANISATION

Consultants bring extra capacity to a project, but they also make demands in terms of time and space. At the outset, you should determine the role of staff (or volunteers), how much time they can and will make available, the lines of communication between the consultant and the person who will be monitoring progress (➤➤ communication). Where several consultants are commissioned together, where a time-scale is short or where tight control is needed, you may appoint a consultant as a project manager in order to achieve cost and time objectives (◄◄ managing the project). You should also determine what access the consultant might have to space, facilities, equipment and administrative support.

Another sort of demand comes later, when you consider the consultant's advice and proposals. You must be prepared to set aside sufficient time for staff and/or Board to consider the consultant's conclusions or recommendations, so that they understand both the thinking and the implications, and so that those recommendations of which they have taken ownership can be integrated into your plans and into any presentations, consultations or submissions. Those parts for which there is little enthusiasm might be set aside, but not without a full understanding of the implications of doing so.

USING AND REVIEWING RECOMMENDATIONS

Where a consultant's report is included as evidence in a presentation, it should constitute a separate appendix. A covering note for the appendix might outline where particular aspects have been set aside and whether this is a short-term expedient or has been rejected on policy grounds, as evidence that you have absorbed its implications and used it for weighing up different options.

Consultants are often commissioned in anticipation of the appointment of full-time staff. Recent Lottery funding has represented such a large proportion of a capital cost that applicants are not prepared to appoint the staff until capital funding is secured. In these circumstances, and because of the support for feasibility studies, it has been normal to appoint consultants on a short-term basis to take the project up to the first important milestone. With the best will in the world, no consultant will set out exactly what a subsequent appointment will want, and an incoming post-holder must have the opportunity to make changes to the Technical Brief and/or Business Plan.

CUP Guidance No. 13, The Selection and Appointment of Works Consultants,available from the **Public Enquiries Unit, H.M. Treasury, Room 89/2, Treasury Chambers,** **Parliament Street, London, SW1P 3AG.** **tel:** 0171 270 4558 **fax:** 0171 270 5244 **web:**www.hmtreasury.gov.uk/pub/ html/docs/cup/cup13.pdf

Museums Association, Working With Consultants, Museums Briefing 16 (December 1997).

design team

THE ROLE OF THE DESIGN TEAM

The design team is a formal grouping of consultants whose tasks relate specifically to the design of the building and the preparations for construction. The members of your Design Team should bring creativity, appropriate professional experience, access to specialist knowledge and cost-effectiveness to the project. They must be able to listen and respond to your requirements and identify with your vision, especially in the way that works of art are displayed, interpreted and handled. You should not hesitate to ask members of the design team to explain matters such as methods of payment, rights of access to the site, snagging, Architect's Instructions, etc.

Before construction, your Design Team is usually responsible for:

- advising you on the options available;
- assisting in developing the technical brief;
- carrying out the actual design;
- costing the plans;
- obtaining approvals;
- advising on the building contract;
- formulating a health & safety plan.

In addition, the Design Team will be concerned with the eventual performance of the completed building and the implications and costs of running it. It will expect to look beyond the construction work, e.g. the Quantity Surveyor will estimate energy consumption and calculate 'life-cycle' costs, in order to demonstrate where long-term savings might be achieved. The Design Team's input into a business plan may not be to the same extent as, say, a marketing adviser or a training consultant, but it is still crucial. The Services Engineer should be expected not only to consider measures for reducing energy consumption and stabilising the internal environment, but also to outline how staff should be trained or recruited to operate and maintain any new plant. Consultants such as a disability advisor or an expert in art handling should ensure not only that the building is designed well but also that policies and procedures are devised to complement the physical provision.

SELECTING THE DESIGN TEAM

In most cases, the members of your Design Team will be appointed using methods similar to those for any other consultants. The main differences will be of degree, since the core members of your Design Team will be appointed for the duration of the project and will have considerable authority delegated to them to act on your behalf. Your Architect's services will normally include administration of the building contract and supervision of the site, and he or she will usually be given authority up to a certain level to make any necessary changes and variations to the design during construction. The Quantity Surveyor will be responsible for monitoring the building work and construction costs and for certifying payments against work completed.

A Design Team is not appointed directly by the client in a design-and-build contract, where the selection of the contractor brings the latter's design team with it. However, this procurement strategy works best for standardised building projects, and would probably not be suitable for an exhibition gallery where quality and fitness for purpose are paramount. You will be concerned that scale, proportion, colour, texture and detail enhance the display and interpretation of art. An architect's response to the visual arts and previous experience of gallery design will therefore be important selection criteria. In most cases, a gallery will go for the normal two-stage process, whereby the Design Team is assembled and a design agreed and costed, before embarking on the second stage of appointing a contractor for the building work (►► project plan).

In some cases, an architectural practice which is multi-disciplinary and includes structural engineers, services engineers, etc. or which has a good working arrangements with quantity surveyors and other professionals will bid for a job as a complete design team. This approach is used in particular for design competitions, which select a design rather than an architectural practice and where a considerable amount of detailed work must be done before selection. Whilst this approach has advantages in terms of a demonstrable ability to work together, it might also bring specialists who have insufficient experience for the areas required by the project. In most small- to medium-scale projects, the client appoints each member of the professional team, according to the particular needs of the project, in a separate competitive interview.

CO-ORDINATING THE DESIGN TEAM

Even if there is a separate project manager, you will normally appoint the Architect as the lead consultant responsible for co-ordinating the design work, with your express authority to act as leader of your Design Team. In this capacity, he or she would then be involved in or even manage the selection of other members of the Design Team, allowing you, the Project Leader and/or Project Manager to participate in the interviews.

Each consultant would agree to act as consultant to you, or to your Project Manager if one is appointed, or to the Architect if the latter has been appointed as Project Manager. You may also appoint the Architect or one of the other consultants as your Planning Supervisor, as required by the CDM Regulations (◄◄ managing the project).

CONSULTANTS ON THE DESIGN TEAM

The following list includes some of the professions that might be represented on a design team. The core of the team usually consists of the architect, quantity surveyor, structural engineer and services engineer, who are employed for the duration of the project. At the outset, each member of a design team will define his or her responsibility and its limitations, normally that part of the work for which he or she has the technical knowledge and experience. Each will analyse the brief in relation to this responsibility, apply current standards, regulations and codes of practice, assist the architect in developing the designs and eventually supply detailed designs and specifications for contractors' use.

You may also specify that particular skills should be represented on your Design Team, in the shape of an access consultant or an artist. Some consultancies might be on a short-term or ad hoc basis for advice on particular requirements.

opposite, page 26 ▶

location:
art.tm, Inverness.

architect:
Sutherland Hussey.

description:
Ground-floor gallery showing the curved shape of the new mezzanine and the hand-rail in plastics by Peter Chang.

photograph:
David Churchill/Arcaid.

overleaf, page 27 ▶

location:
Artezium Arts and Media Centre, Luton.

architect:
Fletcher Priest Architects.

description:
Tim Head's 'Light Rain', located on the inside courtyard wall, is 17 metres high and made up of 6,000 roadside reflectors.

photograph:
Richard Davies, reproduced courtesy of Fletcher Priest Architects.

Whether consultancies are short-term or not will depend on the extent and detail of the advice that is needed, and on the priority given to matters such as access, acoustics, information technology, energy management, fire, landscaping, security, etc. As formal members of the design team, these consultants can help to avoid the delays that result from responding to proposals only after they have been worked up in some detail, and they can instead contribute directly to resolving design problems. In some cases, your staff may be included on the Design Team where, for example, a technician can contribute to options that directly affect his or her work in the new building.

ACCESS AUDITOR

An access or disability consultant is usually appointed to assess existing provision and/or plans for new facilities in order to identify actual and potential barriers faced by disabled people, including those with visual and hearing impairments and people with learning difficulties as well as those with mobility problems. The consultant would review plans against standard requirements for the design of buildings (guidelines of the Lottery distributors, building regulations, standards for emergency egress, etc.) and make recommendations for change where improvements are necessary. As a member of a design team, an access consultant can make an important contribution to resolving design

problems in relation to light levels, surface textures and colours, seating, signs, labelling and other requirements specific to exhibition galleries. In addition, this consultant may advise on policy and training relating to equal opportunities.

ACOUSTICIAN

Acoustics are often a problem in large spaces with hard, echoing surfaces, and an acoustician will often be employed where lecture theatres, education rooms, study rooms, etc. require sound-proofing, and where an exhibition area needs adaptable acoustics for multi-media works using sound, for talks and performances and/or for videos, CD-ROMs and other electronic forms of information and interpretation.

ARCHITECT

On the design team, the architect's responsibility is to act as the client's adviser, design the building and administer the building contract. In the UK, the professional bodies are the Royal Institute of British Architects (RIBA) and Royal Incorporation of Architects in Scotland (RIAS). The RIBA lists a number of basic services that an architect can be commissioned to provide for a client, and its 'Plan of Work' sets out a framework of basic services provided by the architect for the client on a building project (◄◄ planning the project).

ART HANDLING SPECIALIST

Where you do not yet have technical staff with sufficient experience, an art-handling consultant may be appointed to advise on all aspects of the movement, storage and installation of works of art, including such matters as dimensions on the art route, workshop facilities, tools and equipment required, surfaces and loadings.

ARTIST

The guidelines for applications to the various Arts Lottery distributors take the principle of integrating art in architecture well beyond the original concept of Percent For Art, where a proportion of project costs was used for commissioning artists. In part this reflects a feeling that artists and craftspeople can make more useful contributions than simply providing furnishings for a completed building. For exhibition galleries, it also reflects the belief that artists should be involved in and consulted about the design of spaces that are used for showing their work. The Incentive Awards in the RSA's Art for Architecture Award Scheme provide funds for artists to join a design team and to work closely with the architect during the planning and design stages. Although the Scheme is not by any means restricted to gallery projects, it is appropriate that artists can contribute to the overall thinking about a building designed to present contemporary art, acting both as a representative of future users and as another creative input into the overall design and its detailed development.

BUILDING SURVEYOR

A chartered surveyor undertakes structural surveys, produces measured surveys of existing buildings, assesses building defects, advises on remedial work and plans and supervises maintenance work. In the UK, the professional body is the Royal Institution of Chartered Surveyors.

CONSERVATOR

Although heating, lighting and ventilation are the province of the services engineer, a conservator may have an important role on the design team, especially in terms of proposing how a building might be zoned in order to provide control for high-value exhibitions. Preventive conservation is now recognised as more important in the long run than remedial conservation which simply repairs damage without attending to the causes of the damage. Independent conservators will undertake environmental audits, to understand how a building performs under the influence of external weather and internal influences such as heating and occupancy, and to recommend passive and/or active measures to control the internal environment when exhibitions require this degree of control. Independent conservators are included in the directory of consultants in the current **Museums Yearbook**.

DESIGN CONSULTANT

Gallery refurbishments that do not involve structural work are often undertaken by designers who specialise in installations of temporary exhibitions and the internal design of galleries. Interior designers may also work on a project as part of a design team, with responsibility for the detailing of internal elements, including finishes, hanging systems, furniture and fittings. In the UK, the professional body is the Chartered Society of Designers.

IT SPECIALIST

An external consultant in information technology may be required to contribute to the design team where a project proposes to make extensive use of computers for interpretation or where the exhibition programme is to include digital work.

LIGHTING CONSULTANT

Although lighting is one of the responsibilities of the services engineer, hands-on experience of lighting a variety of exhibition installations is crucial to the design of gallery lighting. Within the constraints of the budget available, the dimensions of the space and the equipment currently available, the lighting installation must allow the staff to provide the right quantity and best quality of light for almost any exhibition. Lighting specialists are included in the directory of consultants in the current **Museums Yearbook**.

LANDSCAPE ARCHITECT

A landscape architect would join the design team where the planning and design of outdoor spaces is important. Their work might include a survey of the site, preparing plans and estimates, obtaining approvals and subsequent documentation, from drawings and specifications to contract documents and accounts, and supervising the work on site. In the UK, the professional body is the Landscape Institute.

PLANNING SUPERVISOR

As required by the CDM Regulations, the role of planning supervisor is a responsibility which can be provided by the architect or other member of the design team or even by the client (◄◄ managing the project). This role can also be a separate service provided by a consultant - an architect or engineer - who has undertaken training as a Planning Supervisor. In either case, the aim of the regulations is to incorporate health and safety considerations into the project as early as possible in the design process.

PUBLIC ART AGENT

Public art agents specialise in advising and managing commissions for works of art. Usually, they manage the competition and commissioning process and then supervise the siting of individual works of art. They also devise and administer strategies involving several artists and/or craftspeople.

For a gallery project, a consultant might be engaged to devise and implement a strategy of commissions which range across the fine and the applied arts, include relatively modest as well as grandiloquent pieces, embrace time-based work or film, video and digital media as well as the more permanent 'signposts', and/or involve work that is experienced by the public before and during the construction work as well as after it.

QUANTITY SURVEYOR

After the architect, the quantity surveyor is often the earliest specialist to join the design team. Appointed directly by the client in some cases, the role of the quantity surveyor is to assess, monitor, control and report building costs, in order to achieve the best value for money and avoid unnecessary risk. Early in the planning stages, this person calculates preliminary estimates of the likely cost of the first design proposals and advises on relative costs of each option, guiding the design team towards a design which can be afforded by the budget available. In the Design Phase, the quantity surveyor calculates construction costs and re-assesses them in the light of design changes, and advises the client on contractual methods. He or she prepares bills of quantities for competitive tendering, and helps with negotiating tenders. During the Construction Phase, this person is more concerned with arranging payments and controlling costs. In the UK, the professional body is the Royal Institution of Chartered Surveyors.

SECURITY SURVEYOR

As with environmental control, security for museums and galleries includes special considerations which may also be applicable to exhibition galleries if their policy is to show high-value work and/or take advantage of the government indemnity scheme (GIS). The Museums Security Adviser at the Museums & Galleries Commission offers a free advisory service to museums with collections, and a visit can often be obtained if the exhibition programme is likely to include material from national collections or to be covered by the GIS. Where the gallery does not have a member of staff with direct responsibility and training in matters of security, an independent consultant (i.e. not the surveyor for a company installing an alarm system) will usually be necessary, to undertake a detailed audit of an existing building, draft the relevant parts of the brief, appraise the design proposals and/or devise procedures for the new building, in consultation with the gallery's insurance company and the local crime prevention officer. Taking advantage of such expertise in the design stage can mean that less invigilation may be required, with consequent savings on running costs. It can also mean that later additions of equipment, which are usually more obtrusive than something designed from the outset, can be avoided.

SERVICES ENGINEER

Services engineers assist with the design of mechanical and electrical services and systems relating to lighting, heating, air conditioning and mechanical services. As these services can represent a high proportion of costs in a gallery, appointment at an early stage is always advisable, helping to ensure that these services are integral parts of the design rather than additions that are bolted on later. In the UK, the professional body is the Chartered Institution of Building Services Engineers.

STRUCTURAL ENGINEER

A structural engineer advises on structural matters relating to the site, considers the structural implications of the brief and initial design proposals, assists with the design of the building and calculates the specifications for foundations, walls, columns, beams, slabs and roofs. Appointing a structural engineer in the early stages of the project can be very useful when alternative sites or buildings are being appraised. In the UK, the professional body is the Association of Consulting Engineers.

The **Association of Consulting Engineers** provides a nomination service and publishes guidance on services, conditions of engagement and fees, and can be contacted at: **Alliance House, 12 Caxton Street, London SW1H 0QL**
tel: 0171 222 6557
web: www.acenet.co.uk

Architectural Competitions: A Handbook for Promoters, Department of the Environment/Department of National Heritage, 1996 sets out two basic alternatives. The competitive interview is the method which selects the architect who then goes on to design the building, and is probably the method which will suit most small and medium-scale projects. The other option, the competition to select a design is more expensive and requires a detailed technical brief to be prepared beforehand.

Susan Carmichael, **"The Architect's Role in the Implementation Process",** in Gail Dexter Lord and Barry Lord (Eds.), **The Manual of Museum Planning,** HMSO 1991.

The Chartered Institution of Building Services Engineers (CIBSE) publishes a list of consulting building services engineering firms, obtainable by written request from **CIBSE** at: **222 Balham High Road, London, SW12 9BS.**
tel: 0181 675 5211, **fax:** 0181 675 5449

The Chartered Society of Designers can be contacted at: **32-38 Saffron Hill, London, EC1N 8FH.**
tel: 0171 831 9777

The **Landscape Institute** maintains a directory of registered landscape practices and can be contacted at: **6-7 Barnard Mews, London, SW11 1QW.**
tel: 0171 738 9166
web: www.l-i.org.uk

The Museums Security Adviser can be contacted at the: **Museums & Galleries Commission, 16 Queen Anne's Gate, London, SW1H 9AA.**
tel: 0171 233 4200
fax: 0171 233 3686

Independent consultancies include the **Bureau of Cultural Protection** (staffed by a former Museums Security Adviser), **Barrington House, 13 Aetheric Road, Braintree, Essex, CM7 2NF.**
tel/fax: 01376 322247
email: bcprotect@btinternet.com

Lists of public art agencies and consultants can be obtained from the Regional Arts Boards. See also:
1) Susan Jones,
   Art In Public: What, Why and How,
   AN Publications, 1992,
   ISBN 0 907730 18 3;
2) Nicholas Sharp,
   Commissions Contract,
   AN Publications;
3) Arts Council of England, Lesley Greene,
   Commissioning Art Works,
   Public Art Forum/Arts Council
   of England, 1996, **ISBN 0 7287 0717 9;**
4) Southern Arts Board et al,
   Contemporary Crafts in Museums,
   ISBN 0950 1228 82;
5) Voluntary Arts Network,
   Working With Artists and Craftspeople,
   ISBN 1 899687 02 5.

Both the **RIBA** and the **RIAS** have competitions offices, to help clients to choose the appropriate competitive process, and then to administer design competitions if this course is chosen. The **RIBA Clients' Advisory Service** has a database from which either competitors and/or independent assessors can be identified. Contact the **RIBA** Competitions Office: **8 Woodhouse Square, Leeds, LS3 1AD.**
tel: 0113 234 1335
fax: 0113 242 6791;

or the Competitions Unit:
Royal Incorporation of Architects in Scotland, 15 Rutland Square, Edinburgh, EH1 2BE.
tel: 0131 229 7545
fax: 0131 228 2188
email: EAlborough@rias.org.uk

The Royal Institution of Chartered Surveyors provides advice on professional and technical practice including model terms and conditions of engagement, and can be contacted at:
12 Great George Street, Parliament Square, London, SW1P 3AD.
tel: 0171 222 7000;
or at: **9 Manor Place, Edinburgh, EH3 7DN.**
tel: 0131 225 7078
web: www.rics.org.uk

The **RSA (Royal Society for the encouragement of Arts, Manufactures & Commerce)** publishes an **Art for Architecture Information Pack,** which includes an outline of the scheme, guidelines for applicants, details of Panel members, application deadlines and an application form for Incentive Awards, available from the **RSA** at:
8 John Adam Street, London, WC2N 6EZ.
tel: 0171 930 5115
fax: 0171 839 5805
email: jes@rsa-design. demon.co.uk
web: www.rsa.org.uk

communication

A building project can involve a large number of people, both inside and outside your organisation. Relationships must be clearly defined if conflict, confusion, delay and expense are to be avoided. Equally, information must move smoothly to the people who need to receive it. You must therefore ensure that:

- every individual understands the different roles of client, design team and other consultants, and the specific functions and responsibilities of each member (including themselves);
- clear lines of responsibility and accountability are established and maintained;
- clear lines for communication - instructions and decisions in one direction and reports in the other - are established and maintained.

ROLES OF CONTRIBUTORS

So that everyone in your organisation and on the design team, as well as each individual consultant, understands each person's contribution to the project, a list should be provided of the names, job titles, address/contact numbers and responsibilities of:

- all members of committee and staff involved in the project, including the Project Leader and Project Champion;

- all members of a practice working on the project, noting the partner of the practice or architect looking after the job;
- other members of the design team, with their areas of responsibility;
- all other consultants, with the nature of their contribution or area of responsibility.

ACCOUNTABILITY

In order that everyone in your organisation and on the design team, as well as each individual consultant, understands each person's status and authority, a line-management chart can be provided, setting out to whom each person is accountable. It should include the nature of any ultimate authority or controlling body, to which reference may have to be made and which might influence the nature or timing of the project.

This chart should also include the identities of the Project Leader, Project Manager, lead consultant on the design team, and the extent of delegation to each member of the design team. Individual consultants must take full responsibility for their work, but it should be clear when they have to obtain instructions and approvals and when they can use their own initiative.

LINES OF COMMUNICATION

Communication must be designed for two-way traffic, permitting requirements, instructions and decisions to flow from yourself in one direction, and reports, recommendations, requests and queries to flow back from the consultants in the other direction. Lines of communication can be set out in a diagram which shows how liaison will work between you, the design team and any other consultants.

During the Definition and Design Phases, all requests for information, answers and decisions should be routed through the Project Leader and Design Team Leader (or Project Manager). Board and staff members of your organisation should be alerted to the importance of the formal instruction route. Any ideas or facts which are passed to the design team in discussion or conversation should be recorded and passed to the Project Leader so that, if confirmed, they can be incorporated in the formal instructions to the Design Team.

Regular meetings aid effective internal communication and co-ordination of different contributions. A formal schedule of meetings helps to maintain momentum in the Definition and Design Phases, and to review and control the project during the Construction Phase.

top

location:
Stills Gallery, Edinburgh.

architect:
Reiach & Hall.

description:
'Probe' 1991: the reverse of the
screen pierced with rifles and gun-
sights that faced visitors as they
entered the 'Dominique Blain'
exhibition in Spring 1998.

bottom

description:
'Missa' 1992: Dominique Blain's
installation of 100 military boots in
marching formation suspended by
black thread just above the floor of
the rear gallery.

photographs:
Reproduced courtesy of the
Scottish Arts Council.

Frank Salisbury,
Briefing your Architect,
Architectural Press,
2nd edition, 1998,
ISBN 0 7506 3642 4.

The shorter the project's time-scale, the more frequent meetings will need to be. Meetings should be chaired by the Project Manager or by the Architect, and minutes recording decisions should name individuals and set deadlines for achieving results.

DOCUMENTATION

Building projects generate lots of paper, so it is important to plan for the accumulation and distribution of minutes, reports, drafts, etc., to ensure that everything is not only received but also acted upon. The presence of a formal instruction route should mean that one person is nominated to receive information coming into an organisation or team, to log and file it, and to circulate copies to those within the organisation who need to have it.

The Project Leader should set up a system for absorbing and organising the information which will go into the three documents that will complete the Definition Phase. Word-processing systems allow gradual accumulation, but it is important to log all new information as it becomes available and to have a clear system of recording and dating the different stages of drafts. The Business Plan, Project Plan and Technical Brief will all evolve during the Definition Phase, so all proposed changes should be labelled so that you can agree them and the design team can note them. Each draft should be numbered and dated, ideally with a header which identifies each page as well.

DESIGN AND CONSTRUCTION PHASES

Some form of report - including interim or progress reports on activities of any considerable duration - will usually be a condition of contract with every consultant. The nature and contents of these reports - amount of detail, when required, what summaries, breakdowns and forecasts are needed - should be defined at the outset. A Project Manager will expect to submit to you regular progress reports concerned with balancing quality, time and cost.

Project managers have at their disposal a number of planning and control methods from which they will determine the one most appropriate to the project. In addition, each member of the design team will draw on the standard formats, workbooks, etc., used within their professions. Setting up reporting systems during the Design Phase will help to prepare and test the procedures used during the construction period. As these reports are intended for your information, you must query anything which is not clear and informative.

There should only be minimal changes to the Technical Brief after it is completed and consigned to the design team. Similarly, there should only be minimal changes to the Brief and the detailed designs during construction. Any changes and variations will need to be fully documented and authorised, because of their consequences in terms of cost, time and/or quality.

gathering information

Writing plans and briefs for a new building and/or an expanded operation involves gathering general guidance on types and costs and detailed technical information on aspects of design. Various sources and formats of advice and information can be consulted during the Definition Phase. They include:

- the gallery's staff (➤➤ analysing need);
- published material;
- external bodies;
- visits to other galleries.

PUBLISHED MATERIAL

A search of the available literature can be time-consuming, so it is important to limit the amount of time spent on it, by identifying the information that is required, giving it a priority, noting the level of detail required and setting a deadline for obtaining the answers. References should be kept, since information gathered at the outset may be needed later. You may find three sources of publications of particular interest:

- architectural magazines review new buildings, including exhibition galleries; some concentrate on aesthetic and technical issues, and often do not examine how well the building works, but are useful for identifying which buildings might be visited, and how different architectural practices perform and are regarded within the profession;
- even before the Disability Discrimination Act, disability organisations have been very active in producing guidelines for making buildings accessible;
- museum-related publications cover a wide range of standards and guidance, some of which - e.g. security, environmental control and energy efficiency - are relevant to galleries that do not have collections and show only temporary exhibitions.

EXTERNAL LIAISON

Liaison and consultation with funders, stakeholders and users is a time-consuming but important aspect of the Definition Phase. This is the period when support must be secured from external bodies. It provides information to all people outside the organisation who are drawn into the project, including funding bodies and other 'stakeholders'. The success of a building depends not only on how well you are able to convey your requirements to your Architect, but also how well you can convey your vision - a composite of aesthetic beliefs, aspirations and practical needs - to your stakeholders and persuade them to back the project. Success may also depend on how well the project reflects the known priorities of funding bodies, in terms of access for people with disabilities, energy efficiency, involvement of artists, etc.

top	▲

location:
Whitechapel Art Gallery, London.

architect:
John Miller & Partners.

description:
Meetings Room.

bottom	▼

description:
Lecture Theatre.

photographs:
Anthony Weller, reproduced courtesy of Anthony Weller and the Whitechapel Art Gallery.

You should also determine which constituencies - community groups, groups with special interests or needs, formal education, etc. - should be consulted in order to clarify needs and propose solutions in the capital project (indeed some of these interests might even have provided the stimulus for the project in the first place). This is not a simple one-way process, whereby you inform your market what you intend to do. You may have to give some time to understanding the demography of the locality and devise events and occasions (e.g. special exhibition viewings, outreach activities) which will engage with local people. This exercise may prompt a radical review of what programmes are necessary to ensure that the mission conforms with the desires of the local community. You should consider how consultation can be managed in order to ensure a flow of information in both directions. Methods might include market research, focus groups, presentations, public meetings, special events and informal exhibitions.

ADVISORY BODIES

The Royal Institute of British Architects (RIBA) and the Royal Incorporation of Architects in Scotland (RIAS) each has a Clients' Advisory Service. These can help to identify the right architect for a given project, nominating a shortlist of architectural practices to meet your specific requirements. Each also has a competitions office (◄◄ design team),

and a bookshop with information on working with architects, including the Standard Form of Agreement for the Appointment of an Architect.

The Arts Councils in England, Northern Ireland, Scotland and Wales, the Regional Arts Boards in England and the Crafts Council have an unrivalled overview of the way that gallery buildings actually work and how well they continue to perform in the years after completion. If they know the scale and type of building you propose, they can advise on recent (and not-so-recent) building projects which would be worth visiting, with contact names and addresses and any features - bad as well as good - worth watching out for.

The Council of Museums in Wales, Museums & Galleries Commission, Northern Ireland Museums Council, Scottish Museums Council and the Area Museums Councils in England have a similar overview of collection-based organisations. Their willingness to provide advice and information may be limited if you are not a registered museum. However, organisations without collections are eligible to apply to the government indemnity scheme. The latter is administered by the Museums & Galleries Commission, which takes advice from the Museums Security Adviser and Environmental Adviser. Both of the latter will advise on proposals which may eventually apply to the Government Indemnity Scheme.

FACT-FINDING VISITS

The Project Leader, Architect and appropriate specialist staff and/or users should undertake fact-finding visits to buildings similar to the one proposed. Time and expense will limit these visits, so the destinations must be chosen with care. As far as possible, visits should be made to galleries of a comparable size and similar type to the programme which the project is intended to deliver. Such destinations might be identified in the literature search (which can limit selection to more recent buildings) or by consulting the arts funding bodies (which can restrict the recommendations to specific geographical areas).

The temptation should be resisted to visit recently-opened galleries simply on the basis of keeping abreast of new developments. Very recent experience of the management of building projects can be useful if the purpose of the visit is to understand the overall process and time-scale which raised the funding and designed and built the building. Such visits may be less productive where you want the benefit of hindsight. If the staff of a newly-opened gallery are going through a 'honeymoon period', they may be unable to talk about faults and failures which have not yet surfaced or even be reluctant to acknowledge faults because of their emotional investment in the building.

Even so, visits to new and older buildings provide useful direct experience of how well buildings work, whether there are difficulties such as sound-spill which are easy to overlook. In addition, they will give your Architect the chance to understand why you react positively or otherwise to the space or facilities of the gallery being visited. Such visits are part of the bonding process, which enable you and the Architect to understand better each other's aspirations and attitudes.

Each visit should be treated as a formal fact-finding exercise. The organisation to be visited will need to be contacted for its agreement and co-operation, and asked to arrange access 'below stairs' and to make available relevant personnel for the visitors to question. Each visit should be treated like an audit with a set of standard criteria and

questions on which answers are required - although without losing the possibility that the visit will raise issues that the visitors had not originally considered. A checklist should be drawn up, in order that the visit both covers the full range of design solutions, and assesses - using direct observation and discussion with the local staff - whether the results were satisfactory or otherwise and what alternatives might have been considered.

General considerations for investigation during the visit might include any of the following:

- the process by which the brief was written (e.g. who was involved, and how long did it take?);

- evaluating the resulting building against the brief (e.g. how well does it work, and what are the reasons for any failures?);

- the organisation and management of the project in the Definition, Design and Construction phases (e.g. what would the organisation say, with the benefit of hindsight, about methods used for appointing the architect or contractor, scheduling, etc.?);

- the contribution of consultants (e.g. how they were chosen and how their conclusions were fed into the overall process?);

- successes and failures in fund-raising (e.g. any recommendations on sources and how to make an application?).

For possible subjects for the technical aspects, ►► a checklist of requirements on pages 73-85.

The addresses of the **Council of Museums in Wales, Museums & Galleries Commission, Northern Ireland Museums Council, Scottish Museums Council** and the **Area Museums Councils in England** can be found in the current edition of the **Museums Yearbook**.

For the addresses of the **Royal Institute of British Architects** and the **Royal Incorporation of Architects in Scotland**, see ◄◄ design team

Access Committee for England,
250 City Road, London, EC1V 8AF.

tel: 0171 250 0008
fax: 0171 250 0212
email: Goodclare@aol.com

Access Committee for Wales,
Llys Ifor, Crescent Road,
Caerphilly, CF83 1XL.
tel: 01222 887325

Centre for Accessible Environments,
Nutmeg House, 60 Gainsford Street,
London, SE1 2NY.
tel: 0171 357 8182
fax: 0171 357 8183
email: cae@globalnet.co.uk

National Disability Arts Forum,
Mea House, Ellison Place,
Newcastle upon Tyne, NE1 8XS.
tel: 0191 261 1628
tel: 0191 222 0573

Royal Association for Disability and Rehabilitation (RADAR),
12 City Forum, 250 City Road,
London, EC1V 8AF.
tel: 0171 250 3222

analysing need

You should assess:

- the organisation's own internal needs, as defined by Board and staff;

- the public demand for the exhibitions and other activities that the gallery will provide;

- the facilities required - 'below stairs' as well as 'above stairs' - to meet these needs and demands.

INTERNAL NEEDS

Considerations that are internal to the organisation include a review of its mission and purpose, which sets out the needs that a capital project will meet in terms of rectifying shortcomings and/or meeting new requirements. With an existing gallery, any description of current exhibitions and activities would lead logically to shortcomings or deficiencies:

- an existing building may no longer be available because the lease is expiring;

- it may not fully comply with regulations for fire and health and safety;

- it may have become unsuitable for its activities, perhaps because it has outgrown its exhibition space, is unable to extend its range of work or because lenders are imposing more stringent security or environmental requirements;

- the layout and relationships between the spaces may be unsatisfactory;

- visitor facilities do not come up to contemporary expectations in terms of access, services and educational facilities;

- policy may have been re-written or re-interpreted, especially with the appointment of new staff who have been given a mandate to run the organisation in a different way, e.g. more emphasis might be given to sustaining a viable commercial operation.

A new organisation will set out its needs in terms of providing accommodation for activities which were previously without a home.

EXTERNAL DEMANDS

Other stakeholders - the local community, government agencies, special constituencies - may identify requirements which also have to be addressed in any eventual capital project. The needs of potential users (especially those unable to use an existing facility) might even provide one of the stimuli for the project in the first place. All of the Lottery distributors give a high priority to the need for applicants to show that there is a clear demand and an eventual public benefit from their projects. A preliminary assessment of the market and the public demand for the exhibitions and other activities that the gallery will provide might be based on:

- how the gallery's mission relates to the interests and preferences of the local community and any changes in demography;

- the gallery's experience of public use of any existing facilities and of comparable facilities elsewhere;

- evidence from any previous market research which may have provided a stimulus for the project;

- a start made on gathering evidence from external sources - from officials and representatives, artists and craftspeople, the educational sector, community groups and from the public at large - to test the project's relevance, locally, regionally and/or nationally.

This preliminary assessment might be expanded subsequently in market research as part of a feasibility study, and will lead eventually to the marketing strategy in the business plan

FACILITIES REQUIRED

An appraisal of the existing building can be used to identify how well it serves present purposes, not only in terms of its technical performance but also from an aesthetic or psychological point of view. The eventual result might be a decision to refurbish or extend an existing building or to re-locate to another one. However, the immediate purpose of the appraisal is to use any existing facilities to help to define what does work or what may be necessary to make it work better. Looking at the building from the different points of view of visitor and staff, an appraisal would consider:

- how far present spaces are adequate in size and services;

- whether these spaces do work and, if so, why;

- if the size, shape or aspect of the spaces enhances the experience of the visitor;

- whether access, layout and circulation are convenient, or why there are difficulties or congestion;

- whether there are spaces that are under-exploited, and why;

- how far the facilities meet statutory requirements.

Even where the organisation does not yet have a building of its own, research and assessment of comparable facilities can be used to assess how far these buildings would satisfy the needs of the policy that is envisaged, again from technical, aesthetic and psychological points of view. Such appraisals will help you to decide on preferences and to

define dimensions, configurations and facilities needed to meet the future needs of programme and visitors in a new or refurbished building.

For the staff and Board, a Needs Analysis is not only a general outline of the facilities that are needed to fulfil the mission but also provides a basis for a consensus (◄◄ getting organised). The needs or desires of the staff, influenced by the limitations of any existing building and/or comparisons with other facilities, will lead them to set out their spatial and other requirements. This may be the first opportunity - and most direct way - of engaging the staff and Board in the project.

Each member of staff responsible for a particular activity should be asked to define what facilities are required for that activity in a new or refurbished building and what might be their revenue consequences. An exhibition curator would be horrified if a librarian set out the requirements for an exhibition gallery, and in turn should not expect to define the facilities and location of technical, educational, retail or any other area which is another person's responsibility. Staff who are already in post can outline their activities and how the latter relate to the rest of the building. They should list the

facilities they need and be prepared to justify them in relation to existing activities and future possibilities, in formal discussions or brain-storming sessions.

At the early stages, these 'wish lists' might disregard physical or financial constraints, in order to bring staff into the planning exercise and to stimulate creative thinking. Later, as part of a two-way process, staff will come to appreciate the scale and scope of the final project, and to understand both the impact that improved facilities elsewhere in the building might have on their particular area and the reasons for any eventual scaling-down of their original requirements. It is important for the Project Leader to ask the right questions. Where new education facilities are proposed, for instance, shop staff might be asked to gauge how increased usage by school groups would affect the future ranges of stock and layout of the shop. Staff should also have the opportunity to comment directly on sketch designs. Consultation can also reveal needs beyond the particular requirements of a specialist area of interest, for more congenial office accommodation or for a quiet meetings space. If staff are still to be recruited, they should be appointed as early as possible in the design process and certainly before detailed design is begun (◄◄ consultants).

considering the options

The purposes of an Options Analysis are:

- to provide a systematic way for you to consider a range of alternative ways of taking the gallery forward;

- to use agreed criteria to make conclusions and recommendations, and help you towards the best solution;

- to demonstrate convincingly to outside bodies, not least funding agencies (which often require an options analysis) why this solution has been chosen.

PRESENT PREMISES

Options may range from doing nothing, improving an existing building, acquiring and converting other building(s), to constructing a new building. In the first place, these broad alternatives are measured against the strategic aims of a Vision statement and against the requirements in a Needs Analysis. This first stage would examine present circumstances, in terms of activities, users, location, potential for expansion or growth, etc. It might lead to the conclusion that the existing premises, with refurbishment or extension, are adequate for the need.

Where it concludes instead that these premises are unsuitable, then the same aims and objectives can be used to test a number of alternative locations. Psychological factors should not be ignored: users may be opposed to leaving the present premises, but might be attracted to a building which is innovative or which gives a new use to a symbol of civic pride.

COMPARING ALTERNATIVES

The standard technique for comparing and choosing between alternatives is a 'SWOT' analysis, which tests each option within a standard framework of Strengths, Weaknesses, Opportunities and Threats. The SWOT framework should define the extent to which each option meets the criteria set out in the Vision statement and the Needs Analysis. In addition, it will identify any other implications of particular sites or locations, with their advantages or disadvantages. The fact that a building has been offered at a low rent or sale price, for example, can be set against other factors which might show that this option is not the best answer to the need. New buildings have the advantage that they can be designed to reflect your aspirations but there may

location:
City Museum and Art Gallery, Worcester.

architect:
Worcester City Council Technical Services, with Oscar Faber Consulting Engineers.

description:
Refurbishment of a late Victorian art gallery.

photograph:
Alan Morris, reproduced courtesy of Worcester City Council.

be other constraints - cost, site, planning consents, acquisition - which will get in the way of a successful outcome. Considerations might include:

- location: shape of site, boundaries, adjacent properties, rights of way, etc.;

- access: approach roads for delivering exhibitions, pedestrian access, including for disabled people, car parking, etc.;

- character and quality of existing buildings: layout, listed building constraints and planning restrictions on materials or use, construction restrictions, community pressure groups, etc.;

- site ownership;

- availability of utilities: sewage, water, gas, electricity, telephone, etc.;

- site condition: sub-soil, old foundations, ground-water, etc.;

- landscape requirements, tree-preservation orders, overhead cables, etc.;

- costs and funding issues.

It is important that you do not commit yourself to a building or a site before an objective assessment has been made of its suitability for the proposed activities and before planning, environmental and structural issues have been considered. A formal Options Analysis should lead to conclusions and recommendations which will demonstrate convincingly why the preferred solution is the best response to the need, in terms of improving facilities that are inadequate or offering new facilities. Where refurbishment or conversion of an existing building is being considered,

its layout will exert a significant influence. If it is of historic or architectural interest, its style and the features that must be retained may limit possibilities, and it will be important to assess as objectively as possible the extent to which the building can satisfy the needs that have been articulated, and at what cost. Fire prevention and evacuation measures can, for example, be very expensive in comparison to modern buildings that have been constructed on the basis of contemporary legislation and codes of practice. On the other hand, the character of a particular site or building can clarify the original criteria, e.g. the atmosphere that is required, and give them a different priority.

Although written from the point of view of museums, Harold Kalman's chapter, **"Adapting Existing Buildings as Museums"**, in Gail Dexter Lord and Barry Lord (Eds.), **The Manual of Museum Planning**, HMSO 1991, contains much that applies to exhibition galleries.

Voluntary Arts Network, **Converting Buildings For Arts Use**, ISBN 1 899687 05 X.

feasibility study

PURPOSE

The purposes of a feasibility study are, firstly, to examine in broad terms the strategic rationale, public demand, organisational implications and costs of a project, and secondly to help to set out the strategies and plans which will make the project work. Testing viability should be a continuous process during the Definition Phase, but there may be one or more occasions when time and money are invested in a formal study to obtain more facts and expert advice, and to appraise the technical, logistical, environmental, commercial and financial aspects of something requiring major investment. At its earliest and simplest, the study might be a report written by members of the Board and staff, which gathers together evidence and information that is readily available to help the Board to decide whether to continue to the next stage and how to proceed. A feasibility study can also be an intensive programme of studies, often undertaken by external specialists who are engaged as consultants.

The scale of the study will depend on:

- its purpose;
- the stage at which it is being undertaken;
- the size and complexity of the proposed project;
- the number of options being assessed;
- the amount of new research needed;
- the extent of external assistance needed.

At whatever stage a feasibility study is undertaken, it is crucial that sufficient time is allowed, not only to carry out the study thoroughly, but also to debate and resolve the queries that it raises.

Feasibility studies are also part of the multi-stage application process introduced by the Lottery distributors. In this case, a feasibility study tests purpose and viability before a project proceeds to detailed design and construction, and the resulting strategies and plans will be manifested in the technical brief, project plan and business plan, which close the Definition Phase.

The three most common aspects of feasibility studies are concerned with:

- market relevance
- organisational viability
- technical feasibility

overleaf, pages 45 & 46 ➤

location:
Ormeau Baths Gallery, Belfast.

architect:
22 over 7.

description:
When the hall with the main bathing pool was converted, a new floor had to be inserted, to create upper and lower galleries. A light-well was left which, as well as allowing natural light to penetrate down to the lower floor, permits very large work to be displayed in a tall space. The light-well helps visitors to orientate themselves and understand how the two galleries relate to each other, and has also been very useful for moving very large work up to (and down from) the upper floor.

photograph:
Rory Moore, reproduced courtesy of OBG: Ormeau Baths Gallery.

MARKET RELEVANCE

Market relevance will take its starting point from a Needs Analysis or other sampling and definition of public demand for the exhibitions and other activities which the organisation would like to provide (◄◄ analysing need). It would gather hard evidence, to test the project's relevance locally, regionally and/or nationally, and to demonstrate that there is a market for the project. Improved facilities might be planned for new educational programmes aimed at particular groups in the community or for an improved exhibition programme aimed at attracting visitors from further afield. Drawing on the expertise of marketing consultants enables these proposals to be evaluated objectively. Especially where a new range of activities is proposed, market research might provide:

- statistical evidence about the overall size of the market, its characteristics, trends and prospects for growth and anticipated visitor numbers;

- the preferences of current and potential visitors;

- opportunities and threats, such as how the project's ability to attract visitors compares with the strengths and weaknesses of competing facilities (existing or proposed);

- whether there are gaps in provision which the project might be designed to fill;

- an estimate of the demand for the project, by quantifying the visitors and users who would be attracted by the new facilities;

- a definition of the nature and size of possible target audiences (young or old, visiting as individuals, in family groups or in organised parties);

- the extent to which the public transport system and the road network helps or hinders access from the catchment area.

Such information would subsequently inform the marketing strategy in the business plan for reaching target users within the proposed catchment area. The effectiveness or otherwise of the public transport system would also influence considerations such as the amount of parking space needed to cope with educational groups arriving in coaches or with a large number of private cars for evening previews.

ORGANISATIONAL VIABILITY

Information from market research would also affect:

- the type of facilities and size of spaces required to meet this demand;

- the number of staff and the skills needed to manage the building and its users;

- estimates of income from paid admissions, retailing or catering operation, room hire or group bookings, etc.;

- approaches to funding bodies and sponsors for support for revenue programmes, based on a strategic view of the desirability of the project.

A feasibility study must consider how the building will be staffed and financed after it is completed. A capital project will alter, to a greater or lesser degree, the nature (and even the direction) of the organisation, with changes to its public profile and to the staff needed to manage its activities. A feasibility study will normally predict and estimate these organisational implications. Much of the research on different aspects - marketing, financial management, training, etc. - will be commissioned from consultants, whose conclusions and recommendations will eventually be integrated into the business plan Some of the estimates, not least those relating to the running costs of the building, may be provided by your Design Team.

On the financial side, a feasibility study will make realistic projections of:

- overheads costs of the new building and the staff required to run it;
- the cost of the exhibition programmes and other activities;
- income to be earned from sales, catering, hiring (for conferences, meetings and receptions), etc.;
- grants and sponsorship.

TECHNICAL FEASIBILITY

This aspect of a feasibility study might take as its starting point an earlier Options Analysis which compared a number of possible approaches or actual sites or locations. It must be clear why the preferred option is the best response to the need, in terms of satisfying your requirements and in terms of cost, efficiency, quality and public benefit.

Many of the issues concerning technical feasibility will require the skills of the design team. Appointing the architect early in the Definition Phase can be useful for considering different options and for producing preliminary proposals. Recruiting the quantity surveyor at a similar early stage would also be an advantage for costing not only the building costs but also running costs. A feasibility study corresponds to at least Stage B in the RIBA Plan of Work (◄◄ planning the project). The Design Team's work on the architectural aspects of the feasibility study will not extend to fund-raising considerations, which remain your responsibility. However, a fund-raising strategy will determine when detailed proposals have to be ready and when funds will be available for starting work, so have implications for the Design Team. Equally, the design team will have to take into account decisions and recommendations about the long-term viability of the organisation which affect the building requirements (e.g. the need for more space and staff for educational activities or marketing work).

Technical feasibility might include the following considerations:

- initial response to, and clarification of, the client's requirements;
- commissioning route for detailed design;
- proposals for managing the project;
- proposed procurement route, including compliance with EC procurement legislation;
- site constraints, planning approvals;
- possible time-scale;
- broad estimates of the cost of the project, compared to the target budget and other financial constraints, to assess whether the proposed scale and quality of building is achievable;
- analysis of exploitable resources (property, financial assets, volunteer support);
- sources of finance for the capital programme, possible timing and implications for the time-scale, possible fund-raising strategy.

project description

PURPOSE

The Project Description is a summary of the proposed building, setting out ideas that have been developed and the information that has been gathered during the initial Definition Phase. It brings together in a single document the ideas and research embodied in the Vision statement, Needs Analysis, Options Appraisal and Feasibility Study, amplifying these initial statements in the light of current knowledge.

The Project Description is addressed to everyone involved in the project, whether staff, stakeholders or consultants. It provides the basis for applications for funding and background information for consultants, setting out the significance of the project and its overall requirements.

The Project Description is an interim document, and subsequently the information in it is divided again, and evolves into the detailed business plan, project plan and technical brief. In architectural terms, it is usually known as the outline, preliminary or strategic brief because it leads eventually to the architect's brief. As a preliminary to the Technical Brief, it gives sufficient information to enable the design team to understand what spaces are required, what relationships are important and what the overall feeling of the building should be, and to respond in general terms. The Project Description evolves gradually into the Technical Brief, as parts of the earlier document are incorporated as context and background into the later one and as other, technical parts are expanded into more detailed requirements.

FORMAT

The Project Description and the three documents that evolve from it can share basic introductory material. Formats recommended for Lottery applicants often include the following features:

- title page: this should carry the name and location of the organisation and the name and job title of the author of the document. It might also carry the names of directors or trustees, bankers, financial advisers, auditors and solicitors;

- table of contents: a list of section headings should include page numbers for ease of reference;

- executive summary: a succinct account of the nature of the project and an overview of the rest of the document; if the document has been prepared in support of an application for funding, the executive summary will also summarise the amount of funding being sought from different sources;

- glossary of definitions and explanations;

- methodology;

- references and acknowledgements: a paragraph (or appendix) which records useful sources of information and acknowledges the contribution of other people, both to show that the project has involved those who should have been and to record these sources for possible future use.

location:
Centre for Visual Arts, Cardiff.

architect:
BDP/Robertson Francis Partnership.

description:
Ground-floor gallery.

photograph:
Patricia Aithie, reproduced courtesy of CVA: Centre for Visual Arts.

CONTENT

A Project Description will vary in content and length, but it will set out as clearly and precisely as possible what you expect the project to deliver. Depending on the scale and complexity of the project, it might include some or all of the following:

- background;
- objectives;
- overall requirements;
- schedule of accommodation;
- evaluation.

BACKGROUND

A history of previous activity and a summary of the organisation at present is essentially the background to how the gallery has got to the point where you need to embark on the project. Consultants, not least the Architect, have to understand your nature and character, in terms of what you do, how you do it, whom you employ, with whom you collaborate, how you are involved with outside services, what are your priorities, what is the likelihood of change, how the new building will function, etc. This part might include:

- the purpose, philosophy and policy of the organisation running the gallery, quoting the mission statement and setting out what the constitution or other formal instrument says the organisation should be doing;

- the structure and method of operation, noting governance, staffing, sources of funding and the financial background to the organisation;

- programmes of exhibitions and activities the gallery is actually doing, describing what it does and how it does it, what relationships are important and any special factors;

- any important principles, e.g. whether access is free, the existence of any Friends organisation, the approach to education, research, tourism, etc.

OBJECTIVES

This paragraph is more concerned with the proposed outcomes of the project. The objectives of a capital project are different from the overall objectives of the organisation, but must be consistent with them. Objectives should be precise, comprehensive, unambiguous, understood and shared with stakeholders. This paragraph would extend and amplify the Vision statement and the information in the Needs Analysis, describing the benefits of the project (◄◄ clarifying the vision and analysing need). It should describe:

- artistic policy and vision: your ambitions in terms of the exhibitions and other activities which the project will enable you to provide;

- the market, the nature of the catchment area and the ambience that the project will provide for visitors and other users, actual and potential;

- the quality of the building: what visitors should experience and how users should respond to it; the scale and atmosphere of the exterior and how it relates to its local area, location and site (if a building or a site has been identified, sensitivity to the site and locality might be discussed in the features to be retained in a listed building or be illustrated through scaled plans and photographs of the site with summaries of special planning requirements), its furnishings and fittings, any policy of including artists and craftspeople in the project, e.g. for an artist joining the design team.

- the contribution of the project to the local community, educational work and social and economic development;

- any work done to date, towards achieving these objectives.

OVERALL REQUIREMENTS

This paragraph would extend and amplify the Options Analysis (◄◄ considering the options), taking into account the results of the technical feasibility aspects of the feasibility study. It follows naturally from previous paragraphs by outlining the scale of the building and the physical facilities which are essential to enable you to achieve your aims. The Design Team needs to understand what spaces are required, what relationships are important and what the overall feeling of the building should be. If, for example, the exhibition space is used for different purposes - for a permanent collection, artists' residencies or lectures or performances, as well as for temporary exhibitions - it is important that your Architect is able to understand the relationship between the different activities, their relative priorities and their particular requirements in terms of space and equipment.

SCHEDULE OF ACCOMMODATION

A schedule of accommodation is a list or inventory of all the different types of space - exhibition galleries, circulation spaces, support accommodation, storage - that the project should deliver, with an estimate of the net (usable) area needed for each function. It should set out the spatial requirements for accommodating the target numbers of users, the envisaged programmes of exhibitions and activities and service and staff requirements. This exercise will give an approximate total floor area for the whole project, which can be used to judge how far an available site or building will meet the need. It also gives an overview of the relative amounts of space - and the approximate proportion of building costs - proposed for different aspects of the operation - the balance between art spaces and non-art spaces, the relationship of display areas to storage and workshop facilities, the breakdown of public facilities, etc. Any priorities for particular forms of accommodation - whether storage, upgrading of temporary exhibition spaces, improvements to office - should be described, as should any priorities if spaces are to be shared between more than one activity.

Relationships between spaces, sequences of your normal or anticipated activities and preferred circulation patterns can be described, noting reasons for keeping different functions together. For instance, an education suite or meeting room that is available for receptions and hirings will need to be close to toilets and cloakrooms and any catering facilities, and should have independent access when the rest of the building is closed. A diagram would best illustrate routes and densities of circulation for each type of use.

The minimum facilities and services needed for each activity or function - heating, lighting, air-conditioning, ventilation, sound-proofing, fire detection, security, lift-access, equipment, etc. - should also be described.

EVALUATION

Finally, the Project Description would outline how the success of the completed building will be measured. It would set out the results you hope to achieve in terms of the exhibitions and activities you hope to organise yourself, those you wish to attract from elsewhere, and the ambience you would like to provide for your users (visitors and artists). It would also set out other objectives, e.g. for savings on running costs.

Richard P Dober, **"Preparing the Brief"**, in Gail Dexter Lord and Barry Lord (Eds.), **The Manual of Museum Planning**, HMSO 1991.

project plan

PURPOSE

The objective of a capital project is to bring the building to a successful conclusion, so your planning has to continue beyond the consigning of the Technical Brief to the Architect.

A Project Plan is the overall strategy which brings together within a single framework a number of detailed action plans relating to the different aspects of the capital project. All of these separate documents are normally included as appendices, so that the Project Plan itself can take an overall view of the management and funding of the whole project.

A Project Plan usually embraces two distinct activities:

- liaison with the design team during the design phase and the project management team during construction; and

- managing the gallery during the period of closure, including temporary accommodation for staff and activities at other sites.

FORMAT

The Project Plan is one of the three documents produced by the Definition Phase (the other two are the business plan and the technical brief).

Whilst the Business Plan shows how the completed building will be run and funded afterwards, the Project Plan allows you to demonstrate how the capital project will be managed and financed until completion. It is important not to conflate the two types of plan or to confuse administrative and financial arrangements which are different in nature. In general, the two need to be kept separate, the main exceptions being the combined balance sheet, income and expenditure account and cash-flow statement which show the impact of the project on your cash flow during the period of design and construction.

Because the three documents are concerned with distinct aspects of the capital project, each can be written to complement the other two. However, each should also be written so that it can be understood without reference to the others. This may mean that there will be some repetition, especially at the beginning where the context and background of the organisation are summarised. The Project Plan grows out of the project description, so the format and substance of the introductory parts can follow the structure of the earlier document, expanding on the content where appropriate:

location:
Serpentine Gallery, London.

architect:
John Miller & Partners.

description:
Construction of the new basement.

photograph:
Hugo Glendinning, reproduced courtesy of the Serpentine Gallery.

- title page;
- table of contents;
- executive summary;
- glossary of definitions, explanations;
- methodology;
- references and acknowledgements;
- background;
- objectives.

PREPARATIONS FOR THE DESIGN PHASE

This paragraph would set out arrangements for liaison with the design team and work associated with the capital project that you must undertake during the design phase.

In addition to the activities set out in communication, the former would include:

- making an input into the design process;
- arranging visits with the Architect and others to exemplary projects (◄◄ gathering information);
- identifying and arranging for advisory visits and consultancies to the site.

During the design phase, you may have to undertake other work associated with the capital project, which could include recruiting and briefing consultants and ensuring that their conclusions and recommendations are incorporated into the design team's thinking. The site inspection during an access audit of a existing building and its setting would lead to a report advising on possible solutions to any problems identified. An access appraisal would instead check architects' drawings for implications for disabled people. An audit or appraisal would also influence policy and practice after the project is complete (►► business plan).

Instead (or in addition), specialist staff should be recruited as soon as possible in the design phase, in order to ensure their requirements are incorporated into the design team's thinking. It can be a false economy to delay the recruitment of staff. Changes to the outline proposals will be almost inevitable once the staff actually responsible for programming a space face the practicalities of doing so. The later the changes are agreed, the more expensive they will be, and the longer the building programme will be delayed.

PREPARATIONS FOR THE CONSTRUCTION PHASE

This paragraph would set out arrangements for liaison with the project management team and work associated with the capital project that you have to undertake during the construction phase. It would estimate the amount of time to be devoted to the project by senior management, and how the project is to be managed without disrupting your normal work. The plan would show where key skills are weak or missing from Board or staff, and how they will be filled, e.g. by the use of consultants. Liaison with the project management team would include:

- ensuring that all consents and approvals relating to planning, Building Regulations, Listed Buildings, Conservation Areas, etc. are obtained and that statutory consultations - with English Heritage, Scottish Heritage, CADW, Royal Fine Art Commission, etc. - are arranged;
- setting up a schedule of regular meetings with the Project Manager, design team and contractors in order to monitor progress, to initiate and control any changes in plans and to resolve any other issues (◄◄ communication);
- establishing and agreeing mechanisms for financial control and payment procedures.

PROCUREMENT ROUTE

Procurement routes - the standard methods of buying, purchasing, tendering and commissioning the different services that go into a building project - should be considered at an early stage, since the choice will affect how design is managed. The clients' advisory services run by the RIBA and RIAS will give impartial advice on the different routes (◄◄ design team). Each procurement route has a standard contract and offers different advantages in terms of cost, time and quality.

The three most common methods are:

- Design-and-build, where the contractor assumes all responsibilities for design and construction in return for a lump sum. This method has the advantages of simple management and known price, but gives the client little control over the design process and even less flexibility with changes during the construction phase. Design-and-build works best where the contractor specialises in a particular type of building and/or where requirements can be easily or readily defined. Some Lottery distributors may not fund design-and-build projects.

- Management Contracting reduces the time between design, tender and construction, especially for large and complicated projects, by letting the contract as a series of 'works packages'. Where time is critical, this method allows building to start before design work has been completed. However, substantial unexpected costs can result where design is not completed before work starts on site, and the price will not be known until the final works package is started. In addition, contractor's schedules may not allow adequate time for design.

- Traditional Procurement gives a client the freedom to choose the design team and then to choose the contractor in two separate stages. It allows the design to be developed before the building contract is signed, and ensures that contractors are certain about the project they are tendering on. This method is most likely to lead to the building you want, but it can be a long process, and it may be difficult to determine whether it is the architect or contractor who is responsible for any problems that do arise.

EC Procurement Rules apply to public authorities (including government departments, agencies like the Lottery distributors and local authorities). The rules set out detailed procedures for the award of contracts whose value equals or exceeds certain thresholds. Details of the current thresholds are available from H.M. Treasury.

Appendices would include the following:

- the calibre, experience and skills of the management team;

- use of internal and external advisers.

PREPARATIONS FOR A PERIOD OF CLOSURE

This paragraph would set out all plans and arrangements for the organisation whilst construction is under way. It would include any temporary accommodation for staff. Re-location of staff, furniture and equipment may be a one-off operation if an organisation is moving from old premises to a new building. More commonly, this operation has to be done twice, if an existing building is to be refurbished and has to be vacated during building work. Chaos is bad in one move but is unforgiveable in two.

Although an external contractor may be carrying out the actual move, overall responsibility should be delegated to a senior member of staff, ideally one with technical experience. Depending on the size and complexity of the move, this person might be assisted by a team of other technical and administrative staff.

In addition to the cost of removal itself, the budget for relocation might need to include such items as the rental of temporary accommodation, connection of utilities and any necessary repairs and maintenance or health and safety work, storage and insurance. Redundancies may be necessary.

An inventory of fixtures, fittings, equipment and records should be compiled, and arranged in terms of items for disposal, storage, archiving and relocation, and plans should be drawn up for the storage or disposal of redundant furniture and equipment. When putting the relocation to tender, plans of the site and access to it should be provided. Arrangements should be made to notify Council offices, suppliers, employees, official bodies, etc. of the temporary change of address, and to suspend contracts for gas, electricity, telephones, cleaning, photocopiers, etc.

Temporary accommodation of staff, furniture and equipment should bear in mind statutory requirements as well as the positions of power supplies, telephone sockets, etc. Floor plans for target locations for furniture, equipment, etc. should be agreed with staff. When disconnecting computers, back-up files should be made and transferred separately and securely to the new location. A de-briefing session should identify problems and seek solutions, especially when there will be a second move back into the building after the work is complete.

PROMOTING ACTIVITIES AT OTHER SITES

This paragraph would set out all plans and arrangements for activities whilst construction is under way. The closure of an existing building often provides an opportunity to experiment with a new outreach programme or to expand an existing one by concentrating resources which otherwise would be devoted to the main base. The reasons include maintaining your profile and the loyalty of regular visitors during the building work, reaching and developing new audiences and marketing the new building. Outreach strategies that have been used successfully include:

- a commissioning strategy, usually connected with an educational programme, for a variety of temporary works of art, especially those involving performance, installation or projected light which draw attention to the building and the construction work;

- transplanting at least some of the exhibition programme to locations in the same town which have been made available on a temporary basis (e.g. empty business or retail units), either in the area to which the gallery is to move to help to build up contacts with the local community, or in a completely different area in order to target sections of the population who have been under-represented amongst the gallery's visitors and attract them to the new building;

- enlarging an existing network of artists' residencies and workshops in schools and other community centres in the gallery's catchment area, in order to retain the loyalty of visitors during the closure and to gain access to new audiences which might then come to the new gallery;

- organising and touring a small group of high-profile exhibitions which are designed to publicise the new gallery on a wider stage - regional or national - and timed to arrive back at the gallery for showing there after the re-opening.

RECRUITMENT AND TRAINING

A proposed staff structure should be included as an appendix to the business plan, but this part of the Project Plan would be concerned with the timetable for the recruitment of the full complement of staff to run the new building, additional to people who have been appointed earlier to make an input into the design and/or manage the outreach activities.

It would also be concerned with training. A new building generally involves a degree of re-training of existing staff. At its most basic, this might be no more than ensuring that cleaners do not polish a wooden floor to make a distracting and uncomfortable glare especially for people with visual impairments, or ensuring that staff do not prop open self-closing doors where control of humidity is important. A training plan should be developed and implemented as soon as practicable. Where a building has been designed to make physical access easier, it should be complemented by an Equal Opportunities Policy for the future operation and an action plan which includes staff training in customer care, equal opportunities, disability awareness and emergency egress. Consultants who have advised on particular aspects of the programme might be brought back to undertake training for the staff on their areas of specialism. Some Lottery distributors allow training costs to be included in Lottery applications if the training is designed to help to cope with the management of change or to develop the new skills needed for a capital project. This paragraph would be supported by an appendix with details of the training plan.

LAUNCH OF THE NEW BUILDING

The opening should be an opportunity for re-launching the organisation and drawing attention to its new capabilities, with opening programmes supported by an intensive marketing campaign. This might also be an opportunity to try new forms of publicity, e.g. information might be made available in large print and/or audio formats.

SHAKEDOWN

This section would include planning for the initial occupancy of the building after hand-over and the period when the staff are not only settling in but also getting used to the demands of the new building, developing procedures or being trained to use new equipment. During this period, there would be a series of tests to ensure that the building and its equipment perform as required and to identify faults so that they can be put right during the Defects Liability Period. This period would also be the time to test procedures for access, installation, maintenance and storage (e.g. for lighting, screens) agreed during the design stage, and to improve on them where possible. It would develop procedures for the invigilation of exhibitions (which may vary from exhibition to exhibition, e.g. to meet the requirements of the government indemnity scheme), and for control of the public appropriate to the layout of the building, in addition to any general policies for customer care.

COST PLAN

This part of the Project Plan is concerned with the financial management of the capital project. Those costs relating to the building will be estimated by the Design Team and specifically by the Quantity Surveyor, whose responsibility will have included translating the various design proposals into cost plans and influencing the scale and nature of these proposals in the light of your budget. These estimates should include equipment and fitting-out costs, the fees of the design team, and must make realistic and comprehensible assumptions about inflation, credit terms from suppliers, taxation, etc. Those costs not relating to the construction - commissioning programme and closure and re-location costs - would instead be the responsibility of the Project Leader. In order to provide realistic estimates, these projections would be based largely on models and examples elsewhere of projects and commissions of a similar size and nature. The two groups of financial information would be brought together and summarised in the body of the Project Plan. They would be supported by appendices with:

- a detailed breakdown of projected expenditure;
- monthly projections for the design and construction phases.

FUND-RAISING STRATEGY

Financial projections should also set out the level of sponsorship and grant-aid required to sustain the capital programme and its associated activities, and the current status of funding arrangements. Lottery distributors need to be assured that the necessary level of "partnership funding" has been secured to match any grant, or at least that there is a realistic fund-raising strategy in place. Funding has been secured for gallery developments from schemes such as the European Regional Development Fund, Derelict Land Grants and Inner City Challenge on the basis of the contribution of galleries to social renewal and urban regeneration. In addition to the Arts Lottery, funding can be available from arts-related trusts such as the Foundation For Sport and the Arts, Henry Moore Foundation, RSA

Art for Architecture Award Scheme and the Edward Marshall Trust, especially in relation to specific aspects of the capital programme. Assumptions need to be justified, because there can be a big gap between the likely total cost of the capital project and a credible and achievable fund-raising target. This part will be supported by appendices with details of:

- detailed breakdown of income already raised or promised for the capital project, with the sources of funding;
- applications outstanding, with amounts requested and dates of notification;
- fund-raising strategy, including previous fund-raising experience and any professional support;
- projected balance sheet, income and expenditure account and cash-flow statement for the design and construction phases.

TIMETABLE

This part of the Project Plan would set out the timing of the main activities of the construction phase, and would be supported by appendices with details of:

- an outline timetable;
- cash-flow projections of expenditure and income on a monthly basis for the whole of the design and construction phases.

RISK MANAGEMENT

The purpose of this paragraph is to identify any risks that could prevent the project from achieving its objectives, and to outline the plans or contingencies to reduce these risks. Risk assessment is a standard management practice, which involves identifying all categories of risk that could threaten a project (e.g. delays from poor weather, failure to raise the income required). Each category includes a number of threats, with an assessment of their probability, their consequences or implications, their severity in financial terms, the bearer of the risk (e.g. client, architect, contractor), whether the risk is insurable and how the risk should be controlled or managed. Design teams and contractors will seek to limit their liabilities, but any risk should be borne by those who are technically or professionally best qualified to deal with it. Insurance should cover all needs and eventualities, including third parties.

APPENDICES

Appendices can be used to provide detailed information which has been summarised elsewhere in the Project Plan, and to include relevant reports, references and promotional literature. They might also include plans, diagrams, tables, charts, maps and photographs. In addition to the items listed above, appendices might include the following:

- chart showing the relationship of the design team, project management and client team;

- brief details including qualifications and skills of members of the design team;

- brief details including qualifications and skills of members of the project management team;

- brief details including qualifications and skills of external advisers and consultants, who have contributed directly to the preparation of the project plan;

- any consultants' reports which have been used as source material in preparing the Business Plan, and to which reference may need to be made.

Although intended for procurement by central government, the guidance issued by H.M. Treasury is valuable for starting from the client's point of view and for taking an overall strategic approach. Publications take two forms, a new series of Procurement Guidance, which supersedes in part an earlier series of CUP Guidance, from the Central Unit on Procurement. Of the latter, the following may be particularly useful:

Project Sponsorship (no. 33), Life Cycle Costing (no. 35), Contract Strategy Selection for Major Projects (no. 36), Managing Risk and Contingency for Works Projects (no. 41), Quality Assurance (no. 46), Introduction to the EC Procurement Rules (no. 51), and Programming and Progress Monitoring for Works Projects (no. 52).

Copies are available from the Public Enquiries Unit, H.M. Treasury, Room 89/2, Treasury Chambers, Parliament Street, London, SW1P 3AG. tel: 0171 270 4558 fax: 0171 270 5244 or can be downloaded directly from the Treasury's web-site; web: www.hm-treasury.gov.uk/ pub/html/docs/cup/

business plan

PURPOSE

Your planning should extend not only beyond consigning the brief to the architect but also beyond the completion of the building. The objective of a building programme, after all, is not just to complete the project successfully, but to operate effectively within the new building. The building will be a response to the exhibitions and other activities it is designed to accommodate, but a new or extended building with increased facilities will usually mean that the operational and financial structures have to be revised in order to run it. Planning for the future operation is usually set out in the form of a business plan.

If a substantial application is being made for Lottery funding, a business plan is automatically required by the Lottery distributors, but they may also require a business plan when small amounts are requested if they want to be reassured about the viability of the operation after the building work is complete.

A business plan is essentially the umbrella under which can be gathered the detailed action plans, policies and strategies relating to the different aspects of the organisation - exhibitions, education, marketing,

equal opportunities, fund-raising, etc. All of these separate documents are normally included as appendices, so that the business plan itself can take an overall view of the management and funding of the whole operation.

FORMAT

The Business Plan is one of the three documents normally produced during the Definition Phase (the other two are the project plan and the technical brief). Whilst a Project Plan allows you to demonstrate how the capital project will be managed and financed until completion, the Business Plan shows how the completed building will be run and funded afterwards. It is important not to conflate the two types of plan or to confuse administrative and financial arrangements which are different in nature. In general, they need to be kept separate, the exception being the combined balance sheet, income and expenditure account and cash-flow statement which show the impact of the project on your cash flow for the period of design and construction.

Because the three documents are concerned with distinct aspects of the capital project, each can be written to complement the other two. However, each should also be written so that it

can be understood without reference to the others, which may mean that there will be some repetition, especially at the beginning where the context and background of the organisation are summarised.

Since the Business Plan grows out of the project description, the format and substance of the introductory parts can follow the structure of the earlier document, expanding on the content where appropriate:

location:
Castle Museum and Art Gallery, Nottingham.

architect:
Stuart Hodgkinson for Derek Latham Associates.

description:
Cafe with furniture - doors, counters and other fittings - by Nicholas Pryke.

photograph:
Reproduced courtesy of Nottingham Castle Museum and Art Gallery.

- title page;

- table of contents;

- executive summary, to outline why the Business Plan has been prepared (e.g. in relation to the capital project), to report its conclusions and to present an overview of the rest of the document;

- glossary of definitions and explanations;

- methodology;

- references and acknowledgements;

- background;

- objectives: expanding on the paragraph in the Project Description by setting out, in particular, your aims for growth and change in the short term (the next 5 years), medium term (5-10 years) and long term (over 10 years), in relation to the image you intend to project and the functions you intend to provide, and in relation to your ambitions for the size and future performance of the organisation; it should set out why these objectives are important, what the overriding priorities are, and what might be the alternatives.

PROGRAMMES AND ACTIVITIES

This paragraph would describe the range and scope of exhibitions and other activities (especially where new work is proposed). It would refer to the appendices for details (including costs) of actual programmes, which might include some or all of the following:

- commissioning and/or purchasing works of art after the end of the capital project;

- exhibitions, including touring;

- lending;

- artist-in-residence schemes;

- selling;

- publishing.

THE MARKET

This paragraph might amplify the paragraph in the Project Description, but then set out an overall approach to access, for informing and attracting current and potential visitors and users, referring to the appendices for the specific policies and programmes in relation to some or all of the following:

- customer care;

- educational activities within the building;

- research facilities;

- outreach activities in other sites;

- marketing;

- retailing;

- catering.

It might set out objectives and priorities in the short and longer term for these cultural, educational and social services.

ADMINISTRATIVE IMPLICATIONS

This section would be concerned with the consequences for managing the new facilities, including the staff and procedures required to organise the exhibitions, to administer the building and its services, and to promote and publicise its activities. Extra staff may be needed to use or supervise new education spaces or study areas. A marketing strategy that defines the catchment area from which visitors will be drawn and outlines the methods by which exhibitions and events will be publicised and promoted, must be backed with sufficient human and financial resources to be realistic and credible. This part of the Business Plan would indicate where key skills are already available in-house, where they need to be recruited and when this will be done. It would refer to the appendices for the details of:

- staff structure, present and future;

- job specifications, current and proposed, recruitment policy (e.g. equal opportunities);

- training policy (e.g. customer care, disability awareness, health and safety).

FACILITIES MANAGEMENT

After a major building project, it is usually important to nominate and train an existing member of staff or recruit a building or facilities manager, with overall responsibility for understanding the building, monitoring its performance, ensuring that it works efficiently and implementing a maintenance programme. The Royal Institution of Chartered Surveyors, for instance, recommends that 1% of the value of a building should be spent on maintenance each year. The responsibilities of such a person might include:

- devising a long-term strategy for routine repairs and maintenance as well as one-off renovations and extensions;

- administering a budget for maintenance and renewals, to maintain the condition of a building on which so much has recently been invested, as well as to reduce the risk of disruption and unexpected expenditure on emergency repairs;

- ensuring that there is a good working environment, which matches the culture of the organisation;

- enforcing statutory requirements e.g. for Health and Safety;

- checking the performance of heating and lighting systems against the targets set in the brief, especially where energy efficiency is a factor, and arranging for improvements where necessary;

- monitoring the internal environment, maintaining records and preparing reports for committees or potential lenders, to show that the gallery can provide the right conditions for high-value loans;

- instituting a preventive regime of good housekeeping, to reduce the risk of fire by regular cleaning and waste disposal and by the proper use of equipment;

- training invigilators or attendants, and briefing them before each exhibition, on routine matters as well as emergencies;

- devising a key-holding policy for controlling access, in order to keep visitors from unauthorised access to offices, stores and exhibition areas during turnaround periods, and in order to allow service access to exhibition galleries without compromising other areas;

- devising a closing-down procedure, to identify and eliminate fire hazards, locate members of the public or staff who intentionally or otherwise have failed to leave, ensure that all windows and doors are properly secured, identify wear and tear, etc.;

- keeping an equipment register with maintenance records and inspection certificates;

- preparing a fire precautions manual, which sets out a plan of action in the event of fire in terms of calling the fire brigade, restricting the spread of fire and evacuating the building;

- managing storage, which will never be sufficient if the space is misused.

Security can be a major consideration for exhibition galleries. There is little point in incurring capital expenditure to meet strict requirements during the silent hours, in terms of a strong external perimeter and an effective Intruder Detection System, if the exhibition is vulnerable during opening hours because it is only occasionally supervised by a receptionist, secretary or sales person. Unlike displays from permanent collections, each exhibition begins with a different level of risk - from theft, vandalism, accidental damage, etc. - and it may take some time for invigilators to become fully familiar with an installation and aware of exhibits that are particularly at risk.

COST FORECASTS

This part of the Business Plan is concerned with the revenue consequences of operating the new building, in effect translating the information about activities, users and building into financial projections. It would identify, quantify and evaluate the costs, benefits and uncertainties of operating, maintaining, powering and securing the new facilities. These projections might be based on models elsewhere of organisations of a similar size to the proposed building, in order to provide realistic estimates of the new or incremental costs associated with the new building, its staffing requirements and new or extended programmes. Wherever possible, evidence should be quoted, to demonstrate the basis of estimates. Revenue projections are normally given for a period of five years after the building has opened to demonstrate how the organisation has settled down. This part will be supported by appendices with details of:

- expenditure in each cost centre, perhaps as part of the description of individual programmes;
- five-year budget listing cost centres and producing a total expenditure for each year.

FUNDING ARRANGEMENTS

This part will set out the level of income required from earnings, sponsorship and grant-aid to sustain the building, staff, programmes and services and where this money will be raised. For the Lottery distributors, information on funding arrangements will provide some assurance that resources are available to meet the cost of the building for a reasonable period after the end of the building project. It might compare what happens now and what should happen afterwards. Again, income projections should cover a period of five years after the building has opened, to show that the funding stream is continuing. This part will be supported by appendices with details of:

- income from each activity, again possibly as part of the description of individual programmes, but supported by evidence justifying each assumption;
- five-year budget listing sources of income and producing an estimate of total income for each year;
- fund-raising strategy, including previous fund-raising experience and any professional support.

SENSITIVITY ANALYSIS

Scale and ambition must be balanced with what is affordable, and proposed expenditure will need to be reduced to accord with the resources available. Such reductions may then affect the viability of the organisation and undermine the reasons for the capital project in the first place. A sensitivity analysis, usually set out in tabular form, can be used to identify major uncertainties, possible variations within each uncertainty, the level of risk associated with each and the impact of each variation. In a sensitivity analysis, each key assumption that is subject to uncertainty (e.g. grant-aid levels, income from sales, sponsorship for exhibitions) works upwards from the minimum level needed for the project to be viable.

APPENDICES

Appendices can be used to provide detailed information which has been summarised elsewhere in the Business Plan, and to include relevant reports, references and promotional literature. They might also include supporting data - diagrams, tables, charts, maps and photographs. In addition to the items listed above, appendices might include the following:

- organisation chart, showing the governing body and management;
- brief details of any non-executive directors and trustees;
- qualifications and skills of senior management and key employees;
- list of external advisers and consultants who have contributed directly to the preparation of the Business Plan;
- any consultants' reports which have been used as source material in preparing the Business Plan, and to which reference may need to be made;
- detailed income and expenditure, cashflow and balance sheet projections.

technical brief

PURPOSE

The primary purpose of the Technical Brief is to describe your requirements clearly and simply so that your Architect is able to design a suitable building. This Brief, which is distinct from a consultant's brief (◄◄ consultants), is a description of what the building will be used for and by whom. It sets out the needs that a capital project will answer, in terms of rectifying shortcomings and/or meeting new requirements. The design of the building will be based on and evolve from the Brief. The Brief has additional or secondary purposes: it is used to establish a consensus of client, stakeholders and users and to record their agreement about the sort of building and facilities required; it is used for reviewing design proposals, and it is used for evaluating the completed building.

One of your responsibilities is to choose designers and contractors with the skills to translate ideas into a building of the right quality within an appropriate time-scale and for an agreed and planned cost. Another - and possibly the most important - of your responsibilities is to communicate your needs to the design team. Briefing is this process and is crucial for the design team's understanding of the building which you require.

The Technical Brief is sometimes called the final architectural programme because it contains the precise instructions which are addressed specifically to the architect. It corresponds to Stage D in the RIBA Plan of Work (◄◄ planning the project), and should contain all the available information from which the design team can produce a solution that will give the best balance of quality, cost and time. It will have developed gradually from the project description, whose technical parts will have expanded into detailed requirements. However, despite its title, the Technical Brief will consist of much more than a list of quantitative data. Beyond a mere schedule of accommodation or a factual description of the spaces needed, it must communicate your aspirations and the qualities you require from the building. It will contain many qualitative requirements, developed from the earliest Vision statement and will have taken over much of the background information from the Project Description, so that your Architect appreciates the context and understands the thinking behind your various requirements.

WRITING THE BRIEF

In rare cases, briefing might be completely oral, but it will usually be formalised in writing so that you and your Architect have an agreed set of instructions. These instructions are also available to the wide range of people who are involved in any building project and who all must understand your vision and combine effectively to meet your unique needs.

The written brief needs time and attention, if consultants and contractors are to understand your aims and objectives in order that they can be successfully translated into a design and a building. One person should have sole responsibility for co-ordinating the brief, acting as the main point of contact with all the staff, users (including special needs groups) and consultants. Although the Project Leader should retain overall editorial control, a consultant may be delegated some or all of the meticulous process of listing areas of need, describing them in detail, co-ordinating different inputs and identifying points of conflict. The latter might be an architect whose speciality is assisting clients to determine and describe their building needs. Such a person can make an objective and creative study of your needs and the needs of your users, and will understand their implications in terms of the design of buildings. A short-term consultancy can be the most effective way to interpret your requirements and translate them into a formal brief, especially when a design competition is planned.

Briefs can be vastly different in length and detail. Despite its name, the Brief is rarely a single short document. It may start out on the proverbial back of an envelope but will usually go through many versions, and its detail and complexity will vary from project to project. Developing the Brief is a continuous and iterative process which can be creative and stimulating. However, it can also be disorganised and even chaotic, because of the many different inputs at different times, and may eventually be expensive if important aspects are overlooked. The Brief will be subject to repeated refinements and revisions as the project develops, so it is vital that there is always one authoritative document which records the current state of thinking about all requirements for the new building. Each draft should be numbered and dated, so that those involved can check whether they have the most recent version.

Logically, the Definition, Design and Construction phases would succeed each other, one being completed before the other starts. In fact, the Brief is

rarely completed before design starts, and the architect's proposals can often clarify and amplify the Brief, if early design work helps to refine objectives and criteria and to identify problems. After the Architect has been chosen, the Brief usually evolves over an extended period in parallel to the design process itself, as the Architect responds to more precise instructions from you and as you respond to the proposals from the Architect. During this period, the Architect seeks clarification, explores alternative approaches, and sets out creative and technical solutions. Influenced by budget, site, legal restraints, user requirements, technical feasibility and so on, the Project Description is revised and refined by the design team into a set of instructions which you will eventually be able to approve. The advantages of this method are that it gives time for bonding between yourself and your Architect, helps the Architect to get a feeling for the project and involves you in a process with which creative people usually feel at home. Its disadvantage is that the process after the Architect has been appointed can be time-consuming.

At some point, it will be agreed to "freeze" the Brief, so that detailed design can go ahead. Once the Brief is agreed, the Project Leader should impose stringent controls to prevent later additions or changes of mind, other than the minimal or the absolutely essential.

FORMAT

The Technical Brief is one of the three documents normally produced during the Definition Phase (the other two are the business plan and the project plan). Because these documents are concerned with distinct aspects of the capital project, each can be written to complement the other two. However, each should also be written so that it can be understood without reference to the others, which may mean that there will be some repetition, especially at the beginning where the context and background of the organisation are summarised. Since the Technical Brief grows out of the Project Description, the format and substance of the introductory parts can follow the structure of the earlier document, expanding on the content where appropriate:

- title page;

- table of contents;

- executive summary, presenting an overview of the rest of the document, drawing attention to the significance of the capital project and summarising the main points and conclusions;

- glossary of definitions and explanations;

- methodology;

- references and acknowledgements;

- background.

OBJECTIVES: EXHIBITIONS AND OTHER ACTIVITIES

This would be a more detailed description than that contained in the Project Description, of your programmes after the completion of the capital project, noting the character, scale and special requirements of exhibitions, and the atmosphere required for them. This paragraph should highlight:

- the characteristics of the exhibition programme, e.g. whether it is cutting-edge or (mixing metaphors) mainstream, issue- or personality-based, visitor- or artist-led;

- any changes of emphasis or developments in the exhibition programme and/or its supporting activities which the capital project is intended to deliver;

- examples of particular exhibitions and other activities that will have specific requirements in terms of size, security, educational provision, etc.;

- other factors which have direct implications for the design, e.g. how regularly exhibitions will change, why storage is required, the implications of touring, the relationship with any permanent collection, any activities involving artists or for children, other functions the space(s) may be used for, etc.

OBJECTIVES: THE MARKET

Some or all of the recommendations of an access audit (of an existing building) or access appraisal (of outline proposals) would also be incorporated here.

OVERALL REQUIREMENTS

The following checklist includes a range of factors to be discussed at this stage, if they have not already been discussed in the Project Description.

- any physical or operational constraints, e.g. if the location is already fixed, the size of the site and the layout of existing rooms or buildings and any listed status or planning restrictions;

location:
Centre for Visual Arts, Cardiff.

architect:
BDP/Robertson Francis Partnership.

description:
First-floor: interactive gallery.

photograph:
Patricia Aithie, reproduced courtesy of CVA: Centre for Visual Arts.

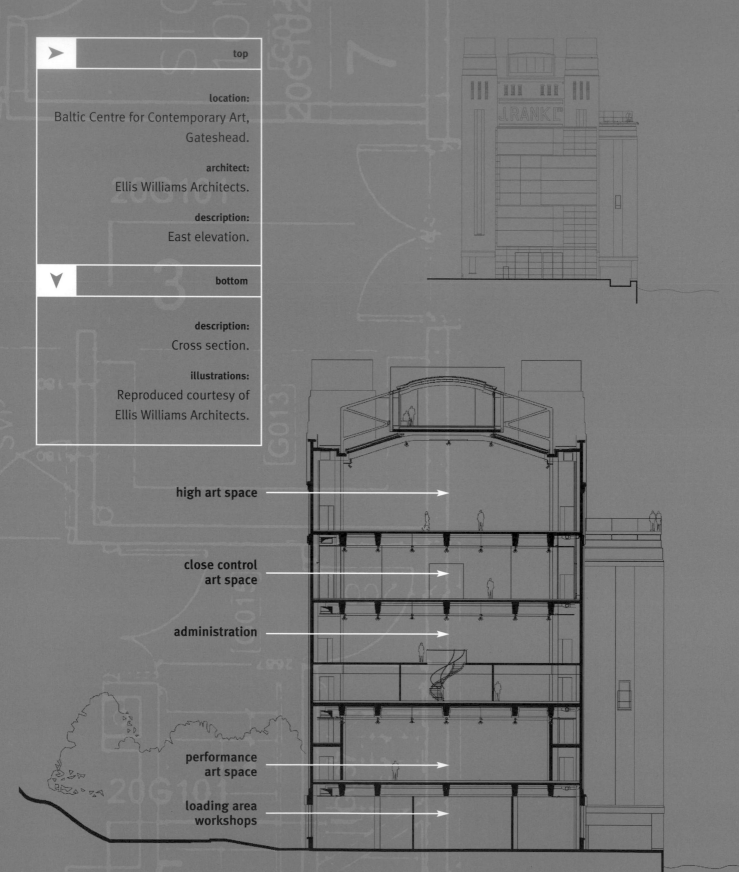

> top

location:
Baltic Centre for Contemporary Art, Gateshead.

architect:
Ellis Williams Architects.

description:
East elevation.

∨ bottom

description:
Cross section.

illustrations:
Reproduced courtesy of Ellis Williams Architects.

high art space

close control art space

administration

performance art space

loading area workshops

- the environmental impact of the building, and the use of external spaces, e.g. landscaping, public art, parking, service access, etc.;

- the general character required of the building, in terms of quality of design, finishes, flexibility, durability, proportions, lighting, security, etc.;

- an inclusive approach to access, so that the building is pleasant and comfortable for all visitors;

- viability, in terms of providing space for services that will help to generate income, e.g. additional space outside the exhibition areas may be required for receptions and functions for the private sector;

- operating forecasts, considerations of energy efficiency or 'life cycle' costs, ease and economy of maintenance, repair, cleaning, minimising the costs of staffing and insurance, possible changes of use over the life of the building;

- time-scale: starting-date and its significance, site availability, milestone dates and their significance, approval process, completion date (whether partial completion or hand-over);

- budget or financial ceiling for the project overall, including fees for initial studies, public art programme, etc., to ensure that all consultants are aware of the finite nature of the capital budget;

- an indication how the project will be financed, e.g. where capital funding is sought from the private sector, an essential requirement for an existing building may be that the project includes an element of prestigious 'new build' which is highly visible and easily accessible from the entrance to the building.

SCHEDULE OF ACCOMMODATION

This section would expand the summary of overall volume and minimum facilities in the Project Description, and would include:

- detailed descriptions of the space for each activity (including occasional and ancillary activities), outlining its purpose and how it might be used;

- indications of shape or layout;

- description of services (lighting, heating, control of humidity, etc.) required;

- standards and procedures for maintenance of the building once completed;

- relationships and links between spaces with related uses, or between public and staff areas, including requirements such as direct access to the outside;

- potential for expansion or extension.

For detailed guidance, ➤➤ PART TWO.

EVALUATION

This paragraph might be based on that in the Project Description.

APPENDICES

Appendices can be used to provide detailed information which has been summarised elsewhere in the Technical Brief, and to include relevant reports, references and promotional literature. In addition to the items listed above, appendices might include the following:

- contact list of project leader, relevant members of staff and Board, plus external advisers and consultants who have contributed directly to the preparation of the technical brief;

- any consultants' reports which have been used as source material in preparing the Technical Brief, and to which the Design Team may need to refer;

- technical specifications;

- relevant diagrams, tables, charts, maps and photographs.

part two: defining the performance
you want from the building

◄ | **opposite**

location:
Surrey Institute of Art & Design

architect:
Snell Associates.

description:
External view of the
Foyer Gallery at night.

photograph:
Max Alexander.

checklist of requirements

The following checklist is arranged in four broad categories - customer care, displaying exhibitions, servicing exhibitions and monitoring and controlling the internal environment.

These categories are not watertight compartments, and considerations in one category will have a consequence in one or another. However, for reasons of space, a question generally only appears once. As a result, a question about the effect of the screens system on the lighting system in the second category is not complemented by a question about the layout of the lighting system taking into account the positions of movable screens in the final category.

The questions are mostly written in the future tense on the assumption that the checklist will be used mainly at the outset, to help you to draw up your requirements and brief your Architect.

The checklist is arranged as a series of closed questions. Each question can be answered with a tick or a cross, but a simple 'yes' or 'no' should then prompt a further question. If the answer is 'no', it should lead you to ask whether this particular feature should indeed be included. It may have been discounted for policy or financial reasons, but the checklist will help you to make an active choice rather than overlook something important. If instead the answer is 'yes', then it should lead you to ask whether you have taken the necessary action and how you will achieve the required result.

Against each question is a page reference, so the checklist provides an alternative way into Part Two of **designing galleries**, whose broad headings are otherwise arranged simply in alphabetical order.

REQUIREMENTS	PAGE(S)	CHECK
PUBLIC PROFILE/CUSTOMER CARE		☑
Has there been any public consultation?	127	
Will the character of the location influence the design of the building and the nature of the activities?	127	
Will the building have an influence on the local environment?	127	
Will planning approvals be necessary?	127	
Will the building be clearly visible?	127 128	
Will the main frontage have a distinctive character?	127	

REQUIREMENTS	PAGE(S)	CHECK
PUBLIC PROFILE/CUSTOMER CARE cont'd...		☑
Will artists help to define how the gallery presents itself?	128	
Will signs be provided outside the building?	127	
Will windows allow passers-by outside to see what is on show inside?	186	
Will any shop be visible from outside the building?	153	
Will pedestrian access be straightforward?	128	

REQUIREMENTS	PAGE(S)	CHECK
PUBLIC PROFILE/CUSTOMER CARE cont'd...		☑
Will access for people arriving by public transport be straightforward?	128	
Will access for people arriving by car, including provision for disabled people and parking, be straightforward?	128 130	
Will the entrance be clearly visible and distinctive?	124	
Will it allow people of all ages and abilities to move easily into and out of the building in normal situations?	122	
Will it have sufficient space for people to enter or leave without encountering congestion?	124	
Will public access be separate from the place where works of art are brought into or taken out of the building and other forms of service access?	145	
Will the design of the space, furnishings and finishes help visitors to orientate themselves?	124 125	
Will the entrance(s) have sufficient information for all visitors to appreciate what facilities and activities are available to them?	124 151-152	
Will toilets/washrooms be sufficient to cope with the maximum anticipated level of use?	117 125	
Will toilets/washrooms be accessible to and usable by disabled people?	117	
Will toilets/washrooms be suitable for children as well as adults?	117	

REQUIREMENTS	PAGE(S)	CHECK
PUBLIC PROFILE/CUSTOMER CARE cont'd...		☑
Will there be baby-changing and feeding facilities for both male and female carers?	125	
Will there be a cloakroom which includes space for removing and replacing outdoor clothing?	117 125	
Will it be able to cope with the maximum anticipated level of use?	117	
If it is to consist of self-service lockers, will they be accessible to and usable by people with disabilities, and suitable for children as well as adults?	117 125	
Will specialist advice be taken on the design and operation of a retail outlet?	153	
Will the layout of the shop allow space between display units for wheelchair-users and parents with pushchairs?	154	
Will material displayed on shelves be easily accessible to visitors?	154	
Will the building be designed for more than one circulation pattern?	152 163	
Will the building be designed to help visitors to understand where they are?	151-152	
Will signs be provided to help visitors to understand where they are?	151-152	
Will public circulation routes throughout the building meet the requirements for inclusive access and independent use by disabled people?	150	

REQUIREMENTS	PAGE(S)	CHECK
PUBLIC PROFILE/CUSTOMER CARE cont'd...		☑
Will changes of level meet the requirements for inclusive access and independent use by disabled people?	150-151	
Will corridors and stairways be wide enough to cope with the expected numbers of visitors?	151	
Will corridors and stairways be designed to enhance the quality of the experience?	151	
Will any door need to be wider and/or higher than standard ?	111, 116	
Will spaces and finishes feel welcoming?	116 124,125	
Will furnishing and fittings be designed for the comfort and pleasure of all visitors?	151-152	
Will there be comfortable seating, suitable for young and elderly people?	125 152	
Will seating be removable, to allow maximum flexibility in the use of a space?	117	
Will there be facilities for guide dogs?	125	
Will there be a low-level public pay-phone?	125	
Will windows be provided to allow visitors to look out?	186	
Will ventilation be adequate for human comfort for the maximum occupancy of each space, especially when doors and windows are shut and blinds are closed?	92 116	

REQUIREMENTS	PAGE(S)	CHECK
PUBLIC PROFILE/CUSTOMER CARE cont'd...		☑
Will doors be designed so that people can see them and be seen from the other side?	111	
Will exhibition area(s) require more than one entrance?	164	
Will entrance(s) to exhibition area(s) provide a comfortable transition between daylight and any reduced light levels in the galleries?	122 124	
Will there be an induction loop system and/or infra-red hearing provision?	116-117 191	
Will there be space to allow educational work and interpretation to take place in the galleries?	113	
Will there be facilities to enable educational work and interpretation to take place in the galleries?	114	
Will cloakrooms, toilets and catering facilities be adequate for group visits?	117	
Will space be designated and facilities designed for educational work and interpretation to take place outside the exhibition areas?	113 116	
Will these designated educational spaces cope with the full range of education activities?	116-118	
Will there be a kitchen or food preparation area for the use of organised groups?	117	
Will there be a space for visiting groups to eat packed lunches?	116	

REQUIREMENTS	PAGE(S)	CHECK
PUBLIC PROFILE/CUSTOMER CARE cont'd...		☑
Will a 'wet' or 'dirty' space be required for educational activities?	117-118	
Will a 'dry' or 'clean' space be required for educational activities?	117	
Will a space be designed for the use of an artist or craftsperson in residence?	118	
Will a library or resource centre be provided for self-motivated study?	118	
Will people of all ages and abilities be able to escape from the building quickly in an emergency?	109 111 133-134	
Will each space in the building be wired for visible and audible emergency alarms?	133	
Will each space in the building be fully wired for the public address system?	116 191	
Will doors be designed so that people of all ages and abilities can move easily out of the building?	111	
Will fittings and equipment help occupants to escape as quickly as possible in an emergency?	133-134	
Will emergency illumination be provided in all public and circulation areas?	134	
Will the content and location of signs for non-automatic fire-fighting equipment, emergency escape routes and fire exits meet local and statutory requirements?	133	

REQUIREMENTS	PAGE(S)	CHECK
PUBLIC PROFILE/CUSTOMER CARE cont'd...		☑
Will emergency escape arrangements be adequate for the estimated numbers of users and for the number of floors?	134	
Will emergency exit doors have push bars or other local release mechanisms?	134	
Will smoke be extracted in the event of fire?	134	
DISPLAYING EXHIBITIONS		☑
Will the proposed exhibition spaces be suitable for the full range of exhibitions envisaged?	163-164	
Has their area and volume been determined by the exhibitions that can be realistically afforded?	163-164	
Will the size and character of the exhibition areas and the treatment of space reflect the gallery's vision?	163	
Will two or more exhibition areas be required?	164	
Will it be necessary to install or dismantle an exhibition whilst another is open to the public?	164	
Will separate exhibition areas be connected or related to each other in some way?	164	
Will flexibility of use be important?	164-165	
Will ease of supervision determine how space is used?	165 167	

REQUIREMENTS	PAGE(S)	CHECK
DISPLAYING EXHIBITIONS cont'd...		☑
Will display materials have inherent fire-retarding characteristics or require the use of appropriate solutions?	182	
Will all surfaces used for display purposes provide a suitable background for a wide variety of works of art?	178	
Will it be possible to fix exhibits directly to all surfaces used for display purposes?	181	
Will all surfaces used for display purposes support heavy loads safely?	181-182	
Will it be possible to paint easily all surfaces used for display purposes?	182	
Will it be possible to maintain easily all surfaces used for display purposes?	181-182	
Will display surfaces be as expansive and uninterrupted as possible?	178 180	
Will external walls incorporate a vapour barrier?	182	
Will the heating system be unobtrusive?	92	
Will sensors be unobtrusive?	95	
Will natural light or artificial lighting be used?	184 186	
Will windows be designed to reduce any security hazard?	187	
Will glass be chosen to maintain the colour rendering of natural light?	184	

REQUIREMENTS	PAGE(S)	CHECK
DISPLAYING EXHIBITIONS cont'd...		☑
Will the components and surrounds of the glazing system be chosen to maintain the colour rendering of natural light?	184	
Will the colour of internal surfaces help to maintain the colour rendering of natural light?	186	
Will windows include back-projection screens which can be used to show projected work.	186	
Will some or all windows be permanently blocked up to create longer lengths of display surface?	178 186	
Will black-out blinds or hinged or detachable panels be used to close windows to eliminate natural lighting, for display or conservation reasons, on a temporary basis?	157 184	
Will movable screens be designed as an integral part of the gallery?	160	
Will they be used to provide additional hanging space?	160	
Will they have surfaces compatible with other display surfaces in the gallery?	160	
Will they be used to divide the gallery into a series of rooms?	160 165 167-168	
Will the screens be designed to look like walls?	160	
Will adequate storage be provided for occasions when the screens are not in use?	161	

REQUIREMENTS	PAGE(S)	CHECK
DISPLAYING EXHIBITIONS cont'd...		☑
Will the screens be easy and safe for the gallery staff to move?	160	
Will they be easy and safe for the gallery staff to install and dismantle?	160	
Will they be stable?	160	
Will their layout take into account the needs of emergency egress?	168	
Will it be possible to maintain high levels of invigilation when the screens are installed?	161 165	
Will their layout take into account the Intruder Detection System?	165	
Will their layout take into account the lighting system?	160	
Will their layout take into account the positions of outlets for power and other wired services?	160	
Will their layout take into account the needs of environmental control?	160 168	
Will the floor be capable of sustaining the weight of likely exhibits?	137	
Will the floor surface in each exhibition gallery be level for self-stable screens, plinths and showcases?	137	
Will the floor include anchor points for fixing the supports for a screen system?	137	
Will the floor surface in each exhibition gallery provide a level, smooth and uninterrupted surface?	136-137	

REQUIREMENTS	PAGE(S)	CHECK
DISPLAYING EXHIBITIONS cont'd...		☑
Will the floor be designed to be a possible display surface?	137	
Will it be possible to screw directly into the floor and to fill the screw-holes and repair the surface subsequently?	137	
Will it be possible to change the colour of the floor surface easily and inexpensively?	137	
Will floor surfaces be scratch – and water-resistant?	137	
Will the floor be wired for power?	137	
Will it be wired for cabled services?	137	
Will it be easy to clean?	136	
Will children be expected to sit on the floor?	115 138	
Will the ceiling function as the background for the display of works of art?	107	
Will it be designed to support safely the weight of exhibits and equipment?	107	
Will it be used for supporting a screen system?	107	
Will the ceiling be wired for power and a variety of cabled services?	107	
Will the boarding material allow dimmers, switches, sockets and cabling to be disguised?	182	
Will switches and controls be secure but conveniently located ?	102-103	

REQUIREMENTS	PAGE(S)	CHECK
DISPLAYING EXHIBITIONS cont'd...		☑
Will it be possible to supply electrical power to any point within the volume of the exhibition space?	189 191	
Will there be space and power to add new equipment as and when required?	191-192	
Will it be possible to supply data to any point in the exhibition space?	191-192	
Will sockets and outlets be designed and located to be as unobtrusive as possible?	189	
Will there be a secure and ventilated control room for electrical equipment that is in use?	192	
SERVICING EXHIBITIONS		☑
Have the gallery's technical staff or external consultants advised on the type of space and equipment required?	193	
Will the building be accessible by roads that are adequate for the likely size and weight of vehicle?	175	
Will access for exhibition deliveries and collections be separate from public access and other forms of service access?	175	
Will there be space outside the building for vehicles to manoeuvre?	175-176	
Will the loading area allow vehicles to approach as close as possible to the building?	145	

REQUIREMENTS	PAGE(S)	CHECK
SERVICING EXHIBITIONS cont'd...		☑
Will there be space outside the building for vehicles to park safely and securely?	175-176	
Will a bell or intercom be fitted at the service access?	176	
Will the loading area be big enough to handle the largest crates that the gallery is likely to receive?	147-148	
Will window openings be designed to allow very large work to be moved in and out through them?	186	
Will any move of works of art from building to vehicle (and vice versa) be protected from the weather?	147	
Will the place where works of art are brought into or carried out of the building be secure, both in use and when the building is closed?	147-148	
Will the dimensions of every internal opening allow for the maximum size envisaged?	104	
Will changes of direction allow for the maximum size envisaged?	104	
Will floor loadings between any starting and any finishing point allow for the maximum weight envisaged?	104-105	
Will lifts, hoists and other provision for changes of level allow for maximum size and weight envisaged?	105	
Will the proposed storage and art-handling areas cope with the full range of the gallery's activities?	170-171	

REQUIREMENTS	PAGE(S)	CHECK
SERVICING EXHIBITIONS cont'd...		☑
Will separate spaces be needed for different aspects of the management of works of art in and out of the building?	170	
Will sufficient space be allocated for storage of works of art?	172	
Will a holding area be required for acclimatisation?	171	
Will a registration area be required for unpacking and re-packing?	171	
Will enough space be allocated for storing crates and packing materials?	172-173	
Will floors be level and durable, for ease of movement of handling and carrying equipment?	170	
Will works of art be stored separately from other materials and equipment?	170	
Will there a secure store for electrical equipment that is not in use?	117 192	
Will sufficient space be allocated for storage of items other than works of art and their packing materials?	170	
Will storage areas be close to the areas where materials will be needed?	170	
Will the layout of storage ensure events and activities are not interrupted if materials have to be retrieved?	117	

REQUIREMENTS	PAGE(S)	CHECK
SERVICING EXHIBITIONS cont'd...		☑
Will the design of the gallery shop allow for the storage of stock?	154	
Will the design of the gallery shop allow for the movement of stock?	154	
Will the design of the gallery shop be planned for the convenience and safety of the staff?	154	
Will there be a cleaner's store, used exclusively for equipment and materials for cleaning, on each floor?	117	
Will all storage areas be actively managed?	171	
Will any activities - education, retail, etc - require a lockable and equipped office area distinct from any central administration?	117 154	
Will the proposed workshop(s) cope with the full range of the gallery's activities?	193	
Will a 'dirty' workshop be required?	193	
Will a 'clean' workshop be required?	193	
Will the proposed workshop(s) meet health and safety requirements?	193	
Will public circulation routes be designed to allow service access to galleries that are closed for exhibition installations?	104-105 152	
Will the loading area be easily accessible to the exhibition spaces?	145	

REQUIREMENTS	PAGE(S)	CHECK
SERVICING EXHIBITIONS cont'd...		☑
Will the floor surface in every exhibition gallery be suitable for access gantries and art-handling equipment?	136-137	
Will any door need to be wider and/or higher than normal, in order to provide access for exhibits?	111	
Will each space in the building be fully wired for electrical power?	116 191	
Will each space in the building be wired into the telephone system?	116 191	
MONITORING & CONTROLLING THE INTERNAL ENVIRONMENT		☑
Will the layout of the building help to reduce the risk of an outbreak of fire?	133	
Will the materials used in the building help to reduce the risk of an outbreak of fire?	133	
Will the management of the building help to reduce the risk of an outbreak of fire?	133	
Will the Fire Detection System detect fire as early as possible?	133	
Will the Fire Detection System set off audible and visible alarms in all areas?	133	
Will the Fire Detection System meet the minimum requirements for the Government Indemnity Scheme?	133	
Will the layout of the building restrict the spread of any fire?	133	

REQUIREMENTS	PAGE(S)	CHECK
MONITORING & CONTROLLING THE INTERNAL ENVIRONMENT cont'd...		☑
Will the materials of the building restrict the spread of any fire?	133	
Will doors be designed to discourage the spread of fire?	111	
Will the fire-fighting equipment control an outbreak of fire as soon as possible?	135	
Will the staff be trained in procedures for controlling an outbreak of fire?	134-135	
Will loans be requested from national collections?	139	
Will applications be made to the Government Indemnity Scheme?	139	
Will the building be designed to meet the basic requirements of the Government Indemnity Scheme?	139	
Will the shell of the building be secure?	130	
Will all windows, including those at high level and roof lights, be provided with security grilles or glazing to deter and delay unauthorised entry?	158 187	
Will external doors, supporting frames and locks be capable of resisting forcible entry?	109	
Will an Intruder Detection System be used to detect an attack on any part of the building?	109 130 187	

REQUIREMENTS	PAGE(S)	CHECK
MONITORING & CONTROLLING THE INTERNAL ENVIRONMENT cont'd...		☑
Will key-holding procedures be designed to prevent unauthorised access?	111	
Will each space in the building be covered by the Intruder Detection System?	116 165 167	
Will circulation areas be designed to avoid hidden corners, unused spaces and dead-ends?	151	
Will each entrance be designed to allow access to be controlled when required?	122	
Will each space in the building be wired for CCTV coverage?	165 191	
Will the security of handling and storage areas for works of art be at least as good as that in the galleries?	170-171	
Will the shop be secure, both in use and when the building is closed?	154	
Will the ceiling include natural lighting ?	107	
Will measures be taken to minimise solar gain?	156 187	
Will light levels be restricted to a specified range?	143	
Will ultra-violet radiation be removed to an acceptable level?	99 142-143 156-157	
Will colour rendering be maintained?	101	

REQUIREMENTS	PAGE(S)	CHECK
MONITORING & CONTROLLING THE INTERNAL ENVIRONMENT cont'd...		☑
Will the duration of exposure to light be reduced?	143 157-158	
Will natural light be controlled using passive methods?	156-157	
Will windows be designed so that light does not fall on sensitive materials?	184	
Are capital resources sufficient to allow natural light to be controlled by mechanical means?	157	
Will revenue resources be sufficient to enable natural light to be controlled by mechanical means?	157	
Will the ceiling be used for the artificial lighting system?	107	
Will light be controlled by manual or automatic means?	102	
Will artificial lighting be the main means of lighting exhibitions, or will it supplement natural light?	99	
Will a uniformity ratio be specified?	101	
Will angles of incidence be specified?	101	
Will lamps be accessible, for cleaning, adjusting and maintenance?	102	
Will other lighting be required, for service and emergency use?	102	
Will light levels be monitored in storage and access routes as well as in display areas?	170	

REQUIREMENTS	PAGE(S)	CHECK
MONITORING & CONTROLLING THE INTERNAL ENVIRONMENT cont'd...		☑
Will lights normally be switched off in storage areas?	170-171	
Will exhibitions and loans depend on precise control of humidity?	95	
Will the building protect the interior from variations in temperature and humidity outdoors?	131	
Will passive features, such as insulation, be considered as well as (or instead of) active measures?	90-95	
Will a "quick-response" or a "slow-response" building be required?	91-92	
Will entrances provide an effective buffer between the external weather and controlled internal conditions?	122 124	
Will windows be sealed and draught-proofed?	187	
Will windows be double-glazed, especially with low-E glass?	187	
Will the environmental conditions for handling and storage areas for works of art be similar to those in the galleries?	170-171	
Will the ceiling be provided with thermal insulation?	107	
Will the heating system be economic to run as well as capable of meeting peak demands?	92	

REQUIREMENTS	PAGE(S)	CHECK
MONITORING & CONTROLLING THE INTERNAL ENVIRONMENT cont'd...		☑
Where precise environmental control is necessary, will the needs of works of art take priority over the comfort of human occupants in the 'art spaces'?	95	
Will the environmental control of spaces used for works of art be treated separately from catering, educational activities, cloakroom and other spaces used for visitors?	92 95	
Will complicated and expensive systems be restricted to areas that need a high level of control?	119 121	
Will different temperature ranges be fixed for different zones?	92 97	
Will different humidity ranges be fixed for different zones?	92 95	
Will doors be designed so that required conditions can be maintained in specific zones?	109	
Will it be possible to maintain required conditions 24 hours a day?	95	
Will the environmental control system take into account lighting, screens and other systems which may have an impact on its performance?	101 160	
Will the ceiling be used for the heating system?	107	
Will the floor be used for the heating system?	136	
Will heat recovery be considered?	92	

REQUIREMENTS	PAGE(S)	CHECK
MONITORING & CONTROLLING THE INTERNAL ENVIRONMENT cont'd...		☑
Will pipe work be kept to a minimum in all art-handling areas?	170-171	
Will temperature and relative humidity be monitored in all storage areas and access routes as well as in display areas?	140 170	
Will temperature and relative humidity be controlled within set parameters in all storage areas and access routes as well as in display areas?	140 170	
Will controls be effective 24 hours a day, whilst an exhibition is on the premises?	140-141	
Will procedures be introduced and staff trained to help to maintain environmental stability?	91	
Will it be possible to make records of temperature and relative humidity available to potential lenders?	95	
Will exhibitions and loans depend on reducing pollutants and particulates in the art spaces?	95-96	
Will the building protect the interior from poor air quality in the external environment?	131	
Will the floor surface be dust-free and cleaned easily without the use of solvents?	138	

REQUIREMENTS	PAGE(S)	CHECK
MONITORING & CONTROLLING THE INTERNAL ENVIRONMENT cont'd...		☑
Will noise levels from lifts, mechanical ventilation and other internal machinery be at an acceptable level?	96	
Will any walls require sound insulation to ensure that there is no sound-spill from noisy activities in an adjacent room?	116	
Will the windows require sound insulation, to control noise from the outside?	116	
Will any doors require sound insulation, to control noise from activities on the other side?	116	
Will the use of sound-absorbent materials be important for the gallery surfaces, to control noise generated by visitors?	107	
Will ventilation be sufficient to cool equipment?	92	
Will ventilation take into account lighting, screens and other systems which may have an impact on its performance?	99 161	
Will the ceiling be used for the ventilation system?	107	
Is energy efficiency a stated aim of the project?	101 119	
Has an energy audit been undertaken of any existing plant and equipment?	121	

REQUIREMENTS	PAGE(S)	CHECK
MONITORING & CONTROLLING THE INTERNAL ENVIRONMENT cont'd...		☑
Will an overall target be set for energy efficiency?	121	
Will there be ongoing energy surveys to assess energy use and to identify measures for cost – and energy – savings?	121	
Will insulation and other low-energy features be introduced to reduce energy consumption and to stabilise the gallery environment?	119	
Will electrical and mechanical equipment and systems be efficient to run?	119 121	
Will a life-cycle approach be taken?	101 119 121	
Has an integrated approach, using a computer-based Building Management System, been considered for security, lighting and heating and for monitoring energy use and consumption?	119 121	
Will monitoring systems receive sufficient investment?	95	
Will sensors be situated to be effective without being obtrusive?	95 180	
Will electrical and mechanical equipment and systems be reliable?	119 121	

REQUIREMENTS	PAGE(S)	CHECK
MONITORING & CONTROLLING THE INTERNAL ENVIRONMENT cont'd...		☑
Will complicated and expensive systems be restricted to areas that need a high level of control?	119 121	
Will electrical and mechanical equipment and systems be simple to operate?	95	
Will electrical and mechanical equipment and systems be simple to maintain?	95 119 121	
Will there be a maintenance plan?	63-64 121	
Will staff be trained to manage and maintain plant and equipment efficiently?	63-64 121	
Will budgets be sufficient to maintain building, plant and equipment?	63-64 121	

expanding the checklist

CHECKLIST

At the beginning of Part Two is a checklist of factors to bear in mind when thinking about the requirements for a gallery. Some of the items may be discounted for policy or financial reasons, but the purpose of the checklist is to ensure that this is an active choice rather than an oversight. Oversights carry the risk of disruptive or intrusive elements - ranging from power sockets to mobile humidifiers - being introduced at a later stage and at a higher cost.

Part Two expands on this checklist by discussing performance requirements for each item. The detail may help your organisation to reach a consensus of what is required before the Architect is brought in, saving the effort and cost of a consultant or the design team having to tease out this information over an extended period of time. Especially where the architect has little previous experience of the design of exhibition galleries, the checklist can also help to ensure that nothing is forgotten. A detailed brief does not guarantee a good building, but it should ensure that the resulting design will do the job you want - or lay the fault at the architect's door if it does not. Part Two should facilitate and shorten the time spent on oral briefings and explanatory discussions, but it must not short-circuit

or eliminate the critical process of bonding between yourself and your Architect.

Part Two does not deal with every possible form of provision. It excludes catering, because this is a specialised area which requires expert advice even more than retailing (which is included). It excludes any consideration of offices and supporting facilities, on the assumption that the staff of an existing organisation or the users of a future one will be asked to set out their requirements which they will know fairly precisely. Within the exhibition space itself, it discusses screens because of their quasi-architectural nature, but it excludes display cases and plinths because these have more to do with the design of exhibition installations. The factors discussed relate only to the visual arts and crafts. If the gallery will be used for other purposes (e.g. for film or performance), then you must look elsewhere for guidance on the facilities that might be required and decide how to reconcile the needs of different functions.

DEFINING PRIORITIES

Much of Part Two deals with the main components of an exhibition gallery (floor, wall, ceiling, doors, windows, etc.) from the point of view of a space shared

overleaf, page 87 >

location:
Kettle's Yard, Cambridge.

architect:
Bland, Brown & Cole.

description:
Installing the 'Antony Gormley' exhibition.

photograph:
Paul Allitt, reproduced courtesy of Kettle's Yard.

by art and people. This integrated approach takes as its starting point an assumption that each of the components will have a number of functions, each of which may be in conflict with one or more of the others. For example, doors need to be designed for disabled access, for security and for fire control; automatic doors can make a building more accessible but can play havoc with the internal conditions, causing discomfort to people inside and risking damage to exhibits. Recognising conflict is a step towards a solution, but there will be no single correct solution that balances all functions. You will need to make an informed judgement about your own priorities where conflicts do appear,

but the expanded checklist will help you by discussing the range of factors that should be considered.

An underlying theme in Part Two is that physical limitations impose restrictions on programme and practice. You need to understand fully the choices available to you, in order to decide whether their implications are worth tolerating in future or whether another location and/or increased capital investment would be preferable. For example, would the extra cost of providing access for works of art that is separate from the public entrance be justified by operational and financial savings, in terms of shorter turnaround periods between exhibitions and a greater degree of flexibility about the times of delivery and collection of exhibitions?

STANDARDS

Some of the models and examples in Part Two may appear too advanced and irrelevant for smaller organisations, but the general principles still hold. For example, a gallery may not have a dedicated loading bay, but it will still have to bear in mind considerations such as dimensions of door openings and changes of level and direction. Moreover, although many exhibitions depend solely on artists, dealers or private collectors, there may be occasions when a gallery will want to step back from the 'cutting edge' of contemporary practice and show less recent works borrowed from a public collection. These might be individual works on loan from a museum but they might equally be exhibitions toured by other organisations which have borrowed from such collections. Either way, museum standards of conservation and security apply, and loans from these sources will not be agreed if the venue cannot satisfy the lenders' requirements. If some of the standards are too high, then Part Two will at least help you to draw the line at the sort of exhibitions you can realistically envisage for your facilities and resources.

White Box	☐
Black Box	■
Strong Box	■

Part Two aims to help you to define what should be your priorities, by setting out examples of how briefs might be written for floor, wall, ceiling, doors, windows, etc. for three types of gallery. These types are characterised as a White Box, for the gallery which might show paintings from the last decades of the twentieth century; a Black Box for a gallery which would show digitally-based work and projected artworks, and a Strong Box for art before the late twentieth century. Many exhibition galleries will combine, with varying degrees of success, two or even all three functions, and you will need to come to your own conclusions about which types of provision you will want from your building project.

Notes ⓘ

The 'White Box', 'Black Box' and 'Strong Box' types are indicative only. They are provided for the sake of contrast and comparison, to illustrate alternatives ways of setting out requirements. It is not intended that you simply choose one type, and then extract the relevant paragraph from each section. In all cases, the different options should be examined in relation to your objectives and resources.

Where quantities and dimensions are quoted, they are for illustration only. They are shown in square brackets simply as a reminder that it must be the needs of the project that determine each and every detail.

REQUIREMENTS, NOT SOLUTIONS

A brief is a series of instructions to an external specialist, whether a lawyer, consultant, designer or - in the case of a capital project - the architect and the design team. A brief is necessary in part because most architects are not familiar with general requirements for exhibitions.

Some architectural practices have carried out a number of gallery refurbishments and conversions, and their experience can make a valuable contribution to the development of a project, but location, personalities, policies and funding make every project different. Even where an architect has already designed several galleries, a brief is necessary to describe in detail the particular needs of the proposed programme and activities, and to help the architect to understand why certain approaches are needed and what priority should be given to different requirements (especially where they overlap or conflict).

The ideal brief is one which identifies and defines all requirements but which yet allows the architect sufficient room for manoeuvre to produce a creative solution. Generally, it is preferable to avoid too prescriptive an approach. As far as possible, you should define the result or performance you require, and not suggest or recommend design solutions. Exhibition organisers who have lived with fluorescent lighting for years have to resist the temptation to specify a system such as track lighting or hardware such as spotlights. Specifying in this way restricts options, and may mean that the design team will be unable to meet the performance or cost

requirements of the brief. In any case, the design team is likely to be better informed about products coming onto the market through the architectural press. You may have only have seen examples from recent buildings which are already slightly out of date.

Your job is to define as precisely as possible what is expected from the building and to describe the purpose and performance of each space. Rather than specify that the walls should be 4.5 metres high, it is preferable to state that the display surfaces should be able to take framed works up to 3 metres in height and still leave ample space between the bottom edge and floor and the top edge and ceiling. One advantage of this approach is that this dimension can then be applied elsewhere, e.g. to the sizes of doors and lift openings. Another advantage is that, because it helps the design team to understand how the space is to be used, it encourages careful attention to detail and avoids the clutter of fittings which have so often spoilt display surfaces in the past.

You should describe spaces and facilities as dimensions and equipment only where there are very precise requirements and/or where there is detailed advice from a consultant

(e.g. on access or new technology). As far as possible, minimum acceptable standards should be quoted. Exact specifications may be necessary where precise control is necessary, and you should only insist on specific conditions where there is no alternative or where there is little latitude. Again, the required performance should be given rather than design solutions. For example, a requirement that light levels should be adjustable down to 50 lux is better than a suggestion that blinds are used on windows and dimmers are used on lighting circuits.

This functional approach allows the architect greater flexibility, and also ensures that statutory requirements can be met. It is then the architect's job to provide a design which will do what you want, with individual spaces that provide the right conditions for particular needs. The architect will advise you if the required performance cannot be achieved - perhaps because of restrictions of space or high cost - and will usually present other options for achieving something close to the brief. In such cases, you would negotiate changes to the brief with the architect, and agree these modifications in writing (◄◄ technical brief).

air handling

When defining requirements for heating, ventilation and other environmental controls in exhibition galleries, you should bear in mind the following considerations:

- the positive influence of the building on the internal environment can be reinforced, and any negative influence can be suppressed;

- the extent to which the internal environment can be controlled may influence what exhibitions and loans can be borrowed;

- where precise control is necessary in the 'art spaces', the needs of works of art take priority over the comfort of human occupants;

- 'non-art' spaces can give priority to human comfort;

- investment in monitoring systems is vital for good performance.

On the assumption that the building will be designed and maintained to be weather-proof, this section is concerned with the temperature, humidity and cleanliness of the air in the exhibition spaces. (For controlling light, ➤➤ **roof lights**). The degree of control over the internal environment may have a direct effect on the exhibitions that can be shown, especially those that contain loans from museum collections. Conversely, ambitions for the programme will establish the degree of control that will be necessary for the internal environment.

For an existing building, an environmental audit can plot variations in temperature and humidity, interpret the causes (e.g. damp penetration, solar gain, draughty doors and windows, central heating cutting on and off) and recommend remedial action to stabilise the internal environment. The audit can also ascertain the amount and type of pollutants and particulates to which a building or site is exposed, and can indicate whether filtration or other control methods might be required.

Conditions suitable for human comfort can apply to the parts of the building where works of art are not kept. As far as possible, the two types of space should be treated separately, especially if the 'non-art' spaces' include catering, educational activities and cloakroom, which are likely to generate high levels of humidity and could de-stabilise the gallery environment or put an unnecessary burden on ventilation or air-conditioning systems.

PASSIVE FEATURES VERSUS ACTIVE MEASURES

Finite resources may mean that only limited control can be achieved, but control will also depend on the extent to which non-mechanical features (e.g. insulation) can be used instead of active measures (e.g. air-conditioning systems) that are expensive to install and run. As far as possible, a building should contribute to stabilising the internal environment by passive means, and heating and cooling considerations should be part of the overall design at the outset, not added subsequently. A draught lobby can make an air-lock between the outside and the exhibition area, preventing cold and dusty air from surging into the building. There is little point in using humidifiers to add moisture to the air if it is removed by condensation on cold windows, so secondary or multiple glazing can help to stabilise humidity levels. A vapour barrier in roofs, walls and floors will discourage the movement of moisture into the gallery as a result of capillary action and wind pressure, helping not only to stabilise humidity levels but also to keep out water-soluble pollutants.

Any system, mechanical or otherwise, must be capable of coping with extremes, and design minima and maxima should be fixed in relation to recorded extremes. Unlike the external weather, it is sometimes possible to anticipate other extremes and to minimise their effects. During exhibition openings it may be necessary to restrict attendance to an agreed number of guests as much for environmental as for safety reasons. The air-handling system must take into account other systems (e.g. artificial lighting and screens) which may have an impact on performance.

You should set out in the brief the degree of your commitment to passive design features. This should state not only an interest in the principle and an appreciation of the financial advantages but also an understanding of the operational implications. At the same time as the design is being developed, you will need to devise procedures for the complete building so that the staff will help to maintain a stable environment and minimise the impact of external influences (◄◄ project plan).

CONTROLLING TEMPERATURE

The norm for heating gallery interiors is 18° C in winter and 20° C in summer, the small seasonal variation being tolerated for economy's sake. As far as works of art are concerned, low temperatures are better because chemical and biological degradation slows down as temperature falls. However, heating strategies in galleries are generally devised for the convenience and comfort of people, and in particular for the comfort of staff. Except for guided and taught groups, visitors will continue to wear outer clothing and keep moving, so will tolerate lower temperatures than attendants and warders. Legislation sets the parameters for heating: the maximum temperature in public buildings should not exceed 19°C and the minimum temperatures in the workplace should not fall below 15.5°-16°C.

INSULATION

Heat loss is a significant problem with thin-skinned buildings, and insulation is necessary to protect conditions inside a building from the effects of variations in the weather outside. Insulation contributes to the stability of the internal environment by providing a barrier which slows down the rate of transfer of heat or moisture from one side to the other. Where there are large expanses of windows and/or roof lights, double-glazing is an obvious expedient. Triple glazing increases the thickness and weight of the window, and similar performance can now be obtained using coated, low-emissivity (low-E) glass (►► windows and roof lights).

Elsewhere, within walls and ceilings, the location of insulation may have a significant impact on a building's thermal performance. A "quick-response" building has thermal insulation and/or vapour barrier towards the inside of the building's mass, so only the volume of air within the building needs to be conditioned, and mechanical systems can be switched on a short time before the arrival of the exhibition that requires this level of control. Non-standard levels of temperature and humidity (e.g. for metal objects) can be quickly provided and easily maintained in such a building.

A "slow-response" building instead has thermal insulation and/or vapour barrier towards the outside of the building's mass, so that the brick and concrete of the structure absorb heat and humidity when the building is cooler and drier than the internal volume of air, and desorb them when the building is warmer and more moist. Exhibition galleries can have extensive surfaces and significant masses of wood- or plaster-board walls and screens and wooden floors which are capable of absorbing and desorbing moisture. Where walls, screens and floors are part of the passive method of control, the use of emulsion paints on walls and wax seals on floors will allow them to act as buffers, whereas a "quick-response" building might seal these surfaces using non-porous paints on walls and sealants on the floors.

Even for galleries without collections, there are advantages in a "slow-response" strategy. Such a building will take longer to bring the environment up to a required level for a particular exhibition, but it will be less susceptible to the daily build-up of heat from lighting or other equipment. It will absorb the effects of any changes introduced from outside (e.g. by opening doors, people wearing damp outer clothes, cleaners washing floors etc.), and it is less dependent on mechanical means for maintaining an equilibrium.

VENTILATION

Air infiltration - the fortuitous leakage of air through a building due to cracks around doors, windows or between joints and imperfections in the structure - is a further source of heat-loss, so draught-sealing around windows, doors, roof lights and other openings will improve performance, reduce cost

and add to occupants' comfort. Ventilation - the air flow resulting from deliberately-provided openings - is then required to introduce fresh air and extract stale air, to meet statutory requirements and to provide comfortable conditions for visitors and staff, especially in warm weather. The CIBSE Guide (Chartered Institute of Building Services Engineers, 1986) recommends 8 litres of fresh air per second per person. Heat recovery systems can help to reduce the cost of heating this fresh air in cold weather, but a more cost-effective approach would be to control the amount of fresh air introduced by using sensors to detect the amount of carbon dioxide in the internal air.

In addition, ventilation is required for cooling down equipment such as video projectors which are installed close to the ceiling, where heat does not disperse easily. Tungsten lights generate heat which must be removed to prolong lamp life. Again heat recovery can help energy conservation. Where air input and extraction are by mechanical means, the control system can be set to extract less than the air supplied, to create a positive pressure in the art areas which will discourage infiltration from the outside and from the non-art areas.

HEATING SYSTEMS

A heating system should be simple and straightforward, of a size appropriate to the building. A heating system designed to meet peak winter-time loads will operate uneconomically for the rest of the year, and it can be more sensible to have a smaller boiler operating continuously at maximum efficiency to cope with normal loads and a second boiler providing extra heat when the demand is high. Standard hot-water central heating systems are often ruled out from exhibition galleries because radiators obtrude into potential display space (➤➤ wall surfaces). Where floor or ceiling cannot be used for heating purposes (➤➤ floor surfaces, ceilings), one option for side-lit galleries is to contain the heat transfer units in screened boxes in window recesses, but fan assistance may be necessary where a heating system is used solely for human comfort and is switched off at night. Linear radiators hidden in skirting features at the bottom of walls are not normally used because of their potentially damaging effect on exhibits positioned immediately above them.

location:
Ikon Gallery, Birmingham.

architect:
Levitt Bernstein Associates.

description:
First-floor galleries.

photograph:
Martin Jones, reproduced courtesy
of the Ikon Gallery.

CONTROL SYSTEMS

For heating to be regulated precisely, monitoring systems must also be effective and user-friendly, supplying information that is easy to understand and raising an alarm when an abnormal situation develops. It is the quality of monitoring and control which defines the performance of the system, so it is worth investing in systems that are accurate and dependable. A computerised Building Management System can help to reduce costs, by monitoring energy consumption, regulating plant times and providing heating in certain zones at different times.

Whilst sensors must be placed to respond to the changing thermal behaviour of each volume of air, care must be taken in the exhibition areas to ensure that they do not obstruct any display surface (➤➤ wall surfaces).

CONTROLLING HUMIDITY

People can tolerate a wide range of humidity as long as temperatures are comfortable. In contrast, objects are sensitive to variations in relative humidity (RH), and humidity levels are therefore controlled for the benefit of works of art (➤➤ humidity). Control aims to minimise any changes and to make them take place over as long a period as possible. For a permanent collection, the ideal is to maintain stable RH levels 24 hours a day, 365 days a year. An exhibition gallery might instead aim to provide stable conditions for the periods that it has exhibitions with loans from museum collections on its premises. Exhibitions depending on loans from artists, commercial galleries and private collectors may not require control within the same strict limits, but protection from the elements and heating and ventilation will be necessary in any case. An energy-efficient building is not only less expensive to run, but is also less subject to external fluctuations in weather, and should have a more stable internal environment. An options analysis might consider how difficult and expensive (using life-cycle costing) it would be to achieve and maintain the required levels on a permanent basis.

Stable conditions for exhibits mean that a heating or air-conditioning system is not switched off at night when the building is empty of people. Indeed, the conditions of the government indemnity scheme require that environmental conditions must be maintained 24 hours a day, 7 days a week throughout the loan period from the time the indemnified material arrives until it departs from the loan venue. Stable conditions are also required for stores, packing rooms, workshops, access routes and any other part of the building where exhibits and their associated materials are kept. The main disadvantage of occasional control is that it does not provide lenders with continuous evidence - in the form of thermohygrograph charts or datalogged information - to demonstrate that particular conditions are being met. As a result, once the building is open, it will be important to collect records which show that any required conditions can be achieved and maintained. Monitoring is essential in any case, since the conditions of the Government Indemnity Scheme require that relative humidity, temperature and light levels in spaces containing indemnified material should be monitored throughout the loan period.

CONTROLLING POLLUTION

Dealing with particulates and pollutants may be a consideration for heavily-polluted sites, in city centres or close to major roads.

Particulates include plant and animal fibres, pollen, skin, sand, industrial and combustion by-products. They cause unsightly dust, which not only requires frequent cleaning of exhibits and causes wear and damage to delicate objects but also attracts acids from pollutants. They are difficult to exclude because people inside a building also shed dust and fibres. Concrete and other construction materials will generate dust for long periods after a building is completed, so exposed concrete must be treated with sealants which are not themselves contaminants. The entry of dust from outside can be discouraged by draught-sealing windows and doors, by installing two sets of doors with a effective mat to form a dust trap at each entrance (➤➤ entrance), and by ensuring that cleaners use equipment and materials that attract and hold dust. Where air is introduced mechanically, fibre filters can be used to remove dust and grit. Electronic filtration is not recommended because it generates ozone (see below). Filters should be fitted with manometers, which will register a drop in pressure as the filters become clogged. Vacuum cleaners used for cleaning the interior should have filters to the same standards as the filters used in any air-handling system.

Pollutants include sulphur dioxide and nitrous oxides, both of which react with water to produce acids that damage textiles and paper. Ozone oxidises pigments and dyes, and can attack any organic matter. The damaging effects of chlorides are most obvious on metal objects where the metal is corroded to metal salts. Draught-sealing minimises the migration of air, humidity and pollution from outside, as does mildly pressurising the interior if air-conditioning is used (see above). Where air is introduced mechanically, it should be drawn from an area away from sources of gaseous pollution such as roads or combustion vents. Air-handling units can be designed to pass incoming air through activated charcoal filters, and even if these filters are not installed immediately, it may be wise to allow for their future incorporation. Sulphur dioxide is the usually the most concentrated and damaging gaseous pollutant, but the need for filtration and the type required will depend on external air quality as well as the stated requirements of lenders. Measurements can either be in parts per million/billion (ppm/ppb) or micrograms per cubic metre. Typical requirements for a gallery are maximum levels for sulphur dioxide and nitrous oxide of 3.5 ppm or 10µg/m³ and ozone of 7 ppb or 0.2µg/m³.

CONTROLLING NOISE

The Noise Rating system is often used in preference to the decibel scale to define what is allowable as background noise, because it takes into account that high frequencies are more disturbing than lower ones. Mechanical systems - for lifts, air-handling, etc. - should be as quiet as possible and their noise levels should be designed to be no greater than NR 30 in exhibition spaces and NR 35 in education rooms, store and service areas. This is particularly important for galleries where surfaces are hard and reverberate strongly, and where white surfaces feel louder than dark ones!

**Environmental Control
for a 'WHITE BOX'**
(see ◄◄ notes on page 88)

Temperatures should be maintained at [17-19]°C in winter and [19-23]°C in summer in all public areas during opening hours, and in all administrative and service areas whilst they are staffed. There should be simple controls for zoning within reception, exhibition areas, storage, education areas and service areas, so that heating can be reduced on days when these spaces are not occupied. The heating system should be simple to operate and maintain, and should be energy-efficient, producing the required levels of temperature with low running costs. Any exposed heating surfaces in the public spaces should be large expanses with low temperatures, but they should not obstruct display surfaces. Circulation pipe-work should not be visible in the galleries, and should be insulated to avoid casual heat loss.

Environmental Control for a 'BLACK BOX'
(see notes on page 88)

It should be possible to control temperatures between [17]°C and [22]°C in the galleries. Because of the amount of electrical equipment and because window blinds will be closed during many exhibitions, ventilation will be required to remove heat from the gallery area, for the comfort of visitors and in the interests of prolonging the life of equipment. Uncomfortable draughts should be avoided where natural ventilation is used, and dust ingress through windows, doors, etc. should be

kept to a minimum. Any mechanical system of ventilation should have a Noise Rating not exceeding NR [30], at any point in the building, even when running at high speed. Mechanical ventilation should include heat recovery. Monitoring and control equipment should be simple to operate. Access for maintenance to all machinery should be straightforward.

Environmental Control for a 'STRONG BOX'
(see notes on page 88)

Irrespective of seasonal variation or weather conditions, it should be possible to regulate relative humidity (RH) at any point within the range [45-60]% according to the stated requirements of lenders to particular exhibitions. Once a level has been fixed, it should be maintained within the parameters of ± [2]% in all areas where exhibits are displayed or stored, for the whole period from the arrival of an exhibition to its departure, with a lead-in time of no more than [3] days. Temperatures in exhibition and storage areas will be allowed to range between [15 and 25]°C in the interests of maintaining RH levels. Environmental stability

must not be compromised by a commitment to minimise energy consumption. As far as possible, construction materials should act as buffers, helping to even out diurnal variations in humidity, especially in the areas where art is displayed or stored. For the whole building, thermal insulation and measures for reducing solar gain are required in the interests of environmental stability and reduced running costs in extreme weather conditions. [95]% of dust particles 1 micron in diameter and [50]% of dust particles 0.5 micron in diameter should be removed from the air in the exhibition galleries. Filtration of gaseous pollutants will be required for about [3] months a year, but would then be required for 24 hours a day, when the maximum permitted levels for sulphur dioxide and nitrogen dioxide is [10] micrograms/m³. While 'non-art' spaces are occupied, a temperature of [19]°C should be maintained during the winter months, and a temperature of [23]°C should not be exceeded in summer. There should be measures for zoning within reception, education areas and office, so that heating or cooling can be reduced on days when these spaces are not occupied.

The Department of the Environment, Transport and the Regions funds the **National Air Quality Information Archive** at AEA Technology plc's National Environmental Technology Centre at Culham in Oxfordshire. This Archive collates information on ozone, oxides of nitrogen, carbon monoxide, sulphur dioxide, particulates and hydrocarbons from monitoring stations around the UK and produces maps of pollution distribution. Detailed read-outs from individual monitoring stations and maps of pollution distribution are available via the internet, at: www.aeat.org

May Cassar, **Environmental Management: Guidelines for museums and galleries,** Museums & Galleries Commission and Routledge, 1995. **ISBN 0 415 10559 5.**

Chartered Institution of Building Services Engineers, **Automatic controls and their implications for systems design,** CIBSE Applications Manual 1, 1985 provides design information on controls and the systems they operate, considering them as integral parts of the overall system at the concept stage.

Chartered Institution of Building Services Engineers, **Guide A: Design Data,** CIBSE 1986 is concerned with the design of heating, ventilation and air conditioning systems. Section A2 is devoted to weather and solar data in the UK, providing data on extremes of climatic conditions in winter and summer and on average conditions likely to be experienced from day to day. It also includes data on daylight availability, solar irradiance and atmospheric pollution.

Chartered Institution of Building Services Engineers, **Natural ventilation in non-domestic buildings,** CIBSE Applications Manual 10, considers issues which the client and design team need to address at the outset of the project.

Chartered Institution of Building Services Engineers, **Selection and application of heat pumps,** Technical Memorandum 11, 1985, introduces the concepts involved in heat pumps and describes practice. A subsequent publication, **Design guidance for heat pump systems,** CIBSE Technical Memorandum 15, 1988, extends the earlier memorandum, reflecting the increasing importance of heat recovery.

The Met. Office provides site-specific weather information for individual requirements. For further information contact: **The Met. Office, Room S1/3, Sutton House, London Road, Bracknell, Berkshire, RG12 2SY. tel:** 01344 856855.

Murray Frost, **"Planning for Preventive Conservation",** in Gail Dexter Lord & Barry Lord (Eds.), **The Manual of Museum Planning,** HMSO 1991.

artificial lighting

You should bear the following issues in mind when considering artificial lighting in the exhibition spaces:

- whether it is the main means of lighting the exhibitions or supplements natural light;
- what range of light levels is required, and how light should be controlled;
- whether ultra-violet radiation should be excluded;
- whether energy efficiency is an issue;
- how access will be achieved for adjusting and changing lamps;
- what other lighting is required, for service and emergency use.

SUPPLEMENTING NATURAL LIGHT

Continuous levels of daylight cannot be guaranteed, and there will be times even in the middle of the day when natural light has to be supplemented by artificial lighting. Variability requires an attentive staff or photocell-driven systems, to operate blinds in order to limit excess daylight, and to switch on lamps in order to supplement fading light outside (➤➤ roof lights and windows). Shorter hours of daylight during the winter months and possible changes in patterns of use in the evenings also require a system of artificial lighting to supplement any natural lighting.

PERFORMANCE REQUIREMENTS

Your role should be to define as precisely as possible the performance required, in terms of where light should be available, what range of intensities are permissible and what quality the light should have. It is better to have an initial design output in excess of the performance required, so that performance can be maintained even as lamps get old and reflectors become dirty (➤➤ energy efficiency). You should also indicate any constraints, such as running costs, maintenance or heat output. The design team's role is to provide a design which is compatible with the power supply and with other systems (◀◀ air-handling and ➤➤ screens) and to select equipment which will meet the brief, in terms of doing a given job within the cost allocated.

Different criteria are used for the performance of a lighting system:

LIGHT LEVELS

For permissible light levels for loans from museum collections, ➤➤ light. Colour discrimination and perception of detail improves with increased light levels, so it should be possible to increase light levels where the effects of photo-degradation are slight,

---

top ▲

location:
Fruitmarket Gallery, Edinburgh.

architect:
Richard Murphy Architects.

description:
The old fruitmarket building with its new roof, with Waverley Station behind.

photograph:
Peter Cook, reproduced courtesy of the Fruitmarket Gallery.

bottom ▼

description:
Photo 98 exhibition in the first-floor gallery.

photograph:
Catriona Grant, reproduced courtesy of the Fruitmarket Gallery.

e.g. with sculpture. For exhibition galleries, it is important to have the flexibility of a range of sizes and types of lamps, in order to have the ability to dim and to focus lamps between wide-angle or narrow beams. High-frequency fluorescent lamps have advantages over older fluorescent lighting, in that that they can be dimmed and also have reduced flicker and noise.

ULTRA-VIOLET CONTENT

For conservation purposes, a continuous spectrum is not an advantage, and fluorescent, tungsten halogen or other lamps with a high ultra-violet content need to be shielded with filters to reduce the UV content of the transmitted light to acceptable levels (➤➤ light).

COLOUR RENDERING

Accurate colour rendering is important, though difficult to measure because the benchmark is daylight, which itself varies with the period of the year, time of day and weather conditions. The standard for colour rendering is the colour rendering index (Ra) produced by the Commission International de l'Eclairage, for which perfect rendering is 100 Ra. Galleries should have lamps with colour rendering indices over 80 Ra.

EFFICIENCY

The efficiency of lamps is measured in terms of the amount of light produced (expressed in lumens) compared to the amount of electricity consumed (in watts). Efficiency varies according to the type of lamp, from 15 lumens per watt for tungsten GLS (General Lighting Service) to 100 lumens per watt for high-frequency fluorescent lighting. Low efficiency means a high energy consumption for a required level of illumination, with the possibility of over-heating and an associated need for ventilation (◄◄ air-handling). Life-cycle costs take into account not only energy consumption but also life expectancy and cost of replacement.

UNIFORMITY RATIO

Lighting of all display surfaces to the same level may be undesirable, especially for people with visual impairments, and small variations in lighting between different wall surfaces will help all visitors to read the shape and volume of the exhibition area. With spotlights, it is relatively easy to illuminate a horizontal band around a room where paintings are hung. Achieving a uniform lighting over the whole height of a display surface is more difficult to achieve. The problem with lighting the full height of a display surface is achieving not a uniform illumination but not too noticeable a contrast between higher illuminance at

the top of the display surface and a lower illuminance at the bottom. In practical terms, this uniformity ratio should be around 2:1, i.e. the level at the brightest part must not be more than twice the level at the darkest part. To avoid a band of distracting brilliance towards the top of a vertical surface means that the light source needs to be as far as possible from the surface.

ANGLE OF INCIDENCE

If the angle of light falling on a framed painting is too shallow (e.g. less than 25° to the vertical), it will cause shadows, especially from the deep box frames used increasingly to protect sensitive early 20th century works. However, deeper angles carry the risks that visitors will cast shadows on the exhibits and that the light sources will be reflected in glazed frames, causing glare in particular for wheelchair users and young people. All directional light sources should therefore be placed in a zone between 25° and 40° to the vertical, measured from a low eye-level on every display surface, including movable screens in their likely positions. If the floor is a light colour, then it will reflect some of the ambient light and help to improve the uniformity ratio, but this gain will have to balanced against reflections in any glazed work and difficulties for people with visual impairments (➤➤ floor surfaces).

ACCESS FOR ADJUSTMENT AND MAINTENANCE

Despite the variety of equipment that is often accommodated in the ceiling space, it is unusual for exhibition galleries to have built-in access to lighting and other equipment, via high-level gantries and catwalks. Consequently, a suitable mobile tower or platform lift must be included in design proposals, for safe and easy access to the lighting system as well as for other high-level work (e.g. painting, hanging items from the ceiling). This equipment should be included in the cost plan, and space should also be identified as close as possible to the exhibition spaces for its storage.

SERVICE LIGHTING

In addition to display lighting, there might be a separate set of service lights, which will provide general illumination, mainly directed downwards onto the floors rather than angled on display surfaces, for cleaning and maintenance and for installing and dismantling exhibitions.

EMERGENCY LIGHTING

Statutory requirements and British Standards govern the provision of emergency lighting and fire-escape illumination (➤➤ fire precautions). The requirement to illuminate emergency escape routes in order to facilitate safe evacuation along defined paths has consequences not only in the design of exhibition galleries but also subsequently in the design of exhibition installations within them.

CONTROLS

Artificial lighting should be switched off when the gallery is not in use, for reasons of conservation and economy. A Building Management System (BMS) can be used to switch lights on and off at opening and closing times, but there will need to be a local override for each room. The BMS should signal an alarm if its settings are overridden, which might be immediate if there is no-one supposed to be on the premises or perhaps after an hour if staff are working. Switches and dimmer controls are normally hard-wired, but remote-control handsets are an alternative which permits security, unobtrusiveness and accurate adjustment.

Artificial Lighting in a 'WHITE BOX'
(see notes on page 88)

Although daylight will be the primary method of lighting the galleries, there will be surfaces and objects which face away from windows or will be in shadow, e.g. because of screens. It should be possible to direct light to all surfaces in the gallery which would normally be visible to visitors but which may not be adequately illuminated by natural means. There will also be times - in bad weather, or winter afternoons or on evening openings - when daylight must be further supplemented by artificial lighting. If controlled automatically, it should switch on and off as unobtrusively as possible. As far as possible, artificial lighting should match the quality and intensity of daylight falling on other surfaces, in the way that it is diffused, in its intensity and its colour temperature. Lamps with a colour rendering index of [90] or higher should be used. Decisions on colour temperature should be subject to tests in situ involving gallery staff. Artificial light should be capable of adjustment between [50] lux and [500] lux over the full extent of every display surface. The uniformity ratio should be [2:1]. In addition to this ambient lighting, there should be a system to provide local highlights of up to [1,000] lux upon any position on any display surface, including screens, plinths and the floor. The area of highlight should be variable from a wide angle down to a tight focus [30 x 30] cm. Neither ambient lighting nor highlighting should be obtrusive or create glare. At full load, there should be no over-heating which would require additional ventilation or air-conditioning. The lighting system should be energy-efficient and easy to maintain. Staff must have easy and safe access, without risk of strain or injury, to lamps, fittings and power supplies in order to maintain and repair the system and to replace and direct or focus lamps.

Artificial Lighting in a 'BLACK BOX'
(see notes on page 88)

Natural light is not required, since most new media emit rather than reflect light. Projected work will require total black out, and displays of computer-based work will require low light levels which must be precisely controlled to eliminate reflection and glare. Any fixed switches and dimmer controls should be discreetly located, if possible off the plane of the display surface.

They should be easily accessible to the staff, and should be clear and simple to operate, but there should be a lockable flap to prevent unauthorised changes.

Artificial Lighting in a 'STRONG BOX'
(see notes on page 88)

General illumination which is variable between [25] and [100] lux should be provided for all display surfaces. There should be transitional spaces between darkened galleries and more brightly-lit spaces elsewhere in the building, to allow visitors' eyes to adjust to the lower levels. In addition to the overall illumination of the gallery, it should be possible to direct light to all horizontal surfaces (floors, tables, plinths, ceilings, etc.) and vertical surfaces (wall, screens, banners, etc.) that

would normally be visible to visitors to the gallery, and to concentrate, without any distracting spill on surrounding surface, an even spread of light on any single work of art, which might vary in height or width from a few centimetres to several metres, and might be displayed at any point in the volume of the gallery. Lamps should be placed to avoid shadows cast by frames and by visitors, and to avoid reflection and glare. The intensity of light falling on any single work of art, of any size and in any position should be controlled to a minimum of [50] lux and a maximum of [200] lux. The amount of ultra-violet radiation to which a work of art is exposed should not exceed [200] $\mu W/m^2$. If controlled automatically, the lighting should switch off when the gallery is closed to the public, but there should be a local override in each room.

Michael Carver, **"Lighting Design and Energy Efficiency in Museums and Galleries"** in **Museums Environment Energy,** ed. M. Cassar, MGC, 1994. **ISBN 0 11 290519 6.**

Chartered Institution of Building Services Engineers, **Lighting for Museums and Art Galleries, Lighting Guide: LG8,** 1994.

BS 8206: Part 2:1992. Lighting for buildings. Code of practice for daylighting includes the design of electric lighting when used in conjunction with daylight, and gives sunlight and skylight data.

BS 8206: Part 1:1985. Lighting for buildings. Code of practice for artificial lighting describes the aims and processes concerned with artificial

lighting design including energy considerations, and deals with the characteristics of various lamps and their control gear, with luminaires and other means of controlling the distribution of light, together with some aspects of installation.

art route

The 'art route' is the path within the gallery which works of art will travel between their initial delivery to the building and their final departure from it. However small the gallery, a consignment will be moved along this route, and some packing materials will have to be stored off it. Along the route there might be spaces designated for various functions (➤➤ loading bay and storage), but its essential characteristic is an uncluttered tunnel.

You should bear the following issues in mind when considering the design of the art route:

- the dimensions of each opening should allow for the maximum size of works of art envisaged;
- changes of direction should also allow for maximum sizes envisaged;
- floor loading between any starting and any finishing point should allow for the maximum weight envisaged;
- provision for changes of level should allow for maximum size and weight;
- maximum size and weight must allow for the box or crate a work of art travels in;
- maximum size and weight must also allow for the trucks and trolleys used to move works of art.

'BELOW STAIRS'

The art route 'below stairs' (i.e. the storage, workshop and service areas to which the public is not admitted) is concerned with clear corridors with the minimum number of changes of direction, to give an easy and direct path between the loading bay and other areas used for storage and handling. What can go along an art route is determined by the smallest opening and the lowest floor loading along it. You must ensure - at the briefing stage and subsequently by carefully checking plans and sections for the proposed route - that potential pinch-points such as doors and corners have the headroom, width and turning space adequate for the largest and heaviest crates that are anticipated. The route should be as short, direct and wide as possible, so that a heavy crate or big painting does not have to be moved unnecessarily, manoeuvred through a series of right angles or carried down narrow corridors. The route should be without steps or ramps, with any changes of level restricted to those between floors (which should be by lift, see below).

CARRYING EQUIPMENT

Crates will usually be too large to be carried safely by hand. Aside from health and safety issues, no owner will be happy if a loan suffers shock and vibration because its crate has to be man-handled and carried, so the art route should be designed for a range of low trolleys and cradles. Pallet trucks, fork-lift machinery, cranes and gantries may be required on occasions. Such equipment should be included in the cost plan, just as much as any fixed hoists or lifts. Smooth surfaces, clear routes and adequate floor loadings are important where wheeled equipment is used to carry crates or display cases. Industrial-standard machinery and equipment will require a higher level of imposed floor loadings (➤➤ floor surfaces), since the weight of the machinery is additional to the weight of work plus any crate, and it will be more cost-effective to invest in customised trucks, trolleys, cradles and lifting frames than to pay the increased building cost of a higher floor-loading capacity.

'ABOVE STAIRS'

The situation 'above stairs' in the public areas is different from 'below stairs'. As far as possible, the art route 'above stairs' should be kept separate from the 'people route' for visitors, for the safety of visitors, the convenience of staff and the security of the exhibits. Some galleries achieve this separation by the simple expedient of closing their buildings to the public between exhibitions. Other galleries, especially those with permanent collections but also those with a policy to run two or more exhibitions at once, may be open to the public whilst an exhibition is being installed or dismantled in other parts of the same building. The latter affects the internal layout and art route 'above stairs', which must be planned to allow for different permutations of galleries open and closed to the public. In each permutation, there must be unobstructed access to 'below stairs' which does not interfere with public circulation.

The interface between 'above stairs' and 'below stairs' is often a large service opening which is covered with a false wall when the exhibition is installed. If this false wall is used as a display surface, there should be some form of secondary access, so that work on show does not have to be removed in order to access 'below stairs' from the exhibition area. This false wall should be secure and solid

(e.g. secured by a series of horizontal beams dropped into brackets on the reverse side and on the walls to each side) so that it cannot be opened from the public side and so that it can be treated like any other display surface in the gallery.

GOODS LIFT

The basic principle is that the art route should be all on one level with a service lift to cope with movement between different floors. The dimensions and carrying capacity of the lift should be compatible with the dimensions and floor loadings that apply to the art route, so that the lift does not compromise the size or weight of crate and machinery that can be moved to upper or lower floors. Conversely, although it is sensible to plan for a size of lift to suit largest and heaviest works conceivable, there is little point in providing an enormous goods lift if it is only accessible by a small opening which cannot be enlarged (e.g. because the building is listed), and some savings might be consequently made. Any quiet spaces for staff or public use that are adjacent to a lift shaft should not be subject to unacceptable noise levels.

For picture galleries, a common alternative to a large lift is to provide a 'picture slot' at the same position in each floor surface, with an electric hoist

at the highest level but capable of being controlled from any one floor, to allow very large canvases to be moved between floors. Galleries situated on an upper floor sometimes have large sliding windows with a hinged or otherwise retractable jib above, to enable large works to be hoisted up the front of the building and in through the windows (➤➤ windows). This method is vulnerable to the weather and cannot be used for material of high value.

Art Route
(see notes on page 88)

Service routes should have as few changes in direction as possible between all 'art areas' (loading bay, storage, exhibition galleries, etc.). All openings and changes in direction should have the headroom, width and turning space necessary to cope with the maximum dimensions of [5] metres long x [4] metres high x [2] metres deep, for crates that might be delivered to the gallery. Floors should be all on one level and surfaces should be durable, easy to maintain, smooth and unobstructed. All 'below stairs' areas (stores, workshops and access routes) must be spacious and well-equipped, to encourage cleanliness and orderliness.

There should be a variety of devices for cushioning, restraining and moving objects, from platform trolleys on shock-absorbing suspension and smooth-rolling wheels to hydraulic fork-lift equipment for lifting and moving heavy crates. Floor loadings should be up to [7.5] kilonewtons per square metre. Humidity and temperature should be controlled to the same levels as in the galleries and stores.

A service lift should serve all floors containing 'art areas'. The size of the opening on car and landings and the internal dimensions of the car should be adequate to cope with the maximum size of crate ([5] metres long x [4] metres high x [2] metres deep) that might be delivered to the gallery. The lift should be capable of carrying [8] tonnes.

left

right

location:
Ikon Gallery, Birmingham.

architect:
Levitt Bernstein Associates.

photographs:
Martin Jones, reproduced courtesy of Ikon Gallery.

description:
Service Lift **(left)**, Passenger Lift **(right)**. The two lifts are new additions to the existing building and are situated opposite each other on the sides of the building, expressing how an old building has been adapted for new purposes and the different requirements of service and public access.

ceilings

The following is concerned with ceilings in exhibition spaces. It is not concerned with the structure of the roof above it nor with ceilings in other rooms and spaces in the building. Like other surfaces (➤➤ floor surfaces, screens and wall surfaces) in exhibition spaces, a ceiling may have to accommodate several different and possibly conflicting functions.

You should consider the priority to be given to the following requirements, for ceilings that:

- include windows (➤➤ roof lights);
- can support safely the weight of exhibits and equipment;
- are used for the heating and/or ventilation system;
- are wired for power and a variety of cabled services;
- provide a suitable background for a range of works of art.

For other aspects of exhibition galleries, ◄◄ artificial lighting, ➤➤ doors and doorways and windows.

THE POTENTIAL FOR CLUTTER

In a gallery which is artificially-lit or lit by windows in the walls, the ceiling is often the surface of the gallery which is least regarded, literally and metaphorically. Because it is not usually in the field of vision, and because of the wish to avoid clutter on walls and floors, it is often crowded with fittings and equipment. For structural or conservation reasons, floors or walls may not be able to carry all necessary services, and the ceiling may have to accommodate many functions. As well as lighting, it might contain ducting for heating (or be a heating surface itself) and ventilation, fire, security and emergency equipment, public address and sound systems, power supply and supporting track or anchor points for screens. For easy access and maintenance, it might even have high-level catwalks. To compensate for hard surfaces elsewhere in the gallery, it might include sound-absorbing materials.

THE IMPORTANCE OF THE CEILING

The ceiling is also a powerful influence on the nature of the space. Its height affects the proportions of the room, and any clutter affects the quality of the visitor's experience. A low ceiling can exacerbate the heating effects of lamps and make the atmosphere feel stuffy. The ceiling might even become a display surface in its own right, against which kites, mobiles and banners might be seen. Careful design is necessary to ensure that the ceiling does not become a dominant feature. In the past, suspended ceilings were inserted in top-lit galleries in order to control light and temperature, but the height and finish of these ceilings were so mishandled that the tendency has since been to sweep away even the baffles that hide high-level machinery and ducting. Designed with care and attention, a suspended ceiling can be used in the same way as wall- and floor-surfaces, to hide services that would only clutter and distract, whilst allowing elements like roof lights to do their job.

Ceilings for a 'WHITE BOX'
(see notes on page 88)

Hanging points should be provided on a [2] metre grid over the whole ceiling, with a maximum loading of [1] kN/m^2, to allow installations, banners, etc. to be hung at any point in the gallery.

Ceilings for a 'BLACK BOX'
(see notes on page 88)

Secure fixing positions should be provided on a [1] metre grid over the whole ceiling, with a maximum loading of [1] kN/m^2, to allow lighting rigs or platforms for slide- and video-projectors to be suspended at any point in the gallery. Concealed trunking should be provided, so that cables supplying power and input can be routed unobtrusively to these points.

location:
ArtSway, Sway (Hampshire).

architect:
Tony Fretton.

description:
Johnny Woodford, '3 Kites'.

photograph:
Gina Dearden, reproduced courtesy
of ArtSway and Johnny Woodford.

doors and doorways

Doors and doorways can have several functions, and their provision and design will be a balance between the different requirements of exhibits and people. You should consider the following requirements, for doors to be designed so that:

- people of all ages and abilities can move easily into, within and out of the gallery both in normal and emergency situations;

- unauthorised access can be prevented to the whole building or to parts of it;

- levels of environmental control can be maintained in different zones;

- the spread of fire is discouraged.

EXTERNAL DOORS

Treatment of external doors is a key part of the strategy of defending the building outside normal opening hours, in terms of reinforcing a potential weakness in the security perimeter and in terms of providing a means of detecting any attack (➤➤ **exterior**). In order to resist forcible entry, external doors should normally be made from solid hardwood or be of solid hard-core construction. In areas of increased risk,

such as the rear of the building, steel doors of varying thickness or laminated security doors with reinforced plastic or steel sheet inserts can be used. All-metal doors should include a layer of insulation and a thermal break between internal and external leaves, to reduce the transmission of heat. Door frames must be capable of carrying the door's weight, and be of equal strength. Hinge bolts should be used, and are essential if hinges are exposed.

Any glazed doors should be supported by a secondary security system, such as steel shutters, retractable gates or laminated security doors inside the outer door. Wrought-iron gates designed by an artist or craftsperson are a more attractive alternative to industry-standard gates and shutters. Horizontal shutters can be successfully accommodated within the cavity of a double brick wall, especially in a new building.

Locks should be to BS 3621, i.e. providing thief-resistant features. Appropriate sensors connected to the Intruder Detection System (IDS) should be used to raise an alarm if the door is attacked or opened without permission.

location:
Harris Museum & Art Gallery, Preston.

architect:
Norman Jones Sons & Rigby.

description:
Disabled access ramp at the main entrance incorporating sculpture by Ian Hamilton Finlay.

photograph:
Norwyn Photographics, reproduced courtesy of the Harris Museum & Art Gallery.

ENSURING THAT DOORS ALLOW ACCESS

Consideration of doors and doorways forms a considerable part of a copious access literature, which aims to ensure that doors do not continue to act as barriers when they are supposed to be open. The Building Regulations and the Approved Document BS 5588 Part 8 contain detailed specifications to ensure that doors are wide and easy to use. An access checklist is part of the application packs produced by the different Lottery distributors. In addition, an access audit is usually a requirement of capital applications, and a disability consultant is often a member of the design team (◄◄ design team). The usual recommendation for doors is an unobstructed minimum width of 0.9 m. These guidelines also recommend that:

- glass doors are marked with safety strips and symbols;
- solid doors are fitted with vision panels to enable people to see and be seen;
- all internal doors are fitted with lever type handles or 'D' pull handles, at a height appropriate to wheelchair users;

- doors - and any automatic door-closing mechanisms - are light enough to be used by people with limited mobility or strength.

SHARED USE WITH THE ART ROUTE

Where doorways are also used as for bringing in or taking out works of art, they will need to be wider and/or higher than openings for people alone (◄◄ art route). This can have consequences for the weight of the door and how easy it is to open, and there may also be difficulties with obtaining fire doors of the required dimensions. Where public access must be shared with service access, the best solution may be to design a section above and/or beside the door which can be removed at exhibition turnaround periods.

FIRE REGULATIONS

The provision of fire-resistant doors and emergency exits is governed by statutory regulation (►► fire precautions). For the security required for high-value exhibitions, emergency doors should be provided with a secure locking device for the silent hours, should have a local alarm to indicate if the door is used when the building is open to the public, and should, if possible, be covered by a CCTV camera.

PREVENTING UNAUTHORISED ACCESS WITHIN THE BUILDING

The brief must ensure that every internal door is protected to an appropriate level. In a multi-purpose building like an arts centre or library, it may be necessary to close the exhibition gallery to the staff and users of the other parts, in which case the entrance has to be treated in the same way as an external door. Otherwise, internal doors are mainly a matter of preventing people who are permitted to be in some parts of the building from having unauthorised access to other parts. This might mean keeping the public out of office or storage spaces, but it might also mean that people using a meetings room or workshop space after-hours do not stray unsupervised into gallery or shop, or that visitors to an exhibition in one space do not gain access to another space where another exhibition is being installed or dismantled. All doorways should have lockable doors. In the past, access was controlled by authorised personnel carrying the appropriate key, but punch-pad systems are more convenient. Swipe-card systems allow door locks to be controlled by a central computer, which can be programmed to allow each person a different degree of access for a specific period and to trip an alarm if there is unauthorised entry.

Electronic tags dispense with the need for cumbersome and obtrusive punch-pads or card readers, because the sensors can be concealed behind the wall-lining material.

Doors for a 'WHITE BOX'
(see notes on page 88)

All external and internal doors should be at least [0.9] m wide with level landings and thresholds, and there should be sufficient space to allow wheelchair users to open them. They should not be so heavy as to be difficult for young or elderly people to open.
Door handles or controls should be distinguishable, accessible and usable. Fully-glazed doors should have safety markings at eye level in a contrasting colour.

Doors for a 'BLACK BOX'
(see notes on page 88)

There must be a high level of security throughout the building, aimed at restricting unauthorised access to expensive equipment, both during opening hours and when the gallery is closed to the public. A light trap will be required at the entrance to the gallery.

Doors for a 'STRONG BOX'
(see notes on page 88)

Security should be to the standards of the Government Indemnity Scheme. Glazed doors across the gallery entrance should be self-closing, to help to maintain environmental stability within, and should be supplemented by a retractable gate or metal shutter for the silent hours. At one time or another, public access will need to be restricted from one or more of the following areas: (Gallery 1, Gallery 2, office, shop, storage, education facilities), whilst allowing access to members of staff and other authorised personnel, and an efficient system of internal control is required. At times when the building is normally closed to the public, it should be possible to have independent access to areas such as the loading bay or education workshops, so the intruder detection system should be zoned to cater for various permutations of part-use of the building.

Access Committee for England, **Towards Better Access**, 1997. ISBN 0 9518948 2 X.

Building Regulations (Part M in England and Wales; Part T in Scotland) and its **Approved Document BS 5588: Part 8.**

Selwyn Goldsmith, **Designing for the Disabled: The New Paradigm**, Butterworth-Heinemann, Oxford 1997. ISBN 0 7506 342 1.

Museums & Galleries Commission, **Improving Museums Security, MGC Guidelines for Good Practice**, Museums & Galleries Commission, 1997. ISBN 0 948630 54 X.

education

For facilities for educational work within the gallery, you should bear in mind the following considerations:

- interpretation may take place in the galleries, in designated facilities or in both;
- designated facilities are difficult to define until education staff are in post;
- an education strategy can include self-motivated study as well as delivered services.

EDUCATION STAFF

The nature of the education space and the facilities it requires will depend on your policy and programmes for education and audience development. Because educational programmes are based on personal skills and interaction, the layout and design of these facilities will depend above all on the people who will be running them. If you already have specialist education staff, they must be directly involved in writing this aspect of the brief, because they will have requirements in every way as particular as a curator's wish-list for the exhibition space. Where such staff have not been appointed yet, they should be recruited as soon as possible so that they can make an input into the facilities they will need. If consultants are used instead, it is very likely that the designs will need to be altered once permanent staff are appointed.

INTERPRETATION WITHIN THE EXHIBITION SPACE

Broadly, there are two approaches to educational activity in exhibition galleries. One is to arrange talks, performances and workshops, generally of a short duration and of a mobile nature, within the exhibition and in front of the works of art themselves. This approach might be simply because space is limited, and there is no room that can be designated for educational use. Equally, it might be for policy reasons, if the organisation takes the view that educational activity should not be restricted to certain areas of the building.

DESIGNATED SPACES

The other approach is to organise lectures, classes and activities of a more sedentary nature, in spaces designated and equipped for these purposes. Designated facilities have the advantage that sessions which might be long, noisy and/or take up a lot of space can be run with minimal disturbance to other visitors to the exhibition and users of the building. By its nature, a temporary exhibition is on the premises for a limited period, and marketing will aim to attract as many visitors from as wide a catchment area as possible. Visitors may be put off if they are unable to approach or contemplate any exhibit because a group is engaged in a practical workshop in front of it. Designated facilities also have the advantages that "wet" or "dirty" activities do not pose the threat of accidental damage or environmental instability to works of art, and that furniture, equipment and materials can be provided appropriate to each activity without cluttering the exhibition area.

The two approaches are not incompatible, and designated education spaces often act as a base of operations, where visiting groups can leave their belongings and from which forays can be made into the exhibition galleries. Proximity of education rooms to the exhibition area can help users to have a direct and immediate interaction with the exhibitions. It can also be valuable for other visitors to be aware of these activities (e.g. through a glazed screen), so that they appreciate that learning happens in the galleries.

The following examples range from the facilities required for informal talks and workshops to those required for formal lectures and classes for young people. Different sorts of educational activity are described as distinct spaces, but the specific circumstances or needs of each gallery may require that one or more are combined.

Educational activity in the exhibition spaces (see notes on page 88)

The basis of our education policy is that education should not be restricted to nominated areas of the building but that discussion and interpretation can take place anywhere where there is a work of art. A flexible use of space is paramount. Apart from the works of art themselves, any materials used for these activities will be in the gallery space only temporarily, so will require storage adjacent to the exhibition space. This storage area should be big enough to

accommodate up to [30] stools/stacking chairs, equipment trolley (e.g. for video cassette player and TV), trolleys with paints and other materials, easels, drawing boards, clipboards with paper and pencils, puzzles and other interactive/hands-on objects, dust-sheets, etc.

Information, orientation or animation area(s) (see notes on page 88)

Integral to each exhibition will be a small, semi-enclosed orientation space, where visitors can drop in for information or orientation on the exhibition or for a pause during their visit, or where parents and carers might wait whilst children are engaged in nearby activities. It should be open and inviting, with comfortable seating for [12-15] users. Its size and location will vary according to the exhibition, but it will generally be close to and within sight of the entrance to the exhibition space, without impinging on corridors or other access routes into the galleries.

Information may take the form of gallery guides, activity booklets or extended labels on paddle boards, for which dispensers will be required. Information may also be presented on illustrated panels. It will generally include newspaper cuttings, recent magazines, current and relevant catalogues, and reference books. It may also comprise one or more video players with headphones showing video tapes of artists in conversation or other exhibition-related videos, or computers with multi-media programmes and/or access to the Internet. The space must be wired for electrical power, for video and computer links, and for CCTV coverage for security of stock as well as general supervision. It should also include provision for questionnaires and other feedback from users and visitors, who might leave their responses and experiences either in a low-tech form (e.g. on pin-boards) or high tech (on computer), to provide other visitors with an alternative to staff-led interpretation.

All spaces designated for educational purposes
(see notes on page 88)

All designated spaces should have independent access, so that they can be used even when the rest of the building is unoccupied, locked and alarmed. External doors should be fitted with a bell, entry-phone and/or door-release mechanism to control entry. If the spaces are not on the ground floor, access should include a lift suitable for disabled people. Since they will take heavy use, all surfaces, coverings and fittings should be durable and easily-cleaned. Walls and doors should have sufficient sound insulation to ensure that there is no sound-spill from noisy activities either into or out of each space. Doors should be double-width, so that they can be left open when 'drop-In' activities are taking place. Ventilation should be provided for occasions when windows are shut and blinds are closed, and should be sufficient to cope with the maximum occupancy of each room. Noise levels from mechanical ventilation should be no higher than NR [35]. All education spaces should be fully integrated into the cabled services - electrical power, PA system, audio loop, telephone, CCTV, computer network, building management system, visible and audible emergency alarms, etc. - of the rest of the building. All sockets should be protected with covers for the safety of young children.

Assembly area
(see notes on page 88)

*An assembly area would be used for orientation, for receiving and marshalling groups, for registering delegates to seminars and conferences, for removing and retrieving outer wear and for eating packed lunches. The following are additional to some or all of the general requirements in the paragraph, "all spaces designated for educational purposes".
The assembly area should be calm, comfortable and attractive to visitors of all ages, cultures and stages of educational development, as well as reflecting the nature and standards of the exhibitions.
Its design should welcome all visitors without specific references to individual cultures.*

It should have seating around the walls, but preferably not bench seating since the space may be used for receptions and formal occasions. It should give access to:

- each education space, so that it is not necessary to go through one to reach another;

- separate stores for each education space, so that people in one of the rooms are not disturbed if materials have to be retrieved from a store during a session;

- a cleaner's store, for all equipment and materials for cleaning the education area;

- toilet/washrooms sufficient to cope with the maximum anticipated level of use, accessible to and usable by disabled people, and suitable for children as well as adults;

- cloakroom facilities, similarly accessible and sufficient to cope with levels of use preferably with individual lockers for coats, baggage and other belongings;

- a kitchen/food preparation area, for storing packed lunches and unpacking and laying out food and drink for groups using the facilities for a half-day or longer; it should have a source of drinking water, sinks with lever taps, and rubbish bins;

- a lockable office space, with a workstation and telephone: if there is a central office area, this space will be used as a short-term base for the person programming the activities, taking bookings, ordering supplies, etc.

'dry' or 'clean' education room ☐ ■ ■
(see notes on page 88)

At one time or another, this space may be used for lectures, video screenings, demonstrations, musical performances, presentations to potential sponsors, training for staff, in-service training for teachers or social workers, outside hire, drama and role-play sessions, reminiscence group work, meetings of trustees or Friends, and receptions. The following are additional to some or all of the general requirements in the paragraph, "all spaces designated for educational purposes".
The 'dry' or 'clean' education room should seat [40] people in comfortable chairs. Movable seating is preferred, in which case an adjacent chair store will be required when the space is cleared. This chair store should also accommodate [5] folding tables and [2] flip chart stands, plus shelved storage (e.g. for teachers' packs) and hanging storage (e.g. for costumes and other props).
If seating is fixed and/or raked, spaces should be reserved for wheelchairs, and there should be access for wheelchair users to any stage or rostrum. Natural light should be available as the main lighting option, with double-glazed windows for sound as much as for thermal insulation. Black-out blinds should provide another option, supported by dimmable lighting. Acoustic control and sound-proofing are essential. The floor surface should be chosen for sound-absorbency, easy cleaning

and user-friendliness, since children may need to sit on the floor.
The room should be wired for sound and video, and there should also be an induction loop system and/or infra-red hearing provision. There should be an adjacent control room for lighting, sound and projection, which might also double as a lockable store for audio-visual equipment, with waist-high shelving for OHP, slide projector, camcorder, video-player and TV monitor, cassette-recorder, tape-recorder, CD-player, microphones, headphones, CD-ROM player, etc. Opposite the control room, there should be a retractable or closable projection screen (or a back-projection screen), and a whiteboard.

'wet' or 'dirty' education room ☐ ■ ■
(see notes on page 88)

This activity room is required for up to [40] people in a range of age-groups, for a programme of practical classes for school children or community groups, object-handling sessions and artist-led workshops which will be part of the interpretation of the main gallery programme. It will help to ensure that our resources benefit the widest possible range of people, particularly groups and individuals who previously may not have had access to mainstream arts provision. The following are additional to some or all of the general requirements in the paragraph, "all spaces designated for educational purposes".

It should have walk-in storage for easels, sculpture stands, tables, chairs, etc. Walls should be covered with a pin-board material, except for a tiled surface around the sinks. There should be wipe-clean work-top areas all round, with lockable drawers and cupboards, to store paper (A1), paints and other consumables. The floor surface should be water- and stain-resistant and easy to clean and maintain. There should be [three] sinks, each with lever taps and double-drainers: one large art sink, one accessible to small children and one accessible to wheelchairs. They should be separated to avoid congestion and there should be a hand-drying facility next to each one. Furniture will include easily-cleaned tables and chairs or stools of different heights and sizes, paper-towel dispensers and bins, and a lockable cupboard for toxic and/or valuable materials.

Studio

(see notes on page 88)

*This space is for the use of an artist or craftsperson engaged to carry out a residency for a period which might range from a few days to several months. The following are additional to some or all of the general requirements in the paragraph, "all spaces designated for educational purposes".
The studio should be adjacent to the 'wet' or 'dirty' education room, so that the artist can lead workshops if required. It should also be adjacent to the exhibition areas, so that work can be moved easily from one space to the other and so that the public can have access to the studio on occasions. There might be a glazed partition, to allow the public to see into the space, but this should have blinds or shutters for privacy and control of light. It should have a floor area of approximately [45] m^2 with an additional [25] m^2 of secure, walk-in storage. Walls should have wipe-clean surfaces. The floor surface should be water- and stain-resistant and easy to clean and maintain. There should be a sink. A lockable area for computer and telephone and lockable storage for the artist's personal belongings would be advantageous.*

Library/resource centre

(see notes on page 88)

There should be a small art library storing the gallery's archive of books, videotapes, CDs magazines, archives, etc for use by a maximum of [8] readers, who might be students, researchers or visitors wanting more detailed information on current exhibitions. The following are additional to some or all of the general requirements in the paragraph, "all spaces designated for educational purposes". The library should be quiet and self-contained, and it should have daylight, supplemented with task lighting (up to [300] lux) at the tables and adequate lighting (at least [150] lux) on the book shelves. Finishes should help to create a warm, informal and relaxed atmosphere, and the floor surface or covering should be chosen for sound-absorbency and easy cleaning. The librarian's work-station should be located by the entrance, supervising tables for study and research. Comfortable seating should be provided, since individual researchers may use the library for long periods of study. There should be [15] m^2 of floor area devoted to open access racks and shelves for published material (magazines, catalogues, books, videos, CD-ROMs) and a similar area, but closed and lockable, for storage of exhibition archives and other unpublished material. In addition to the supervisor's computer, there should be [3] computer workstations, [1] reserved for directories and indexes and [2] with headphones for readers to access multi-media programmes and the Internet. All tables, workstations and shelves must be designed to take account of the needs of disabled people. Noise levels from computers, mechanical ventilation and other equipment should be no higher than NR [30].

energy efficiency

ENVIRONMENTAL BENEFITS

Energy efficiency is part of a larger environmental agenda concerned with the effects of pollution on personal health and global warming, as well as with the availability of fossil fuels and their rising cost. It is often associated with other environmentally-friendly policies and practices, such as the use of timber products obtained from sustainable forests. Energy efficiency is one of the performance criteria used by all the Lottery distributors, following instructions laid down by HM Government.

ECONOMIC BENEFITS

After staff, energy is often the largest cost in a gallery, and financial constraints are a major stimulus towards savings. Inefficiency is not always obvious in an existing building, and you should undertake an energy audit to find out how energy is currently being used, and to understand where a capital project can make savings.

A lighting system should give good viewing conditions for visitors, but automatic controls can be introduced to switch off lights when the exhibition is closed to visitors and to switch or dim them when natural lighting is adequate. Energy consumption can be further reduced by using more energy-efficient options than conventional tungsten lamps and by directing lower wattage lamps directly on the exhibits instead of reflecting a brighter light from another surface.

STABILISING THE INTERNAL ENVIRONMENT

Energy efficiency means reducing a gallery's dependence on plant and equipment that have a high energy consumption. This brings benefits in terms of reduced operating costs, but it also avoids the risk of dramatic changes when the mechanical system fails. Simple low-energy features can often be introduced in a new building or renovation which insulate the interior from extreme weather conditions outside. The process can help to stabilise the gallery environment, to the benefit of the exhibitions and the loans you can attract (◄◄ air-handling).

PASSIVE MEASURES

Passive measures are non-mechanical solutions, which involve working with the building to take advantage of free resources like daylight, whilst reinforcing the building's ability to protect its contents from extremes of weather. This approach avoids the use of unnecessary technology by making the building as efficient as possible. Where energy efficiency is a stated aim

location:
Stills Gallery, Edinburgh.

architect:
Reiach & Hall.

description:
The cafe on the mezzanine inserted above the rear gallery.

photograph:
Gavin Fraser.

of the project, the design team should be encouraged to investigate design solutions that reduce the need for electrical or mechanical systems for lighting or environmental control.

ACTIVE MEASURES

Where electrical or mechanical systems have to be used, they should be energy efficient, reliable, easy to maintain and easy to operate. Complicated and expensive systems should be restricted to areas that need a high level of control. For example, if air conditioning is introduced for precise environmental control for works of art, it should be limited to exhibition and storage areas. Where there are large variations, as with demand for heating, one boiler working

close to its operating capacity to meet normal requirements and another switching in for abnormal demand are more efficient than having a large boiler working at a fraction of normal capacity for much of the year. A life cycle approach can be used to justify high initial expenditure. For instance, the cost of high-frequency fluorescent tubes might be affordable seen in the context of the extended life of these lamps. A computer-based Building Management System can monitor and control all systems, taking an integrated approach to security, lighting and heating, and monitoring energy use and consumption.

TARGETS

Architects can be set targets for energy efficiency. Lamp performance is measured in terms of output in lumens compared with the input in watts of electrical power (◄◄ artificial lighting). Insulation is measured as a U-value, expressed in terms of watts per square metre K (►► exterior). An holistic approach is preferable in order to take into account heating and power requirements. Energy efficiency for a building is measured as kilowatt-hours/m² per annum. A target of 120 kilowatt-hours/m² per annum is not unreasonable for a new gallery with air-conditioning.

OPERATIONAL IMPLICATIONS

Energy efficiency is an opportunity to invest in capital equipment that will help to reduce running costs, but it should not be just a consideration at the time of building. It also has implications for the operation of the completed building. Energy efficiency requires effective operation and management. Low efficiency may itself be the result of inadequate maintenance. For example, dirty light fittings will mean that illumination levels have to be higher, so increasing energy costs. Equally, low efficiency may be because the design was too complicated for the management and maintenance skills and budgets available (◄◄ business plan). Energy audits and surveys are vital to good management, assessing energy use and identifying measures for cost and energy saving, and should be undertaken regularly, using the results of routine energy monitoring.

Michael Carver, **"Lighting Design and Energy Efficiency in Museums and Galleries"** in May Cassar (ed.), **Museums Environment Energy**, HMSO, 1994.

Chartered Institution of Building Services Engineers, **Contract energy management**, CIBSE Applications Manual 6, 1991, offers guidance for organisations considering employing the services of a CEM company, and includes detailed sections on evaluating proposals, financial appraisal techniques and important aspects of CEM contracts.

Chartered Institution of Building Services Engineers, **Energy audits and surveys**, CIBSE Applications Manual 5, 1991, provides guidance on developing an appropriate strategy, conducting an energy audit or survey, assessing results and implementing options.

Energy Efficiency Office, **Introduction to Energy Efficiency in Museums, Galleries, Libraries and Churches**, 1994, from: **Energy Efficiency Office, Department of the Environment, Blackhorse Road, London, SE8 5JH.**

Royal Institution of Chartered Surveyors, **Energy efficiency in buildings: energy appraisal of existing buildings: a handbook for surveyors**, Royal Institution of Chartered Surveyors, in association with the Energy Efficiency Office and the Building Research Energy Conservation Support Unit, 1993, is intended for use by surveyors in carrying out energy appraisals and relating the results to commercially-realistic recommendations.

entrances

The design of public entry and egress will be a balance between different needs. You should bear in mind the following considerations, for the public entrance to the building to be designed so that:

- people of all ages and abilities can move easily into and out of the building both in normal and emergency situations;
- the space, furnishings and finishes feel welcoming, and encourage visitors to meet, orientate themselves and gather information;
- it provides an effective buffer between the external weather and controlled internal conditions;
- it provides a smooth transition between daylight and lower light levels in the galleries;
- it allows access to be controlled when required.

For the approach to the building and for security issues, ➤➤ **exterior**. For emergency egress, ➤➤ **fire precautions**.

REMOVING PHYSICAL BARRIERS

The removal of physical barriers from existing buildings and the design of new buildings that are barrier-free are covered extensively in access literature. Current legislation and guidelines aim to ensure that no-one is prevented from entering and using a building because of uninformed or bad design. The Disability Discrimination Act 1995 has a very broad definition which includes people with limited dexterity, little strength or poor comprehension, and it also recognises handicapping conditions, such as age, size, advanced pregnancy, mental distress, and psychological disturbance.

The access checklists provided by some Lottery distributors summarise requirements in terms of the dimensions and design of parking bays reserved for wheelchair users, and the provision of drop kerbs, tactile non-slip surfaces and the maximum gradients for ramps. A locked or unattended entrance should be provided with a bell or an intercom, at a wheelchair-accessible height, clearly labelled for visually-impaired people. Links to CCTV, minicom or video would also be useful for deaf visitors.

DRAUGHT LOBBY

Automatic doors are ideal for people who cannot, for whatever reason, easily open or close large and unwieldy doors, and they are often installed to make the point that the gallery welcomes everyone. Automatic doors must remain open for sufficient time for a person moving slowly to pass through them, which can allow surges of cold and wet air to enter the building. Where environmental stability is important for the art spaces, the entrance should be provided with two sets of sliding doors, with sufficient clearance for a wheelchair or group of people, and with appropriate sensors and controls to ensure that both sets are not open at the same time. A draught lobby will also act as a dust trap to inhibit the movement of particulates into the building, especially if it has a recessed mat or grille (◄◄ **air-handling**).

FOYER

Alternatively, the entrance foyer itself can act as a draught lobby if there are other doors from the foyer into the galleries. In this case, an unshielded reception desk must not be placed so close to the external door that the staff are exposed to draughts in cold weather, and staff will need to be instructed to close internal doors which should not be propped or wedged open (◄◄ **project plan**). As well as a buffer against the external weather, the foyer

location:

Surrey Institute of Art & Design.

architect:

Snell Associates.

description:

Entrance to the Foyer Gallery, Farnham campus.

photograph:

Glenn Millington, reproduced courtesy of Positive Images.

will act as a transitional zone for lighting, helping visitors to adjust to any changes in light between, for example, a sunny day outdoors and the low light levels required for an exhibition of watercolours or digital works.

REMOVING PSYCHOLOGICAL BARRIERS

In the past, museums and libraries reinforced the sense of arrival at a place of dignity and grandeur by flights of steps and heavy doors, whose institutional feel at least meant that they could be read as public buildings. Other spaces for contemporary art - notably converted industrial units which have nondescript exteriors - can give the impression that these are private

spaces. For both, a prime design consideration will be how to eliminate the psychological barrier between inside and outside. First impressions matter, and the entrance and reception area is perhaps the most important space in the whole building for making visitors feel welcome. It has to be a generous space that attracts people inside, whether they are arriving for the first time or as regular visitors. Once inside, visitors should feel comfortable and reassured in what may be an unfamiliar environment.

DESIGN FOR MOVING TRAFFIC

The entrance is a corridor which has traffic moving in both directions. As far as possible, moving and static traffic must be kept separate, and space should be sufficient to enable people simply entering or leaving to do so without encountering congestion from other people who might be at the reception desk, cloakroom or shop, looking at information or simply waiting for friends and relatives.

DESIGN FOR STATIONARY TRAFFIC

An entrance is also a place where visitors stop to understand what facilities and activities are available to them. It must have information, plans, signs and other materials and services designed and located for their

convenience, to help them to orientate themselves and to be in control of their visit. The brief should indicate what types and quantities of information will be available in the foyer and how it will be displayed or otherwise made available. Particular attention might be given to multi-lingual facilities in the languages of local communities and/or of principal tourist groups, or to interpretation by audio guides or by the use of Braille, large print or tactile signs.

RECEPTION

The reception/enquiries desk should have clear space in front of it, so that it does not create congestion. It should have a low-level section with a recess to enable wheelchair users to approach. The presence of a TV monitor at the reception desk would help to advertise the fact that the exhibition is covered by closed-circuit television (CCTV), whilst the purpose of a CCTV camera in the reception area would be to help to identify people who might have been recorded at a distance in a gallery.

TICKET SALES

If there will be paid admission to the building as a whole or to the occasional exhibition or event, the design of the entrance should ensure that:

- the perimeter between spaces which are freely accessible and those which will be by paid admission can be covered by the minimum number of control points;
- visitors can queue under cover and without causing congestion;
- there is a enclosed and lockable sales desk which includes an induction loop for partially-deaf visitors.

FITTINGS AND FURNISHINGS

The entrance should be furnished, equipped and lit for the convenience and enjoyment of the variety of individuals who will use the gallery. It might include some or all of the following:

- comfortable seating (suitable for young and old people);
- low-level public pay-phone;
- signs in clear lettering;
- toilets in sufficient numbers and suitable for all users;
- baby-changing and -feeding room;
- facilities for guide dogs.

CLOAKROOM

A cloakroom is important not only for the comfort of visitors but also for security and environmental control, because it helps to keep out of the galleries bags and coats where a small exhibit could be hidden, as well as wet umbrellas and outer clothing which would destabilise the internal environment. A gallery which cannot afford to staff a cloakroom should consider lockable coat-racks and lockers, in a range of sizes so that large items (e.g. rucksacks and pushchairs) can be accepted as well as small ones. Lockers take up more space but an attended cloakroom requires space instead for the staff, a counter and for the public to queue. Also ➤➤ retailing.

Entrance to a 'WHITE BOX'
(see notes on page 88)

The location of the entrance must be clearly visible and distinctive. Its design should relate to the frontage and mass of the building, and to the internal layout, and should express the image of the gallery. It should be accessible, with entry in a straight line and on one level. Doorways should be wide enough to cope with entry and egress of anticipated numbers without creating congestion. The entrance should create a sense of arrival and anticipation of first-hand contact with what is new and exciting in contemporary art. The foyer should include a split-level reception desk slightly off the main route into and out of the building, for control purposes as well as to welcome and help visitors. Information for visitors will include a plan of the building for orientation, the poster for the current exhibition and press reviews in glazed boxes. There should be an area with comfortable seating for visitors to wait and meet. Finishes should be attractive and durable, easy to clean and maintain. Flooring should be non-slip, and should not show dirt.

Entrance to a 'BLACK BOX'
(see notes on page 88)

The public foyer and reception should be a dynamic and exciting space, where marketing and branding will reinforce the identity of an integrated "one-stop" service, sales, information and meeting point for visitors. Lighting should provide visitors with a comfortable transition between external conditions and the controlled lighting within the galleries. Finishes should be durable and set the tone of the

Centre as a welcoming place that is also of international significance. Trained staff will offer visitors accessible programme information from a counter with a split level so that it does not put people in wheelchairs or young children at a disadvantage. The counter should accommodate a CCTV monitor, PA system control, computer, and there should be a small separate connecting office which will contain any controls and switches for the current exhibition. This introductory/orientation space should provide information on how to use the building, including a plan of the building for orientation, details of the current exhibition on wall panels and TV monitors showing the exhibition area.

Entrance to a 'STRONG BOX'
(see notes on page 88)

There should be a single public entrance, for easy and secure control. Where automatic doors are used at the entrance, a second set should be installed either at the entrance to create a draught lobby or between the foyer and the environmentally-controlled spaces. A reception/information desk

should be visible on entry, and the visitor should be aware immediately of the existence and function of the facilities that the gallery has to offer. Information for visitors will include a plan of the building for orientation, a notice board for posters and other information on exhibitions in the gallery and elsewhere, and leaflets in a dispenser. As there will be paid admission to occasional exhibitions, there should be provision for a secure and lockable box office, which should also be clearly visible on entry. There should be the minimum number of control points for entering from the free area (comprising box office, information area, reception desk, cloakroom, seating, toilets, telephones, shop and cafe) into the paying area. Box office and reception desk should have minicom facilities. A CCTV camera in this area should be dedicated to recording visitors in high definition. A self-service cloakroom should be provided for visitors' outer clothing, bags and pushchairs.

Building Regulations and its **Approved Document**, BS 5588: Part 8.

James Holmes-Siedle, **Barrier-Free Design, A Manual for Building Designers and Managers**, Butterworth-Heinemann, 1996.
ISBN 0 7506 1636 9.

Museums & Galleries Commission, **Guide to the use of closed circuit television in museums and galleries**, May 1998.

Gail Nolan, **Designing Exhibitions to Include People with Disabilities**, National Museums of Scotland Publishing, 1997.

exterior

When defining requirements for the exterior of the building, you should bear in mind the following considerations:

- the influence of the building on the local environment;
- the character and visibility of the building;
- access for people arriving on foot, by public transport and by private vehicle, including parking;
- service access;
- protecting the interior from the weather;
- protecting the contents from loss and damage.

SETTING

The ideal location is somewhere where people go normally and is convenient for current and potential users in terms of pedestrian access, public transport, car parking and/or other nearby attractions. To some extent, location determines the kind of institution people understand and expect it to be: museums are monuments of civic pride which are usually in prominent locations in city centres, whilst a rural location suggests a different character. Each location will have positive characteristics or associations that the design will need to reinforce, as well as negative factors which have to be neutralised. For example, a city-centre site can be under more regular surveillance and be more quickly reached by emergency services, than can a rural site which may need extra security as a result. A school or a country house which is converted to arts use will also carry some of its previous associations which the architect may need to emphasise or suppress.

Sensitivity to the impact of the project on the immediate locality should be considered, and the nature of any consultation process - with the public through exhibitions, open meetings, focus groups, etc., and with historic buildings agencies, amenity societies, etc. - should be agreed. Architects will expect to take into account the contribution that an existing building makes to street frontages and vistas and the potential contribution that a new building might make to urban renewal. These considerations might include any historical significance of the site, and any elements or surfaces (e.g. walls, cobbles, etc.) that should be retained. They might include the relationship to other buildings of note, any height restrictions because of adjacent buildings, and the location and sensitivity of the frontage in the street or square. The building should be expected to enhance the character of the area, respect the surrounding buildings and enhance the quality of the townscape in terms of scale, massing, materials, colour, texture, rhythm, light, transparency, etc. You might indicate requirements in terms of surface finishes or any restrictions in terms of the type of stone, brickwork, etc., of the surrounding area which might limit the colours on one elevation (but you might also note where there may be opportunities for a wider range on others). Cleaning and maintenance should not create revenue problems.

IMPACT OF THE BUILDING

The exterior should have a strong character which is welcoming at the same time that it announces the quality of the experience within. A well-designed frontage can help to raise the organisation's visibility. Signs can also help, if they are designed and located to be visible, i.e. perpendicular to normal directions of pedestrian and vehicular traffic. Views into the building and its activities are frequently used to impart an air of familiarity to contemporary art spaces, and a shop with a window display or a café can help the uncommitted person outside the building to cross the threshold. Advertising its availability and visibility can lead to illuminating the exterior and/or the interior at night, to be visible by people on foot and in moving cars. Views into exhibition spaces present problems for security, unless anti-bandit glass or security gates are used (▶▶ windows).

SHARED USE

Defining and promoting a separate identity is a challenge for galleries within buildings largely devoted to other functions (e.g. library, museum, arts centre), and the size and style of entrances off the shared entrance must be designed to be noticeable and welcoming to potential visitors, preferably with glazed doors if they have to be kept closed because of fire regulations and/or the requirements of environmental control. Galleries in educational institutions also need to assert their separate identities where there has been little or no tradition of access to or use of the building by the local community or the general public.

ARTISTS' COMMISSIONS

The brief should describe how the gallery wants to present itself and how the exterior of the building will contribute to this end. The traditional way of declaring the cultural or imaginative nature of the building is to commission an artist to add a 'signpost', which might be a monumental piece of sculpture or which might take advantage of lighting technology to draw attention to, or subtly modify the appearance of, the building. The role of an artist on the design team might include not only what type of spaces and facilities are provided inside but also how the gallery presents itself to the outside.

VISITORS ARRIVING ON FOOT

Pedestrian access should be safe and easy. The eventual position of pedestrian access to the building (if different from any present access) will need to be identified, along with any opportunities for the use of external spaces such as courtyards. Access should relate to existing thoroughfares and exploit the known direction and flow of pedestrian traffic. The architect will need to be informed of any requirements to retain vehicular and/or pedestrian routes and any proposed pedestrianisation or traffic management measures. There may be opportunities or requirements for enhancing existing routes or creating new ones which will need to be designed to be safe, accessible and

unaffected by the closure of the building. The boundaries of the site will need to be defined, especially where emergency escape routes may have to be negotiated across other properties.

VISITORS ARRIVING BY VEHICLE

Access for visitors (and staff) arriving by vehicle should also be safe and easy. A drop-off point as close as possible to the entrance is important for school-groups, and people arriving or leaving by taxi as well as people with impaired mobility. The Department of the Environment, Transport and the Regions sets standards for parking bays for orange badge holders and other outdoor provision for disabled people. The location of convenient parking should be identified, and the number of car-parking spaces required for expected attendances should be estimated to see whether existing or planned provision is adequate, especially when a large number of people might be expected for a special event on a rainy evening. The basis should be clear for calculating the amount of car parking needed: the rule-of-thumb of one car space for every four visitors (based on the assumption that 50% of visitors arrive by car and that each car carries two people) will vary according to whether the gallery is in

a city centre or in a rural location, and an events or education programme will require provision for parking for coaches for groups and parties. The possibility of promoting other forms of access should be considered, e.g. by providing a number of well-designed cycle racks in a prominent location. Signs should be discussed with the local authority's planning and transport departments.

For service access, ➤➤ vehicle access and loading bay.

SECURITY CONSIDERATIONS

Galleries have to operate two quite distinct security strategies. Outside opening hours, security depends on a strong building, a detection system and the prompt response to any alarm. When the building is open to the public, these defences are largely neutralised, and a new strategy has to come into action which depends on monitoring visitors in the public areas and ensuring that they do not gain access to other areas (◄◄ doors and doorways, ➤➤ space).

The security strategy outside normal opening hours will concentrate on defending the building, with metal shutters on doors, grilles on windows, roof lights etc. and other measures to prevent unauthorised persons from gaining access. This should include the less obvious openings, such as sewers, tunnels, basement areas and air ducts. An Intruder Detection System (IDS) is then used to complement these physical defences and to detect any attack on them using magnetic contact detectors, inertia switches, vibration sensors and break-glass detectors, as well as camera surveillance with recording facilities. Neither replaces the other. An efficient IDS may identify an intrusion promptly and set off an alarm, but it offers no form of resistance in itself, and its value is limited if an intruder can enter and escape before the police arrive. If the physical strength of the building cannot defeat an intruder, then it should at least buy time for the police to respond. Tender documents should require the IDS installer to provide training and written instructions on the installed system.

The government indemnity scheme (GIS) sets the standard for physical security, and the Museums Security Adviser at the Museums & Galleries Commission will carry out a security audit if the gallery applies to the GIS or if loans are requested from a national museum (◄◄ gathering information). Any IDS alarm must be transmitted automatically using a monitored line (e.g. BT RedCARE) to an alarm-receiving centre which in turn will alert the police. The IDS should meet the standards set by the National Approval Council for

Security Systems in order to be eligible for Level 1, Immediate Response, as set out by the policy adopted by the Association of Chief Police Officers.

PROTECTION FROM THE WEATHER

The external environment also poses threats to works of art from dirt, pollution, heat, cold, moisture and light, for which the fabric of the building provides the principal line of protection. Existing buildings may be inefficient barriers, but it is more cost-effective to work with the building, not against it. It should not be assumed that environmental control always requires active measures such as air conditioning. Draught-sealing of all openings can discourage the infiltration of outside air and air-borne pollutants; multiple glazing can help to reduce heat-loss; and a vapour barrier can discourage the penetration of moisture and water-soluble pollutants (◄◄ air-handling, ►► windows).

**Exterior for a
'WHITE BOX'**
(see notes on page 88)

The project will create a centre for contemporary art of international significance which will also play a key role in the future regeneration

---

and cultural personality of the city. It should be a symbol of a partnership between the arts, the local authority, educational institutions, business community and community groups. The gallery is not an isolated development and its creation will have a broad impact on the surrounding areas. The design should be instrumental in the regeneration of the immediate locality, and should demonstrate the contribution that contemporary architecture can make to an historic urban fabric. It should lead to a building of architectural significance, paying great attention to its location, proportions, sense of space and light and detail. The building should be welcoming and accessible to all. Public spaces should be formed in front of the building which might be used as extensions of the gallery spaces for external displays, special events, performances and exhibitions (but not for car parking). These spaces should have a strong appeal, in order to draw people to the space and encourage them into the building. Public art, defined in its broadest sense, may be appropriate for inclusion in these outside areas.

To identify the building and advertise the exhibitions, there should be external signs and provision for banners and/or other devices, which must be easy to access and maintain. There should be a drop-off point for people arriving by coach or taxi, and [2] parking bays reserved for people with orange badges should be provided adjacent to entrance.

**Exterior for a
'BLACK BOX'**
(see notes on page 88)

The design must stand as a work of architecture which contains the best of contemporary art. Situated next to a residential area, the gallery must be sensitive to the surrounding area in architectural terms and must be aware of its effect on the local residents. Gallery policy and facilities should encourage alternative means of transport to the car, but there should be space for the increased parking caused by previews. A high thermal performance is required, reducing heat-loss in winter and heat-gain in summer, in order to lower energy usage, maintain environmental stability and prevent condensation. Walls should have a maximum U-value of [0.45] W/m²K and glazing systems a maximum U-value of [1.9] W/m²K. The external fabric should be well-sealed, with particular attention given to the construction of glazing elements and to the lobbying of external doors, to reduce the rate of uncontrolled infiltration of air. To reduce solar gain, windows should be externally shaded and/or provided with appropriate glazing. Use should be made of the window frontage to draw attention to the building and its contents and, in particular, to advertise the exhibitions.

Exterior for a 'STRONG BOX'
(see notes on page 88)

The preferred site is shown on the plan. The outlined area is thought to be the maximum which could be included, but might be changed if the design team puts forward other options which can satisfy the brief requirements. The fabric of the building should be of a construction substantial enough to resist forcible attack. Pipes, ledges and buttresses should be located so that they do not provide easy access to doors, windows and roof lights. Walls and roofs of adjacent properties should also be considered from this point of view. Any party walls with an adjacent property should resist attack, by being bricked up to at least the same structural strength as the surrounding wall, keyed in and reinforced if necessary. Slated roofs

should be strengthened by expanded metal or timber boarding under the slates, and should have thermal insulation and a vapour barrier. Any openings in this outer shell should be reduced to the minimum necessary for access, lighting and environmental control. There should be substantial doors and locks at all entrances, and other openings should be strengthened, to resist a determined physical attack for as long a time as is needed for the police to respond. Security lighting will be required externally, and the site should be secured with locked gates at front and rear. Opportunities for concealment - vegetation, porches, recessed doors, projecting adjacent properties - should be avoided. An intruder detector system should be activated by any attack on the security perimeter.

Bryan Dovey, **"Planning for safety and security"**, in Gail Dexter Lord and Barry Lord (Eds.), **The Manual of Museum Planning**, HMSO 1991. **ISBN 011 290483 1.**

Chartered Institution of Building Services Engineers, **Security engineering**, CIBSE Applications Manual 4, 1991, includes guidance on risk assessment, vandalism, methods of physical protection, detection and alarm systems, and security control rooms.

Museums & Galleries Commission, **Improving Museums Security, MGC Guidelines for Good Practice**, 1997.

Museums & Galleries Commission, **Guide to police response to automatic intruder detection systems**, May 1998.

fire precautions

Like any building, an exhibition gallery has to be designed to:

- minimise the risk of fire;
- restrict the spread of fire;
- detect fire as quickly as possible;
- ensure that occupants can escape as quickly as possible;
- control an outbreak of fire as soon as possible.

MINIMISING RISK

In addition to installing gas, oil, mechanical, electrical equipment and their wiring and controls in accordance with the appropriate regulations, a gallery must ensure that it uses fire-retardant materials and paints. Otherwise, minimising the risk of fire is largely an operational matter in terms of enforcing fire-prevention measures, including a strict non-smoking rule, especially where empty travelling crates and packing materials can be a significant fire risk.

RESTRICTING SPREAD

Building codes require parts of a building to be isolated into distinct fire compartments, and gallery display and storage areas should be insulated to provide one hour's protection against areas of risk, such as workshops, kitchens, plant room, paint stores, etc. Fire doors can be difficult to open and close by people in wheelchairs or by those who have limited strength, especially where extra large doors are required because service access is shared with public access (◄◄ **doors and doorways**).

FIRE DETECTION SYSTEM

An automatic Fire Detection System (FDS) should be provided, which sets off an alarm if it detects fire and/or smoke in any part of the building. Sensors can be smoke- or heat-detectors or a more sophisticated air-sampling system. Smoke detectors tend to be preferred because they react earlier - especially VESDA (Very Early Smoke Detection) systems - but fire detectors may be necessary where smoke detectors might lead to false alarms. The standard for galleries is set by the minimum requirements for the **government indemnity scheme**. The latter's security and environmental conditions require that:

- the FDS covers the whole building;
- the FDS has been fitted by an alarm company approved by the National Approval Council for Security Systems (NACOSS); and is serviced annually and maintained in good working condition;
- unless it is monitored internally by security personnel, the FDS transmits an alarm automatically, using a monitored line such as BT's RedCARE, to an alarm-receiving centre which in turn alerts the fire brigade.

Whilst there are people on the premises, the FDS must also signal audible and visual alarms and release locks and open automatic doors on escape routes.

EMERGENCY EGRESS

The architect should ensure that statutory and local requirements are met in the following areas:

- the FDS should set off audible and visible alarms in all areas, including toilets and other enclosed spaces where a disabled person might not hear or see a general alarm;
- the content and location of signs for non-automatic fire-fighting equipment, emergency escape routes and fire exits should meet local and statutory requirements; locations of alarm bells, emergency signs, break-

glass door releases, fire extinguishers etc should be discussed at an early stage with the local Fire Officer, to ensure that these items do not intrude unnecessarily into display surfaces (➤➤ wall surfaces).

- emergency egress must be adequate for the estimated numbers of users and for the number of floors: in addition to escape staircases, a building on several floors may need a fire-protected lift and fire refuges if the number of wheelchair users allowed on upper floors is not to be restricted; requirements for emergency egress must not compromise the security of the building and its exhibitions. e.g. emergency escape routes should not be through an exhibition space, if at all possible;

- emergency illumination has to be provided in all public and circulation areas, in the event of a mains failure, with a battery of sufficient capacity to provide lighting for a period of three hours; the light levels recommended in BS5266 are considered inadequate for visually-impaired people, and a minimum of 30 lux should be provided along the centre line of an escape route, but

any power to emergency lighting must be controlled in normal conditions, so that light levels do not exceed those required for an exhibition; on any loss of mains power, they should automatically switch to full output on the emergency circuit;

- for emergency exits, doors can have push bars and other local release mechanisms, but electro-magnetic locks, which release when the fire alarm sounds or the power fails and which also open any automatic doors, are preferable. All emergency exits should have sensors to detect when they are opened and also to indicate if the doors remain locked whilst the building is occupied (◄◄ doors and doorways).

- the purpose of smoke extraction is to help people escape in an emergency, to help fire-fighting and to minimise smoke damage.

To complement this physical provision, staff will need training to ensure that emergency egress, including the special needs of disabled people, is managed safely and effectively (◄◄ project plan).

location:
Spacex, Exeter.

architect:
Nicholas Gilbert Scott.

description:
Half-hour fire doors: entrance to gallery and new flight of stairs to studios upstairs.

photograph:
Warwick Sweeney, reproduced courtesy of Warwick Sweeney.

CONTROLLING AN OUTBREAK

The local Fire Officer will advise on numbers, types and locations of extinguishers and other control equipment.

Although automatic sprinkler systems can now give a very localised response, museums and galleries are often reluctant to use them because of the risk of accidental discharge. However, this risk is balanced by the use of less water than would be the case if any fire had chance to spread, and museum conservators regard a limited amount of water damage as a lesser evil than widespread smoke or fire damage. The risk can be further reduced by using a "pre-action" system which only allows water into pipes supplying the sprinkler head that a fire has activated, although this system is more complicated and slower than traditional sprinklers.
To avoid the risk of rusty or dirty water, pipe-work should be in stainless steel or similar corrosion-resistant material. Sprinkler heads should also switch off when the temperature drops, in order to limit water damage. Even so, it is still possible for some lenders to insist that a sprinkler system is de-activated whilst their material is on the premises, and smoke detectors will be necessary as a back-up in this eventuality.

BS 5445: Components of automatic fire detection systems: Part 7:1984, sets out requirements, test methods and performance criteria for re-settable smoke detectors using scattered light, transmitted light or ionisation.

BS 5266: Part 1:1988, Code of practice for the emergency lighting of premises other than cinemas and certain other specified premises used for entertainment, considers the level of hazard and the degree of familiarity of occupants with the premises, covers safe evacuation along defined routes allowing for changes in floor direction and level; and provides guidance on the illumination of fire alarm points and fire fighting equipment.

Chartered Institution of Building Services Engineers, **Emergency Lighting, CIBSE Technical Memorandum 12**, 1986, complements the British Standards, with recommendations on illuminance, glare and duration and information on planning; equipment and installation; commissioning and servicing.

Chartered Institution of Building Services Engineers, **Fire precautions: sources of information on legal and other requirements, CIBSE Technical Memorandum 16:1990**, brings together information on both legislative requirements and non-statutory codes and standards related to fire precautions.

Fire Protection Association, **Heritage Under Fire**, Aldermary House, Queen Street, London EC4N 1TJ **tel:** 0171 248 52222.

Murray Frost, "Planning for Preventive Conservation", in Gail Dexter Lord & Barry Lord (Eds), **The Manual of Museum Planning**, HMSO 1991

G M B Webber, M S Wright & G K Cook, **'Emergency Lighting and Wayfinding systems for Visually-Impaired People'**, BRE Information Paper IP 9/97.

floor surfaces

The following is only concerned with floors in exhibition galleries, and not with other rooms and spaces in the building, nor with a floor's structure. You should bear in mind the following considerations, for floor surfaces that:

- are easy and comfortable for visitors to move across;
- are durable and capable of sustaining the weight of likely exhibits;
- might be used for the heating system;
- are wired for power and a variety of cabled services.

For other aspects of exhibition galleries, ◄◄ doors and doorways, ►► roof lights and windows.

FINISHES

You should resist the temptation to state a preference for polished concrete, hardwood, quarry tiles, carpet squares or any other surface finish. Decisions about the material and the colour and texture of the surface will derive from all of the functions the floor is expected to accommodate. Like other surfaces (see ◄◄ ceilings, ►► wall surfaces) in exhibition spaces, the floor can have many functions where walls or ceilings may not be able to carry all necessary services for structural or conservation reasons. The character, strength, texture and colour of the floor will also influence the nature of the space and the type of works of art that can be seen there.

DESIGN FOR PEOPLE

Because it is the surface upon which visitors move, the floor must be as easy to use and as comfortable as is compatible with other requirements. Its texture and colours must help disabled people, although there may be difficulties with reconciling some needs. For example, people with visual impairments find textured surfaces helpful, but these surfaces are uncomfortable to wheelchair-users. The choice of floor surface will determine how comfortable the gallery feels to people who are walking, and will affect the acoustic properties of the space. Light-coloured hardwood floors are currently popular, and help to make the best use of available light, especially where levels have to be controlled. On the other hand, visitors on a bright floor can be reflected in glazed paintings at some viewing angles (◄◄ artificial lighting).

Some contrast between floor surfaces and walls, screens, plinths, etc. is useful for people with visual impairments, but too dark a tone can have a negative effect, because the extent and generally uncluttered nature of a gallery floor makes it a powerful influence on the character of the space. An old building may have a wooden floor which it may be difficult not to strip and seal, but the final colour and tone must be tested for its effect on the space. Unless instructed otherwise, cleaners will invariably polish a wooden floor, and the resulting reflection can create a distracting and uncomfortable glare - especially for people with visual impairments - as well as alter the colour rendering of the light.

HEATING

Where the priority is to avoid the clutter of radiators and pipes on wall surfaces, heating elements are often located in the floor. Electric under-floor heating, using night-time tariffs and the storage capacity of concrete floor slabs, is invisible, but it may be difficult to regulate output to match requirements each day. More satisfactory is the provision of grilles set into the floor for hot-water or air-conditioning systems.

DESIGN FOR WORKS OF ART

The floor is frequently a display surface in its own right, e.g. for sculpture and installations. If hardwood floors are popular for collection-based galleries, more experimental galleries often prefer the less precious and more industrial feel of polished concrete, which will tolerate heavy sculptures and paint spills, and can be drilled and bolted into. On the other hand, a suspended floor has the flexibility to be broken into and used for installations.

FLOOR LOADING

The floor of the exhibition space must be considered part of the service access between delivery point and installed position in an exhibition (◄◄ art route). Imposed floor loading should be adequate for the heaviest sculpture that it would be possible to bring into the gallery. Structural engineers measure loading in terms of the force acting on the floor, in kilonewtons per square metre, instead of the simple measurement of mass used, for example, for the carrying capacity of a lift which is measured in units of thousand kilograms. The conversion rate is approximately 1 kilonewton = 100 kilograms, so the recommendation that all museum floors should support a distributed load of 4.5 kilonewtons per square metre is equivalent to less than half a ton per square metre. For the exhibition organiser, it is more important to know the maximum load that a particular point of the floor can bear (i.e. the maximum of weight for an individual piece of sculpture, plus its carrying equipment) and the total load that a floor can bear (i.e. the maximum of weight for all the sculptures and visitors in that room or on that level).

WIRING AND CABLING

A recent use of suspended floors is to enable cables for power and data to be routed to any position in the gallery, for display cases requiring electrical supply and for free-standing exhibits requiring co-axial or computer cabling. As artists explore the possibilities afforded by new technologies, galleries need to be designed so that it is not necessary to hang cables down from the ceiling or to route them along from the walls (►► wired services). Proprietary raised "computer floors" are one of the possibilities for concealing cables, for laying down new ones to cope with different needs and technological change, and for supplying equipment without a cable being visible or creating a trip hazard in a darkened room.

DESIGN FOR EXHIBITION STRUCTURES

A level floor can be a major consideration and expense when converting an old building, but a sloping and uneven floor is uncomfortable and inconvenient for people with mobility problems, and can also make difficulties with self-supporting screens, especially in travelling exhibitions which have an integral screen system, and - to a lesser extent - with plinths and display cases. In addition, the floor may have to include anchor points corresponding with similar points immediately above them in the ceiling, for fixing the supports for a screen system.

**Floor surfaces
for a 'WHITE BOX'
(see notes on page 88)**

The floor should provide an uninterrupted surface for the display of works of art, whether large sculptures or installations that are free-standing or smaller works shown on plinths and platforms or in display cases. It should be level and smooth, both for the easy movement of large works of art and for the stability of plinths, screens, etc. It should be capable of sustaining a point load of [4] tons per square metre and a total load of [25] tons. It should be water- and scratch-resistant, hard-wearing and easy to maintain. The ability to screw directly into the surface, and to be able to fill the screw-holes and repair the surface subsequently would be an advantage. It should be possible to change the colour of the surface easily and inexpensively.

location:
Glynn Vivian Art Gallery, Swansea.

architect(s):
Swansea City Council.

description:
School group in the 'Emrys Williams' exhibition.

photograph:
Paul Newcombe, reproduced courtesy of Glynn Vivian Art Gallery.

**Floor surfaces
for a 'STRONG BOX'**
(see notes on page 88)

The floor surface should be quiet and comfortable for visitors, attractive and light-reflecting. It should be as dust free as possible and easily cleaned without the use of solvents.

**Floor surfaces
for a 'BLACK BOX'**
(see notes on page 88)

The floor surface should be attractive, hard-wearing and easy to maintain. It should supply a number of cabled services preferably by concealed trunking, to which access should be possible at almost any point in the gallery.

BS 6399: Part 1, 1984, recommends that museum floors should support a distributed load of 4.5 kilonewtons per square metre, and that additional allowances, up to 7.5 kilonewtons per square metre, may have to made for heavy exhibits or the weight of screens and partitions.

Centre for Accessible Environments, **Specifier's Handbook 4: Internal Floor Finishes: improving access for all.**

government indemnity scheme

PURPOSE

The Government Indemnity Scheme (GIS) is a scheme whereby museums and galleries can apply for a Government-backed indemnity in place of commercial insurance for temporary exhibitions. In effect GIS makes available on a short-term basis the sort of cover that H.M.Treasury operates for the Tate Gallery, National Gallery of Scotland, Ulster Museum and other national museums and galleries in the UK, with the important difference that the Government undertakes to reimburse lenders for the value of lost, stolen or irreparably-damaged work. Requirements are stringent in order to minimise the risk of loss and damage, and GIS applicants have sometimes discovered that they were spending more on extra supervision or additional security measures than they would have paid had they taken out full commercial insurance.

IMPLICATIONS FOR EXHIBITION GALLERIES

The lesson for buildings is that, if there is a real possibility of applying for Government Indemnity Scheme (and/or for borrowing work from national collections), the building should be designed from the outset to meet basic GIS requirements. Actual requirements will vary from exhibition to exhibition, according to the assessment of risk, but a building can be designed to satisfy basic requirements in terms of strengthening the physical fabric of the building and providing appropriate electronic systems (◀◀ exterior). The design can also ensure that exhibition spaces can be effectively invigilated for exhibitions covered by GIS, although supervision may be at a lower level for the rest of the programme (▶▶ space). GIS requirements also extend to environmental control (◀◀ air-handling).

location:
Castle Museum and Art Gallery Nottingham.

architect:
Stuart Hodgkinson for Derek Latham Associates.

description:
Window grilles by Michael Johnston.

photograph:
Reproduced courtesy of Nottingham Castle Museum and Art Gallery.

For the general conditions of the GIS, contact the **Capital Taxes Officer, Museums & Galleries Commission, 16 Queen Anne's Gate, London, SW1H 9AA. tel:** 0171 233 4200 **fax:** 0171 233 3686

humidity

RELATIVE HUMIDITY (RH)

Humidity is important because moisture-sensitive materials such as paper, wood and textiles react by expanding if conditions become more humid and by contracting if conditions become drier. As well as putting the material itself under stress, this movement can damage or destabilise any pigment and binding medium resting on it.

Relative humidity (RH) is a measure of the amount of water vapour in the air, expressed as a percentage of the total amount that will saturate the same volume of air at the same temperature. A hygrometer is used for measuring RH; a thermohygrometer measures both temperature and humidity; and a thermohygrograph records temperature and humidity. Increasingly, electronic sensors are being used to supply data, either by wire or by telemetry, to a computerised monitoring system and into an automated Building Management System.

RH is usually a consideration if the exhibition gallery is attached to a museum or when it wishes to borrow material from a public collection. In these cases, the objective is to keep RH stable in all spaces where exhibits are kept for even short periods of time. As well as display areas, storage and access routes need to be monitored, and controls and procedures have to be provided to maintain stability within strict limits. There are two sorts of variation which exhibition galleries need to be prepared for:

- differences between the conditions at the lender's premises and those at the borrower's;
- lack of stability at the venue itself.

DIFFERENCES BETWEEN THE LENDER'S CONDITIONS AND THE BORROWER'S

The conditions at the lender's premises are the most important guide for the borrower, because the work to be borrowed will have stabilised at these conditions. The recognised norm for paintings on canvas and works on paper in Europe and North America is a RH of 55% ± 2%, but other materials have different needs, e.g. metals require drier conditions (less than 40%), whilst ivory or lacquer ware may require moister conditions (up to 60%). However, applying textbook figures could cause damage if they are different from the conditions in which an object has been kept and at which it is now in equilibrium. The first aim of environmental control is therefore to stabilise the conditions to an optimum level for the works being borrowed. Lenders will often specify parameters for their material, and they will expect the borrower to demonstrate that conditions can be maintained within the required limits, usually by providing records of RH measurements in the exhibition spaces for a similar time of year to the period of the proposed exhibition. In this case, a parameter is an acceptable range, normally expressed in terms of a target figure and tolerance either side shown as a "±" figure. This does **not** mean that a temperature of 19°C ± 1°C has a thermostat set at 18°C for night-time and at 20°C during the day. Instead it means that 19°C is the target which building and its control strategy is attempting to maintain at all times. Fluctuations are inevitable (e.g. a large number of people at a private view will create heat and humidity) but the strategy will try to anticipate and mitigate them.

LACK OF STABILITY AT THE VENUE

Because of the relationship between temperature and RH, the most common cause of variable RH in a gallery is heating for the benefit of staff and visitors during the day, which is often exacerbated by solar gain and heat from tungsten lighting. As air warms up, its RH drops. This increases its capacity to absorb moisture, which it takes from the objects - including the works of art in an exhibition - with which it is in contact. Cooling at night, if a heating system is switched off and heat is lost through windows, roof lights, etc. increases the RH. The air has less capacity to hold the moisture it has absorbed, which it transfers to objects with a lower RH. If there are surfaces which are colder (e.g. windows which are themselves contributing to the cooling process), then condensation can form and water can drip on exhibits. Daily variation of this kind - and the relationship between temperature and RH - can be measured using a thermohygrograph which plots RH and temperature on a graph on a rotating drum over a 24-hour or 7-day period. Environmental control aims to ensure that any variation takes place over as long a period as possible, over weeks and even months rather than days, so that materials do not undergo stress from rapid and continual movement.

METHODS OF CONTROL

A common way of controlling humidity is to use mobile units - humidifiers when the galleries are warming up and de-humidifiers when they are cooling down. However, controlling temperature can be a more effective way of stabilising RH. Instead of humidification during the day, cooling can be used to stop the air from becoming dry. Instead of dehumidification at night, temperature levels are maintained by keeping the heating system running. This regime involves using humidistats instead of thermostats for controlling the temperature in the galleries. It also requires improved insulation (e.g. double-glazing) to cope with the lower night-time temperatures outside, to save energy costs and to prevent condensation.

Where the gallery's environmental control cannot cope - or where there are loans of different materials from different sources, all requiring different RH levels - the usual course of action is to provide micro-climates in the form of sealed frames and display cases. In these instances, general control of the internal environment assists whatever is maintaining the micro-climate.

With a non-mechanical system using hygroscopic salts, it extends the life of this buffering material so that it does not need conditioning quite so quickly. With mechanical systems, it reduces noise levels, power requirements and running costs.

light

Protection from the damage caused by light:

- applies to all works of art containing organic materials;
- is particularly important for loans from museum collections;
- is achieved by a combination of removing the shorter wavelengths and reducing the intensity and duration of exposure.

WHICH WORKS ARE SENSITIVE TO LIGHT?

All works of art that contain organic substances are sensitive to light. Particularly sensitive are those that contain unprotected organic substances, such as watercolours, drawings, manuscripts and textiles. Works are partially sensitive to light where the organic substances they contain are protected in some way. For example, the oil medium in oil paint offers some measure of protection to pigments of organic origin. The only works not sensitive to light are ceramics, stone, glass, metal, enamel, etc. that contain no organic materials.

Contemporary works are as sensitive as their historical equivalents composed of the same materials, but protection from the effects of exposure to light is often only a consideration after an object has been acquired by a museum. Many objects have suffered the damaged from exposure to light before entering a museum collection, and curators have these constant reminders before them of the need to prevent damage. New acquisitions become immediately subject to the museum philosophy which makes preservation for the long term a primary objective. It follows that, if an exhibition gallery wishes to borrow material that has entered a museum collection, then it must abide by the precautions that the museum has established for the preservation of that work.

The damage caused by light is irreversible. The principal chemical reaction induced by exposure to light is oxidation of pigments, but - since it is impractical to exclude oxygen - it is light that is subject to control. The amount or rate of fading is accelerated by warm and damp conditions (as well as causing other forms of deterioration, ◄◄ humidity), but galleries have also to take into account the comfort of visitors and staff. As a result, the normal strategy for museums to minimise photo-degradation is a combination of:

- removing the shorter wavelengths;
- reducing the intensity of light;
- reducing the duration of exposure.

An exhibition gallery wishing to borrow light-sensitive material from a museum collection should be able to duplicate this strategy for the period that the loan is on the premises.

REMOVING THE SHORTER WAVELENGTHS

The extent of deterioration depends on the spectral characteristics of the light falling on an object, with most damage caused by the short wavelengths in the ultraviolet range of the spectrum. UV radiation is defined as wavelengths between 280 and 380 nanometres (nm), although wavelengths shorter than 300 nm are filtered by the atmosphere's ozone layer. However, there is nothing safe about staying the 'right side' of the dividing line between ultraviolet and visible light. Wavelengths longer than 380 nm can provoke almost as much damage, but the range between 400 and 440 nm can be detected by the human eye. Filters giving protection up to 440 nm have a yellow tint, since they remove some of the violet end of the spectrum, so they are usually only used where colour rendering is unimportant. For exhibition galleries, the aim is to remove progressively more radiation as wavelengths become shorter and more destructive. Garry Thomson's specification is that transmission at 400 nm should be less than 50% of the transmission in the middle of the visible range 550 nm, and transmission of wavelengths between 320 nm and 380 nm should be less than 1% of transmission of that at 550 nm.

In practice, UV is filtered by using plastic films laminated between glass (including security glass) in new glazing or by applying such filters in the form of acetate, acrylic or polycarbonate sheets to existing glazing. (➤➤ rooflights, windows) Manufacturers will normally guarantee a life expectancy according to the type of film and its location, but it is up to the gallery to monitor its performance. UV has been measured as a proportion of an amount of visible light transmitted through a window or emitted by a light source, using instruments scaled in terms of microwatts (μW) of UV radiation per lumen of light output. A window or a lamp which exceeds the accepted norm of a maximum of 75 μW/lumen should therefore have its filter replaced. (➤➤ rooflights, windows) More recently, there has been a move to fix a maximum for the amount of UV radiation actually falling on a surface, which is more directly relevant for

sensitive material, and a maximum of 20 μW/m² is becoming accepted. Consequently it might not be necessary to replace or filter the lamp or a window with a output reading of over 75 μW/lumen, if the work of art is far enough away to for it to receive less than 20 μW/m².

REDUCING THE INTENSITY OF LIGHT

Since it is not practicable to remove all the damaging radiation, it is still important to control overall light levels. The extent of deterioration depends partly on the intensity of light falling on objects, and the conservator's aim is to reduce exposure to the lowest levels that are compatible with visibility. In practice, this means shading windows and dimming artificial lights either by controls or by replacing bulbs with a lower output. There are two basic methods of measuring light. The lumen is the lighting engineer's measure of the output from a light source. Lux is instead the conservator's unit of measurement of the level of illumination on an object. For oil paintings, a maximum of 200 lux is generally recommended, whilst a maximum of 50 lux has been adopted for objects sensitive to light, including prints, drawings, manuscripts, gouaches, watercolours and textiles. Although 50 lux is frequently quoted as if it were some sort of magic figure, the fact is that all light damages, and

location:
ArtSway, Sway (Hampshire).

architect:
Tony Fretton.

description:
Ann Carrington, 'Coca-Bossa Nova'.

photograph:
Gina Dearden, reproduced courtesy of ArtSway and Ann Carrington.

exposure at 49 lux is only moderately better than 51 lux.

REDUCING THE DURATION OF EXPOSURE

Finally, the extent of deterioration depends on duration. The effect of light is cumulative, so an exposure at 50 lux for 2 hours is equivalent to 100 lux at one hour. Consequently, light should be excluded from galleries when it is not needed, e.g. before and after opening hours in summer.

Garry Thomson,
The Museum Environment,
Butterworths,
second edition 1986.
ISBN 0 408 1536 5.

loading bay

This section uses the term "loading bay" to signify the delivery and collection area of an exhibition gallery. At one end of the scale, this might be little more than a door close to which a truck can be parked, whilst at the other, a loading bay might be a fully-enclosed dock big enough to take a vehicle. ◄◄ art route, ►► storage and vehicle access.

The lifeblood of an exhibition gallery is the continuous movement of exhibits and exhibitions in and out of the building, so you should bear in mind the following considerations, for a transition between building and vehicle which should be:

- separate from public access and other forms of service access;
- protected from the weather;
- big enough to handle the largest crates that the gallery is likely to receive;
- secure, both in use and when the building is closed;
- equipped with appropriate handling and lifting equipment;
- easily accessible to the exhibition spaces (◄◄ art route).

LOCATION

Wherever possible, external access for exhibits should be separated from access for people, for the safety and convenience of visitors and passers-by (►► vehicle access). The public entrance to the building should be inviting and welcoming, but delivering or loading through this entrance can mean that public access to the building has to be restricted. In addition, public entrances are often on main thoroughfares designed for people, and delivering or loading across a busy pavement is inconvenient and potentially dangerous to passers-by.

Separate access for exhibits is also for the safety and security of the exhibits and for the convenience of staff. One of the most vulnerable moments for an exhibition can be when it is loaded and unloaded from a vehicle. If a site does not allow for separate access, then the gallery must be prepared to exclude the public from the building during deliveries and collections, which can be a problem for exhibition galleries within a museum, arts centre or library building. Stand-alone galleries can be closed to the public between exhibitions, but it is not unknown for deliveries to be made before an exhibition has closed or for collections to be made after an exhibition has opened.

location:
Fruitmarket Gallery, Edinburgh.

architect:
Richard Murphy Architects.

description:
Part of the entrance facade.

photograph:
Peter Cook, reproduced courtesy of Fruitmarket Gallery.

A loading bay should be located to give an easy, direct route to areas used for storage and exhibitions. In conversions or restricted sites, the location of a loading bay is often determined by external road access rather than by the proposed layout of the gallery, but you can at least indicate your preferences in terms of ideal internal layout, perhaps illustrating in diagrammatic form how different functions (loading, holding, storing, moving and displaying) should relate to each other.

PROTECTION FROM THE ELEMENTS

Ideally, a loading bay would provide a protected environment for loading and unloading of exhibitions, reducing the risk of damage from the weather, providing comfortable working conditions, improving physical security and allowing the safe use of lifting and carrying machinery. Reversing the vehicle into a loading bay is preferable to an unsheltered situation where the vehicle parks parallel to the building and the consignment has first to be exposed to external weather - e.g. a large painting being affected by high winds - and risk of theft or damage before it can be moved back into a protected environment. However, reversing does require an apron outside the loading bay, with sufficient space for the maximum size of vehicle to be able to manoeuvre to the required position (➤➤vehicle access).

EXTERNAL SHUTTER

The size of the opening of the loading bay should be dictated by either the maximum size of the crates that the gallery can receive or - if the vehicle can reverse into the loading bay - the maximum height and width of vehicles delivering a consignment. High-value or vulnerable works will often travel in crates which are significantly larger than their contents, and this size plus any trucks and trolleys required to move them should be allowed for in all doorways between the loading bay and the exhibition area. There is little point in providing high-grade travelling crates and air-conditioned spaces if the external door is too small to admit a crate, and the work must be unpacked in the hot sun or in the pouring rain. To provide a greater degree of protection, vehicles need to be able to reverse, wholly or in part, into the loading bay. The flush type of loading bay used by commercial operators - whereby a vehicle reverses up to the edge of a loading platform that is flush with the outside wall of the building - is impractical for galleries because of the great variety of sizes of vehicles that might deliver or collect exhibitions.

To accept a vehicle, the minimum opening should be 3.67m wide x 4.6m high. Although vehicles are not normally wider than 2.5m, an opening narrower than 3.67m risks damage to the building's security doors and to the vehicles' tail-lift mechanisms, and requires extra time in manoeuvring. The loading bay opening will also need to be high enough for fine art transport which, in order to carry very large works of art, frequently has a box that is higher than a standard vehicle. For high security, this opening would require a heavy-duty steel shutter, preferably an insulated sandwich, provided with appropriate locks and sensors. Internal doors leading from the loading bay into the gallery should also have alarm sensors on them, and the loading bay should be covered by a space alarm. The loading bay should be a separate zone within the security system, so that deliveries can be made in the early morning or late evening without switching off the alarm system and compromising the rest of building.

CAPACITY

The floor area of the loading bay will depend on whether it is designed simply to receive and handle the contents of a vehicle, which could require a volume of up to 60 m³ for the largest trailers or whether it is designed to fully enclose a vehicle, which would require an area of up to 150 m² for an articulated lorry. Clearly, driving the vehicle into the building and securing the outer doors would be ideal from the point of view of security and protection from external weather. Independence from external weather would be more efficient, as well as being more comfortable and healthier for staff. Fully-enclosed areas are adaptable to a wide variety of vehicles, e.g. side-loading, and make the use of overhead equipment possible. However, this is an option only for the largest building projects or the most exposed (e.g. seaside) positions, because it is expensive on space, heating and lighting and has additional design requirements (e.g. to reduce engine running time, to extract the exhaust fumes and to drain away any snow and rain brought indoors on the vehicle). If only part of the vehicle can be reversed into a loading bay, a dock shelter might be considered. This adjusts to different heights and widths

of vehicle body to provide a weather-proof seal between building and vehicle. Where environmental control is critical, there might be a holding area immediately adjacent the loading bay (➤➤ storage).

For ease of manoeuvre of large items, the space within the loading bay should be designed to be open and unobstructed. For the same reason and also for security, the loading bay should not be used for purposes such as deliveries of fuel oil, foodstuffs, publications, or for the removal of refuse from a catering facility. Floor surfaces have to be smooth, durable, easy to maintain and on one level, so that crates on piano wheels or platform trucks can be moved with little effort and without undue vibration or shock to the exhibits. The ceiling needs to have sufficient clear height, allowing for light fittings, ducting, etc. to cope with the highest crate or vehicle envisaged.

EQUIPMENT

Except for the smallest vehicles, most fine art transport is now equipped with tail lifts, so that a loading bay does not need to have a platform at approximately the same height as the vehicle bed, and the floor of the loading bay can be all on one level, without

steps or ramps. Where there is a raised platform, it should be set sufficiently back within the loading bay, to allow the tail lift to operate under cover. The disadvantage of a tail lift is that large crates may not fit on the platform and heavy crates can cause the vehicle to rise at the front, possibly requiring greater clearances. In these circumstances - and for vehicles not provided with a tail lift - the solution can be a scissors lift or hydraulic lift table in the floor of the loading bay.

The loading bay should also include an area designated for the storage of mobile equipment used for lifting and transporting crates and works of art, e.g. hydraulic fork-lift, pallet truck, mobile gantry, platform trolley, piano trolley.

Loading bay for a 'WHITE BOX' or a 'BLACK BOX' (see notes on page 88)

Service access should be separate from access for the public, and be secure, sheltered and controlled. The loading bay should be designed for vehicles up to [15] metres long, [2.5] metres wide and [4] metres high, to back up to the opening. It should allow crated and uncrated work, with maximum dimensions [5] metres long, [2] metres wide and [3] metres high, to be manoeuvred safely in and out of vehicles, using a range of handling equipment, both powered and unpowered. Lighting should be artificial, with general illumination up to [500] lux, supplemented with robust directional lighting for lighting within vehicles when required. There should be a high level of power service. The loading bay should be protected from the elements for the comfort of staff as much as the safety of the exhibits.

Loading bay for a 'STRONG BOX'
(see notes on page 88)

The loading bay must comply with the standards of the Government Indemnity Scheme for security and environmental control and should be reserved for the purposes of delivering and removing exhibitions. The external door or shutter should be resistant to attack and be locked and provided with tamper alarms, with the loading bay treated as a discrete security zone within the alarm system. There should be space alarms within the loading area. There should be space for safe storage of lifting, carrying and handling equipment.

Although intended for commercial applications, The **Loading Bay Design - How, Where, When?** is a useful 20-page, illustrated booklet.
It promotes the concept of the vehicle as an 'extra room' which, although only temporarily attached to a building, deserves the same considerations of access, security, health and safety and environmental control that apply to the permanent structure.
It is available free from:
R.S. Stokvis & Sons Ltd., Pool Road, West Molesey, Surrey, KT8 2HN.
tel: 0181 941 1212
fax: 0181 941
email:info@stockvis.co.uk
web: www. stockvis.co.uk

'people route'

For the design of circulation routes through the building for members of the general public, you will need to bear in mind the following considerations:

- statutory requirements to implement inclusive access and independent use by disabled people;

- the capacity of a building to handle people efficiently depends more on the width of its corridors and stairways than on its area or volume;

- corridors and stairways are more than physical means of connecting one part of the gallery with another, but are also psychologically valuable for relaxing and preparing the visitor and can enhance the quality of the experience;

- buildings may need to be designed for more than one circulation pattern;

- orientation throughout the building should be designed for all types of user.

For emergency egress, ◄◄ fire precautions. For the movement of works of art, ◄◄ art route.

INCLUSIVE ACCESS

The Disability Discrimination Act (1995) requires all areas of a building to be accessible to disabled people.

Every decision about the design of the building must therefore be assessed for the impact it may or may not have on people with physical or sensory impairments. It is not enough for everyone to be able to enter 'through the front door', but the building should be designed so that there is unrestricted access - subject to security requirements - to different levels and floors including staff areas. Signage and information should be provided (eg. using audio guides, and Braille, large-print or tactile signs) on the same principle of giving full access to all forms of activity and information. Most visits to galleries are self-directed, so information and signs must be welcoming, simple and clear. Signs should incorporate symbols and directional arrows. Floor plans indicating layout and features should be in raised tactile lettering. The aim should be independent access and use, so that a disabled person is able to move through the building and to use its services without assistance. The complexity of provision means that a specialist consultant should be involved in the project from the outset (◄◄ design team).

location:
Tate Gallery, Liverpool.

architect:
Michael Wilford and Partners.

description:
Entrance foyer: view past the plans and other information for visitors into the exhibition galleries.

photograph:
Richard Bryant/Arcaid, reproduced courtesy of the Tate Gallery.

MINIMUM PROVISION FOR CHANGES OF LEVEL

The Building Regulations and Lottery checklists set out requirements for both physical and sensory access. For changes of level, they include:

- stairs that are well-lit, preferably from the side; with a nosing strip in a contrasting colour to the tread and with the solid risers in a different colour;

- ramps with firm non-slip surfaces and shallow gradients;

- both stairs and ramps with level landings at top and bottom that are clear of opening doors, with changes of direction only at landings, and with handrails at two heights for their full length and extending at top and bottom.

For the convenience of all users, services would be better all on one level, and lifts should be provided where this is not possible. A lift designed for independent use by a wheelchair user is large enough to allow a wheelchair to turn round and has controls and emergency telephone and alarm at a suitable height. For visually-impaired people, the controls should also have tactile and Braille markings, and the lift should be equipped with voice announcement.

Any quiet spaces for staff or public use that are adjacent to a lift shaft should not be subject to unacceptable noise levels.

CORRIDORS

Access guidelines recommend an unobstructed width of not less than 1.2 metres for corridors, but these are only minimum requirements for wheelchairs. Narrow corridors and stairways form choke points and can cause crowding and discomfort, and a more suitable basis would be provision adequate for a family group, for which the width of any part of the circulation route should be not less than 2.1 metres. The character of these routes should be generous, welcoming and without awkward corners. Finishes and lighting should enhance the visitor's experience, e.g. matt finishes will help to reduce glare for all visitors - not just those with visual impairments. Provision for people with impaired vision will have an impact on internal appearance in terms of the use of lighting, contrast of colour (e.g. visibility bands on glazed panels, door handles) and of texture (e.g. tactile pathways and indications of changes of level), and choice of fittings (e.g. visible as well as audible alarms).

Hidden corners, unused spaces and dead-ends should be avoided, to reduce the possibility of thieves concealing themselves during opening hours to break out after closing time. Circulation areas should be covered by the Intruder Detection System, e.g. by sensors responding to movement and heat which would detect a potential thief emerging from hiding after the building has been vacated and trace his or her progress through the building.

location:
Dundee Contemporary Arts.

architect:
Richard Murphy Architects.

description:
View towards the main entrance looking down the foyer.

photograph:
Reproduced courtesy of Richard Murphy Architects.

REST AREAS

Circulation routes should be designed for moving traffic, and more width should be allowed where these spaces have additional functions, such as an information area with notice-boards, casual seating for visitors to rest during their visit, or simply a place to pause to look out of the building. Seating and furnishings should be located and designed for convenience and comfort, especially for frail or elderly people who will need such seating but who may find low seats without arms difficult to use. Windows in the circulation route can provide relief from the enclosed conditions of the exhibition galleries, without compromising the low light levels and the precise environmental control needed for the exhibitions. Windows can also aid orientation without the necessity of resorting to numbers or names for distinguishing levels and rooms.

IDENTIFYING CIRCULATION PATTERNS

A gallery is open to the public at large, but may serve many different communities, each of which will use the building in a different ways and make different demands on circulation areas. It can be a useful exercise to identify what different visitors might expect and/or should be able to do during a visit, and draw diagrams of the various ways that individuals or groups of adults or children, artists and curators or 'lay' people, with and without disabilities, will move through the building at different times. Friends/member organisations, researchers, school groups, private functions, commercial receptions, shops and catering, performances or lectures, etc. will all

have different requirements in terms of where and when access will be required. Such diagrams can help to identify where public circulation overlaps with service access (◄◄ art route), what by-pass arrangements will be necessary for rooms that are closed to the public, and what provision needs to be made for access to catering facilities and toilets when the galleries are normally closed.

INDEPENDENT ACCESS TO PUBLIC FACILITIES

Although they should be close to the art areas, it can be advantageous for public facilities - meeting rooms, lecture theatre, catering facilities, shop, toilets, etc. - to be able to operate independently. Educational facilities may also be used by groups before and after normal opening hours (◄◄ education). Other areas must be securely-locked and alarmed (►► space).

Circulation for the Public
(see notes on page 88)

It is important that the quality of the architecture enhances a visitor's experience. Dimensions, proportions, lighting, signs, the textures and colours of finishes and the style of furnishings and fittings of all public services should be designed to enhance the visit for everyone, including disabled people. The layout of the building should be comprehensible so that

orientation is easy, whilst at the same time allowing opportunities for surprise and delight so that the visitor enjoys moving across and between floors. Circulation areas and routes should have generous proportions, but be welcoming and human in scale. Comfortable seating should be available at frequent intervals throughout building, and views out of the building should be used to make links between the gallery experience and the outside world. The building will be used for lectures, films, meetings and other functions outside normal opening hours, and there should be access to catering facilities and toilets without compromising the security of closed areas and without incurring costs on staffing, heating and lighting the whole building when only part is being used.

Building Regulations and the Approved Document, BS 5588: Part 8.

James Holmes-Siedle, **Barrier-Free Design, A Manual for Building Designers and Managers**, Butterworth-Heinemann, 1996. ISBN 07506 1636 9.

Museums & Galleries Commission, **Improving Museums Security, MGC Guidelines for Good Practice**, 1997. ISBN 0 948630 54 X.

retailing

When considering a retail outlet in a gallery, you should:

- take specialist advice;
- make location a priority;
- ensure that fittings are designed for the purpose;
- allow for the movement and storage of stock;
- plan for the convenience and safety of the staff.

THE NEED FOR SPECIALIST ADVICE

Whether a space be for exhibitions, education, a cafe or a shop, it ought to be the person with the responsibility of making the space work who writes the brief and vets the design proposals. If the relevant person is not yet in post, then a consultant should be commissioned to advise on the proposed retail operation and the brief for the design of the shop (see ◄◄ consultants). It is crucial that people with direct experience of retail contribute to decisions on location, layout and design. Shops often appear to have been slotted into a design as an afterthought, and involving the relevant member of staff or retail consultant at an early stage can make all the difference between a shop which generates the expected levels of income and a backwater where the odd visitor

can browse without disturbance. A potential franchisee may lose interest if the location is wrong or if the area set aside is too small. Even if they decide to go ahead with a franchise, their expenditure on fitting-out may be limited by their estimate of turnover.

LOCATION

Visibility is vital. The best location for a shop is at the exit, so that visitors pass in front of the shop as they leave the building. If the entrance and exit are one and the same, so much the better. For the retailer, the very best option is making visitors pass through the shop as they leave, but clearly there is a potential conflict between optimum visitor flow and a retailer's wish to slow down and stop potential customers (◄◄ 'people route'). For a shop manager, the congestion created as people stop to look at shop displays may be a 'high-class problem', but crowding and jostling also carries the risk of alienating and losing customers. The shop might have its own independent access from the street or be otherwise accessible when the gallery is closed. A shop that remains open between exhibitions provides a user-friendly enquiry point for passers-by whilst the rest of the gallery is closed.

DESIGN OF FITTINGS

Although the appearance of the shop must reflect the identity and aspirations of the gallery that contains it, it must also function as a retail unit, with fittings which can safely accommodate the required stock and which do not allow a stack or a display to collapse once two or three items have been withdrawn. Where the shop is part of a larger building project, the latter would naturally include signage for the shop, but the design of packaging might be a discrete task for a graphic designer. You should define the different types of material the shop will sell, the broad requirements for their storage and display, and the numbers of different items which might be on sale at any time. A gallery shop might sell a wide variety of stock, including slides, videos, toys, mugs and other gifts. It might sell small craft objects such as jewellery in locked display cabinets, larger craft objects such as pottery on shelves and open display, hangings mounted against wall or other surfaces, and scarves, ties etc., displayed on free-standing racks. It should be possible to suspend objects (e.g. banners, mobiles) from the ceiling. Statutory requirements should be planned into the early stages, and the Fire Officer should be consulted about the design proposals.

STORAGE

Storage can be provided under display units, but this should only be for small quantities for topping-up the displays during the day. For bulk deliveries of stock, this form of storage is inadequate, since it would only be accessible when the shop is closed. Boxes and pallets would still have to be stored somewhere until closing time, and unpacking would require out-of-hours working.

STAFF CONVENIENCE AND SECURITY

As well as being planned for the convenience of staff and visitors, the sales counter must also ensure that tills are secure and out of reach, to allow no opportunity to the potential thief. A shop needs an enclosed office, so that staffing matters and administrative work (including ordering and controlling stock and cashing-up at the end of the day) can be done in confidence and security. It should be separate from the gallery's office, especially where the shop is franchised rather than directly managed by the gallery. An office directly adjacent to the shop is important where staff might be required on the shop floor at a moment's notice.

Gallery shop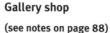

(see notes on page 88)

The shop should be visible and accessible from the gallery foyer. It should also be located so that it is visible from outside the building, to encourage visitors to enter the gallery as well to look round the shop itself. A window display would be an advantage, but both display and windows must be accessible for cleaning purposes. The shop should have its own independent access from the street, so that it can operate when the rest of the building is closed. There should therefore be a retractable gate or shutter between gallery and shop, which can be closed and locked when the gallery is shut, and the shop should be a distinct zone in the alarm system.

The area required for the retail unit (including office and store) should be a minimum of [25] m². The layout of the shop area itself should be uncluttered, with aisle widths allowing sufficient space between display units for family groups, wheelchair-users and parents with pushchairs. The sales counter should be split-level, so that wheelchair-users can be served by other wheelchair-users, whilst standing customers can be served, write cheques, etc. without discomfort. The cash desk should be secure, out of reach and lockable. In front of the sales counter, there should be space for queuing and clear views of the display units (without blind spots) to discourage shoplifting. CCTV cameras should monitor the whole area, and be connected to a CCTV monitor and video-recorder in the office. The lighting should be flexible and easy to maintain.

The shop should have an attractive and welcoming atmosphere, with clear spaces and a controlled use of colour. The style and quality of fixtures should be consistent with the design of the gallery, reflecting its identity and aspirations. Materials should suit the overall context, visually and physically, and should be renewable where possible, whilst meeting budgetary and statutory requirements. All fittings should be easy to maintain and replace, and should be without sharp corners and edges. Shelves, hooks, supports and other fittings must be strong enough to sustain the likely loads. Self-service stock on shelves and display units must be accessible to children, elderly people and wheelchair users. Locks on cupboards and display cabinets should be robust. Fittings should be provided on the basis of the following types, quantities and display methods:

postcards, [150] different images in flat, wall-mounted displays (i.e not revolving);

cards in non-standard formats and greetings cards, [50] different images in flat, wall-mounted displays (i.e not revolving);

soft-back catalogues, [50] different titles displayed on inclined racks;

hard-back books (often large format), [25] different titles on shelves for both frontal display and stacked spine outwards, plus some table-top display;

posters [10] framed display items, with ready-rolled sales items in pigeon holes.

Most deliveries of stock will be heavy and bulky, often shrink-wrapped on pallets requiring the use of a platform truck, so service access should be short, direct and on the one level if possible (any changes of level should be by lift).

In order to cope with peak demand, there should be a secure store equivalent to [a third] of the cubic capacity of the shop. Within this store, there should be: shelves and racks which are low and shallow so that stock can be moved and/or reached without risk of strain or injury; a plan chest for storing posters and prints; an open space for unpacking and checking boxes and packages; and a docking position for trolleys and trucks. In addition, there should be an office space large enough for [two] people, with workstation, telephone, CCTV monitor and video recorder, etc. There should be at least two telephone lines, one serving the office and the other designated for credit cards.

roof lights

You might consider top-lighting of exhibition galleries for display purposes in the following circumstances:

- in conversions of existing buildings which already have roof lights,
- in new buildings where the control of natural light is unimportant;
- in new buildings where capital and revenue resources are sufficient to introduce controls.

BENEFITS

A large area of roof lights is the traditional and most effective way of exploiting a free and high-quality source of light. This was especially the case for the art galleries built by local authorities above their libraries, but top lighting can also be available in conversions of industrial buildings. Top-lighting has been used in recent new gallery buildings, and remains an option especially where the roof is not needed for other purposes, whether for plant or even for a roof-top restaurant. For the aesthetic and economic reasons for using daylight, and for colour rendering, ◀◀ ceilings, ▶▶ windows.

REDUCING SOLAR GAIN

Heating from solar gain can be a real problem for galleries that have large expanses of windows facing any direction but north. High temperatures can be uncomfortable for visitors and staff, but an increase in temperature also lowers relative humidity and affects objects sensitive to moisture. Light-absorbing glass or films can be used to reduce the transmission of light, but are permanent additions that restrict the transmission of light even on dull days when every lumen is required. The most effective measures are those which intercept excess sunlight before it penetrates the glass - after all, the original "greenhouse effect" is the capacity of glazing to trap solar radiation at the infra-red end of the spectrum - but which can be adjusted to reflect downwards as much light as possible when light levels are low.

CONTROLLING LIGHT LEVELS BY PASSIVE METHODS

Optimum viewing conditions have to be balanced against conservation requirements if the exhibition gallery is attached to a museum or when it wishes to borrow material from museum collections. Daylight has a major drawback in that many of the materials and pigments used in works of art are damaged by exposure to light (◀◀ light). As a result, many galleries have in the past dispensed with natural lighting in exhibition spaces, and give visitors variation and orientation by using daylight only in circulation areas. Natural light can be controlled to some degree by using passive design features, such as paints that contain titanium white pigment (which absorbs ultra-violet radiation) combined with roof-lights that face north or internal coving that reflects the light coming through near-vertical glazing downwards into the exhibition galleries. Ensuring that all daylight is reflected once before it enters the exhibition area can be used to eliminate solar gain, reduce the level of light overall and remove the most damaging radiation.

Passive measures to control daylight require height. The traditional top-lit gallery is in effect a deep light-well which allows reflected - rather than direct - light to penetrate to the display areas. This might be the traditional central lantern with services around the walls, or the more recent central services unit supplying air and artificial light which has natural light spilling down two or more sides. One advantage of this light-well is that the upper part of the space is a buffering or mixing zone, absorbing solar gain from above and heat from lamps and people below, and evening out variations. Its disadvantage is the height that is required, especially for the second type (because a services unit that is low in relation to the width of the space can create a pool of shadow below it).

ULTRA-VIOLET FILTERS

Ultra-violet penetration can also be filtered by using special glass sandwiches or by applying films to external glazing. Filters on roof lights can be a heavier grade than those used for side windows where views in and out are important (➤➤ **windows**). Heavier filters can reduce light transmission to a quarter, and reflect almost two thirds of solar energy. Films applied to the outside are less durable than those applied to internal faces, and will need to be renewed more frequently.

ACTIVE MEASURES FOR PRECISE CONTROL

For optimum viewing conditions, light needs to be precisely managed. It has to be controlled in order to avoid glare and reflection especially when looking at work behind glass, whether paintings or objects in cases. Perhaps the greatest difficulty with using natural light is its variability. The ideal design would take maximum advantage of the light available on a gloomy winter's day but limit excessive penetration during the summer, and cope with every variation in-between. Shutters and blinds can be adjusted to intercept and reflect direct sunlight, either using manual controls which require a degree of training and commitment on the part of the people staffing the gallery or using photocell-operated motorised controls. The latter are more expensive to install, but are probably cheaper and more effective than the former. It is also possible that lenders who are looking for precise control would not be convinced that manual control is adequate.

Automatic control systems for daylight which are effective for display purposes but which limit the exposure to light, are complicated to design, and the architect would normally resort to models to predict how a particular design would perform in a new building. In an existing building, photocells can be located on different display surfaces to monitor the light falling on them, so that the pattern of exposure can be assessed and so that control regimes can be tested. Controls might include motorised Venetian blinds, which raise, lower and tilt, to protect from direct sunlight and to vary the amount of light reaching the exhibition.

More sophisticated again, probably only acceptable on new buildings, are adjustable external louvers pre-set for the sun's position in each hour of the day which stop sunlight from penetrating and reflect light to remove UV radiation, but allow visitors to be aware of the weather outside.

BLACK-OUT PROVISION

Simple black-out measures, such as shuttering held by pegs against the glazing bars, are suitable for small windows that can be easily reached. Because they require a tower or access gantry, adjustments can only be made during installation and dismantling periods, so such measures are only suitable for exhibitions where natural light needs to be reduced or eliminated completely at the outset.

Since duration of exposure is one of the factors in photo-degradation, the most straightforward method of reducing damage is to black out the exhibition spaces when they are closed to the public, especially in the summer months when it is light for several hours before and after normal opening times. Opaque fabric blinds are more suitable for this frequency of use. They should be motorised, since mechanical systems depend on springs that can lose their tension and on long wires which can jam or break. Motorised blinds can be closed and opened by manually-operated switches, but where blinds are opened at the beginning of the day and closed at the end, the surest and most efficient method is to have the controls completely automated and controlled by a Building Management System. Motorised or otherwise, the mechanism must be accessible for adjustment, maintenance and repair.

SECURITY CONSIDERATIONS

Even very high windows and roof lights can be security risks, if they can be reached from adjacent roofs and ledges. To satisfy the security conditions of the government indemnity scheme, there should be security grilles with bars less than 0.18 m wide on all roof lights, especially where access to the roof is possible. Security provision can be combined with light control, by mounting pivoting sun blinds on metal bars which are in effect hidden within the aluminium louvers.

Secondary glazing may be an acceptable alternative. These physical defences should be supported by alarm sensors which will register an attack on the external perimeter and any movement subsequently within the gallery.

Roof lights for a 'WHITE BOX'
(see notes on page 88)

As far as possible the lighting design should make maximum use of daylight, to give good viewing conditions. Daylight should be controllable between [250] lux and [1,000] lux, and should be supplemented with artificial lighting when and where appropriate. Roof lights should minimise solar gain and heat loss, and be easy to clean, maintain and repair. The colour rendering of natural light should be preserved as much as possible.

Roof lights for a 'BLACK BOX'
(see notes on page 88)

It should be straightforward and inexpensive to eliminate daylight as and when required for particular exhibitions, to less than [10] lux with full sun outside. Roof lights should be fitted with blinds or controllable shutters that are easy to operate and maintain.

Roof lights for a 'STRONG BOX'
(see notes on page 88)

As far as possible the lighting design should make maximum use of daylight when the gallery is open to visitors, but it should be totally excluded when the gallery is closed and when required for particular exhibitions. Most of the ultra-violet radiation with wavelengths less than [400] nm should be removed. An active control system should be used to monitor the external light conditions and to operate louvers or blinds automatically. This system should be energy-efficient, fully controllable and easy to maintain. It should be possible to set this system for each exhibition, to control the amount of light allowed into the gallery so that a set level between [50] lux and [200] lux is maintained. No direct sunlight should fall on the display surfaces. Physical protection and alarm coverage of roof lights should satisfy the security conditions of the Government Indemnity Scheme.

location:
Whitechapel Art Gallery, London.

architect:
John Miller & Partners.

description:
Upper Gallery during the 'Thomas Schutte' exhibition.

photograph:
Anthony Weller, reproduced courtesy of Anthony Weller and the Whitechapel Art Gallery.

Manufacturers in the UK of light-reducing films, ultra-violet filters and motorised blinds include: **Sun-X (UK) Ltd. Madeira Parade, Madeira Avenue, Bognor Regis, West Sussex, PO22 8DX.**
tel: 01243 826441
fax: 01243 829691
email: sun-x@argonet.co.uk

Manufacturers in the UK of light meters which measure both visible light and ultra-violet radiation include:

Littlemore Scientific Engineering (ELSEC), Railway Lane, Littlemore, Oxford, OX4 4PZ.
tel: 01865 747437
fax: 01865 747780
email: sales@elsec.co.uk;
and
Novatron Ltd, Unit 34, Southwater Industrial Estate, Southwater, Horsham, Sussex, RH13 7UD.
tel: 01403 733012
fax: 01403 733311.

For manufacturers of anti-bandit, ultra-violet filtering and heat-reflecting glass, ➤➤ windows.

screens

You should bear in mind the following considerations, for display screens, movable partitions or demountable walls that:

- provide additional hanging space;
- divide the gallery into a series of rooms;
- reconcile stability and mobility;
- are provided with adequate storage for when they are not in use;
- can be handled and installed by gallery staff;
- have surfaces compatible with other display surfaces in the gallery;
- are tailor-made as an integral part of the design of the gallery.

SCREENS AS INTEGRAL TO THE DESIGN

Movable walls, partitions or screens are often needed for the extra display area they can offer to spaces with little usable wall surface, and they can also be used to divide a space and to change its character. Unless an exhibition area is very small or narrow, screens should be considered at the design stage. They may not be needed or wanted, but their exclusion should be a deliberate decision and not an oversight. If they are wanted, the design stage is the time to decide what will look best and do the job. One or two

demountable walls that are designed of a piece with the gallery are likely to be much more satisfactory than a panel system bought off the shelf after the building has opened. Their structure and layout can take into account lighting, power and air-handling systems and ensure that one system does not compromise another.

SCREENS-THAT-DON'T-LOOK-LIKE-WALLS

There are two approaches to screens: broadly, those that look like walls, and those that don't. Screens-that-don't-look-like-walls are usually used where there is an interesting wall or historic structure that must be left visible, where many of the external walls are glass or where walls are used for shelving or other purposes. They are normally lightweight panels which often do not extend to floor or ceiling and which are supported on wires or poles. To maintain stability, pole systems may have obtrusive bases or feet or depend on a zig-zag configuration. Such systems are adequate only for very small and/or light exhibits in informal exhibition areas, and are not suitable for a wide-ranging exhibition programme.

SCREENS-THAT-LOOK-LIKE-WALLS

By and large, screens-that-look-like-walls are preferred when the walls are also used as the main display surface. In this case, they need the same consideration as the wall surfaces themselves, with which they should share a consistent approach to proportion, composition of board, colour and texture of surface finish, frequency of maintenance, hanging system, etc. Screens-that-look-like-walls can be used effectively instead of walls in buildings which might have short wall-lengths or large expanses of windows, to manipulate a large space and create smaller environments, provide adequate amounts of display surface, and even to control light by obstructing windows.

TRACK-MOUNTED SYSTEMS

Stability and mobility are key requirements that are difficult to reconcile. In side-lit or artificially-lit spaces with lower ceilings, a common approach is to use screens which are moved on a track fixed to the ceiling. Such systems can be simple and convenient to use, but they need a level floor and the layout of the track must be designed to cope with the most useful configurations - which are not necessarily the most convenient ones for a modular system. Such a track system can also support other functions, e.g. CCTV cameras and video monitors for multi-media installations. Ready-made screens need a storage point which is close to the exhibition space and which is large enough to take all the screens, if an exhibition requires the gallery to be completely open. Because such screens are often used in lines of two or three, or are installed to create small bays, installations can look cluttered and insubstantial. Security, emergency egress and environmental control also can be a problem where screens are used to create a large number of small spaces.

SPECIALLY-DESIGNED DEMOUNTABLE WALLS

In high, especially top-lit galleries, free-standing screens can often be anchored to existing pillars or columns. In spaces where there are relatively few anchorage positions, installations have to be designed to take into account this degree of inflexibility, and a few, very large screens might be built for each exhibition. An alternative allowing more flexibility is the use of vertical stanchions which are braced between specially-designed anchor points set into both floor and ceiling. Constructed on a timber framework and finished to high standards with junctions between the boards that are taped over, and then painted like the walls, they have the scale and appearance of a wall, suit the proportions of the space and are excellent for the display of very large exhibits.

Their disadvantage is the time and effort needed to build a completely new panel structure at every - or perhaps every other - exhibition changeover period.

Demountable partitions for a 'WHITE BOX'
(see notes on page 88)

Each gallery should be conceived as a single space, but a movable wall system should be devised to produce up to [50] metres of extra display area and to break up the space. The movable walls should match the walls in scale, performance and appearance and respect the character of the space.

Demountable partitions for a 'BLACK BOX'
(see notes on page 88)

Most exhibitions will require the gallery space to be sub-divided into [4-6] self-contained rooms, each one for a separate multi-media installation, projection piece, etc. A partition system should be devised which matches the walls in scale and appearance. The surface material should be sound-absorbent, but it must be possible to fix at any position shelves for projectors, TV monitors and other equipment weighing as much as [50] kg. It must also be possible to feed cabling within the structure, to supply power and data to such equipment.

Demountable partitions for a 'STRONG BOX'
(see notes on page 88)

A system of wall-height display panels will be needed to provide an additional [50] metres of hanging space. It should be possible to install these panels at any position within the gallery and at any angle relative to the walls. It must be possible to drill directly into the surface and provide a firm purchase for security screws. It should also be possible to change the colour of the surface easily and inexpensively. Wall finishes should be as dust free as possible and easily cleaned without the use of solvents. They should be easy to move and simple to install. Provision should be made for their storage when some or all of them are not required.

Manufacturers of temporary exhibition display systems include: **Panelock Systems Ltd, Hamilton House, 17A Cedar Road, Sutton, Surrey, SM2 5DA. tel:** 0181 770 7543 **fax:** 0181 770 9212 As well as its track-mounted system, Panelock has recently developed the Panelock Gallery Display System 200, which are mobile walls based on a demountable aluminium framework.

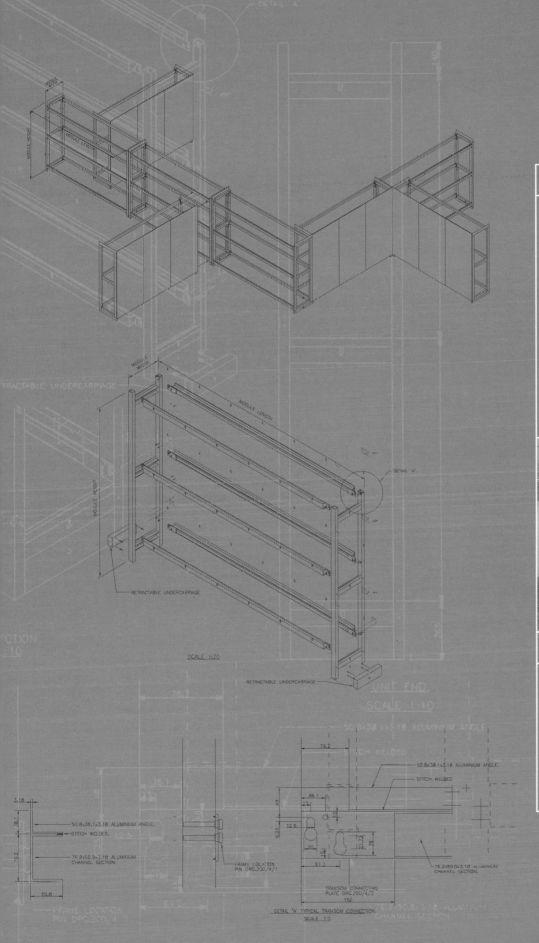

DETAIL 'A'

MODULE HEIGHT

MODULE LENGTH

RETRACTABLE UNDERCARRIAGE

MODULE WIDTH

MODULE LENGTH

MODULE HEIGHT

DETAIL 'A'.

RETRACTABLE UNDERCARRIAGE

RETRACTABLE UNDERCARRIAGE

SCALE 1:20

UNIT END.
SCALE 1:10

50.8x38.1x3.18 ALUMINIUM ANGLE

76.2

STITCH WELDED

50.8x38.1x3.18 ALUMINIUM ANGLE.

38.1

STITCH WELDED

12.5

FRAME LOCATION
PIN. DRG.200/4/1

TRANSOM CONNECTING
PLATE DRG.200/4/2
150

76.2x50.0x3.18 ALUMINIUM
CHANNEL SECTION.

DETAIL 'A' TYPICAL TRANSOM CONNECTION.
SCALE 1:2

3.18

50.8x38.1x3.18 ALUMINIUM ANGLE.
STITCH WELDED.

76.2x50.9x3.18 ALUMINIUM
CHANNEL SECTION.

50.8

FRAME LOCATION
PIN DRG.200/4/1

below

title:
Ferens Art Gallery, Kingston
upon Hull.

description:
Movable screens in Gallery IV

photograph:
Reproduced courtesy of Kingston
upon Hull City Museums and Art
Galleries.

main illustration

description:
Panelock System 200.

illustration:
Reproduced courtesy of
Panelock Ltd and Jumatec.

space

When defining the size and character of exhibition spaces, you should bear in mind the following considerations:

- the treatment of space will be the clearest expression of the gallery's vision;

- measurable requirements for area and volume will be fixed as much by the exhibitions that can be afforded as by the capital budget;

- the degree of flexibility required must be determined at the outset;

- security can be a major determining factor in how space is used.

For the treatment of surfaces, ◄◄ ceilings and floor surfaces, ►► wall surfaces.

MIXING SPACES

Exhibition galleries are public spaces which people share with works of art and where people experience art in a more or less controlled way. The balance between people and art will vary from gallery to gallery, according to each organisation's overall policy. At one extreme, the exhibition area may be a public space that is designed to be comfortable and relaxing, where the art appears to have been slipped in almost as an afterthought. At the other, the area may be treated as a laboratory where the artist has been experimenting and to which the public has been granted access as a concession. In galleries devoted to temporary exhibitions, the balance between people and art will vary from exhibition to exhibition, according to the intentions of the artist or organiser.

SCALE AND PROPORTION

After lighting (◄◄ roof lights), scale and proportion are the most important considerations in the design of galleries. They affect not only how exhibitions are installed but also how visitors will regard the work on show. Proportions may be dictated in part by the height of the works that the gallery intends to show, but high ceilings might be required even for small-scale work, for environmental as much as aesthetic reasons (◄◄ air-handling). The traditional art gallery is at least as high as it is wide and was designed to inspire respect, if not awe and reverence. The large historical narratives for which it was originally designed have contemporary parallels in scale and even subject matter, so a gallery should be able to show large work, although preferably in spaces which are less daunting.

If the total exhibition area is or will be permanently sub-divided into two or more separate rooms, then the proposed relationship between the spaces and the directions(s) of visitor movement should be indicated. A discussion of the relationship between the spaces might include whether different types of exhibition are envisaged for the different spaces and how far differences in scale or atmosphere - and different experiences for the visitor - are required. It might indicate whether the spaces should be directly adjacent to each other and capable of being used together, whether movement from one to the other should be direct, through generous openings, or whether they should be separated by doors and corridors. The treatment of galleries on different floors may need to be compatible if it is possible that a single exhibition will extend over two floors.

PROGRAMMING CONSIDERATIONS

The exhibitions policy will influence scale and layout, since large paintings have different spatial requirements from small craft objects. The size of the exhibition space will be dictated by realistic ambitions for the programme, in terms of the exhibitions that the gallery will be able to afford to organise itself and attract from other sources. Where there have already been collaborations with other galleries or where such collaborations might be realistically expected in future, the size of exhibition spaces at these other galleries may also be a guide to the spaces required.

For marketing and other reasons, some exhibition galleries will schedule two or more exhibitions to open and close at the same time. Other galleries, especially those with permanent collections, may be open to the public whilst an exhibition is being installed or dismantled in other parts of the same building. A venue usually has limited control over the exact dates that a touring exhibition will be available, and staggered dates might also be preferable in relation to the technical resources available. Whatever their reason, staggered showing periods affect internal layout and the art route 'above stairs'. They require each exhibition area to be securely closed off and accessed and serviced without interfering with public access to the areas that are still open (◄◄ art route). Separate entrances not only ensure that the public can have access to one space whilst another is closed, but also make for better working conditions, the safe use of tools and equipment and the security of exhibits during installation and dismantling. Separate galleries should always be distinct zones in the Intruder Detection System, so that the system can be activated to protect a closed space.

FLEXIBILITY

Traditionally, art galleries have been large spaces making few concessions to the visitor's feelings or comfort. Although there have been recent moves towards a more human scale, two strong inducements remain towards large open spaces in exhibition galleries. The first inducement is what has been called the flexibility fallacy. "Flexibility" has meanings almost as elastic as the requirement itself. Clearly, some degree of flexibility is crucial for galleries that show temporary exhibitions, since the size, character and other physical requirements will vary from one exhibition to another. In the longer term too, a degree of "loose-fit" is needed so that galleries can be adapted economically to respond to changes of attitude, different media and new forms of expression.

Within limited resources, total flexibility is impossible, and an ability to change the layout of movable walls will usually be the main form of flexibility. For larger, well-resourced organisations, a single large and unobstructed space within a weatherproof shell may be preferred. Anonymous and featureless on the inside, this space usually needs the services of architects or designers, not so much to furnish and otherwise complete the interior, but rather to provide a succession of temporary

alternatives, each one a completely new environment designed specifically for a particular exhibition. The disadvantage with this approach is the time and expense associated with designing and building new free-standing environments for each exhibition.

At the other extreme is the gallery designed as one or more spaces whose character and proportions are by and large unvarying. This approach is often dictated by the character and layout of an existing building, and any modification of the exhibition areas for particular exhibitions is minimal, perhaps restricted to a single large screen to draw attention to a particular exhibit. Recent high-profile art museums have helped to reinforce this approach, but there is a clear difference between a museum where the spaces can be specifically designed to display particular works of art, and an exhibition gallery which must be adaptable to many different types and sizes of work. A more valid reason is the trend for artists to create installations and site-specific pieces in dialogue with a building which has a strong character of its own. For mixed exhibitions, this type of gallery relies on the staff's familiarity with the character of the space and their ability to locate each exhibit most appropriately and effectively.

Somewhere between the two extremes is the 'universal box', whose inner walls are designed to be part of the display surface but whose internal layout can be varied using movable partitions (◄◄ screens). This middle way seeks to avoid the high cost of designing and building a new free-standing environment for each exhibition, whilst introducing both variable amounts of display area and variety into the way that exhibits are presented. Its ideal is endless flexibility, but the design of such spaces demands the greatest care of all, since the result can so easily become an oppressive box with uncomfortable proportions and low ceilings where exhibitions look fragmented and lifeless.

SECURITY CONSIDERATIONS

The second inducement towards large open spaces in exhibition galleries is the need for ease of supervision. The general conditions for the government indemnity scheme (GIS) state that, unless an acceptable alternative is agreed, all indemnified material must be displayed so that it is invigilated by at least one trained person in each room. A large open space can feel unwelcoming, and it can look monotonous when the exhibition consists of work of small scale and/or similar sizes. However, dividing up the space with screens can interfere with sight-lines and create hidden corners, so negating the original reason for the open space. The exhibition space should be designed to ensure that it can be effectively invigilated for exhibitions covered by the GIS, although supervision may be at a lower level for the rest of the programme.

Invigilators should therefore be located within each exhibition installation, and not placed outside by the doors or off to the side at a location which is convenient for a desk or work-station. In design and planning terms, this may mean that no single invigilation point is 'plumbed in' but that a number of possible locations are designed - with cable outlets for intercom, alarm system, CCTV, etc. - so that those with the best field of vision can be activated for each installation (►► wired services). CCTV can be used to extend the range of supervision, especially where exhibition spaces are sub-divided, by allowing a visitor to be tracked in otherwise hidden areas. Applying the same considerations of field of view and maximum coverage, each space should also be planned for alternative locations for cameras and sensors connected to the Intruder Detection System.

A strategy which is frequently recommended for augmenting invigilation during opening hours is to deliberately plan staff routes through the galleries so that exhibitions benefit from incidental supervision. The disadvantage of this approach is the extreme case of an exhibition space which is the only link between several administration areas: members of staff jangle keys as they open doors; light floods into an exhibition which might have been designed to have low

top ▲

location:
Ffotogallery, Cardiff.

architect:
Peter Bodoano.

description:
A staircase links two first-floor galleries with an exhibition gallery and a bookshop on the ground floor.

photograph:
Marc Arkless, reproduced courtesy of Ffotogallery Wales Limited.

bottom ▼

location:
Jerwood Gallery, The Jerwood Space, London.

architect:
Paxton, Locher.

description:
Gallery 1, the largest of a suite of three exhibition spaces, has sliding windows which open onto an external sculpture space.

photograph:
Richard Bryant/Arcaid, reproduced courtesy of The Jerwood Space Limited.

light levels; doors slam shut; and two or more members of staff chat all the time they make their way through the exhibition, with ladders, trolleys or other equipment.

SECURITY CATEGORIES

The level of security required will depend on your ambitions and resources and may even vary from exhibition to exhibition, according to the stated requirements of the lenders and the vulnerability of the exhibits. On the one hand, it is sensible to err on the generous side when it comes to specifying security, in order to anticipate the worst case in terms of lenders' requirements. On the other hand, it is not sensible to try to achieve security up to the highest standards if the exhibition space is too small or inadequately funded ever to attract high-value loans from the national museums.

There is widely-held misconception that galleries are categorised according to their levels of security. In fact, there is no formal status of "Category A Gallery" or any other category of gallery. Security categories were introduced by the Victoria & Albert Museum when it had a whole department devoted to touring, and continues to be used by National Touring Exhibitions from the Hayward Gallery. They were an approximate indication of the extent of security provision required for a particular exhibition. A small gallery in a library or arts centre without any supervision and with limited physical protection would know that it should look mainly at Category C exhibitions and possibly

aspire to Category B if it made a special effort. Inevitably such a gallery would come to see itself as a 'Category C Gallery', but this shorthand had no formal status, and has been rendered meaningless by recent developments.

Category A, the band with the most stringent requirements, was associated with security to national museums' standards (in this case, the "national museums" are those like the National Museum and Gallery of Wales, the Scottish National Gallery of Modern Art, the Tate Gallery and the Ulster Museum, which are funded by national government). This category has largely been overtaken by GIS requirements which now set the standard for physical security and invigilation. The Museums Security Adviser at the Museums & Galleries Commission will carry out a security audit of a gallery which requests loans from national museums or which applies to the GIS. However, security is only one of the considerations in GIS applications. Environmental considerations are increasingly important, and the Museums & Galleries Commission has an Environmental Adviser to parallel the security role. Even with security, there is no simple prescription, since the risk associated with each loan varies according to its size and portability, physical vulnerability, financial value or disposability, likelihood to cause offence or controversy, etc. A gallery which has been granted an indemnity for one exhibition may not therefore obtain it for another exhibition with a different level of risk.

For the detection and control of fire and for emergency evacuation, ◄◄ fire precautions.

| Space for a 'WHITE BOX' (see notes on page 88) | ☐ |

There should be two exhibition galleries capable of presenting innovative and ambitious exhibitions of contemporary art of an international standard, in media which will range from small works on paper and large paintings, to sculpture and installations. The larger space of approximately [300] m² should clearly be the main one and should be rectangular in shape, whilst the smaller space of approximately [100] m² should be rectangular or square. The aim should be to create exhibition spaces that are notable for their simple, classic proportions, sense of light and spaciousness and ability to enhance the art on display. At the same time, the galleries must be functional: they must have floor and wall surfaces which can be drilled into and subsequently repaired with relative ease, and they must have hidden sockets for electrical power. Natural light should be used, although not at the expense of reducing the length or height of wall surfaces, where display is the priority. The galleries should be able to display - with adequate space all round - large-scale works up to

[3] metres high and [5] metres wide. There should be a generous amount of space above visitors and exhibits. The two spaces should have separate entrances, so that each can function whilst the other is closed. However, some exhibitions will require both spaces, so visitors should be able to move directly from one to the other without having to return to the entrance. Whilst taking into account security requirements when closed, entrances and exits should be inviting in scale and in proportion to the galleries. Consideration should be given to inviting visitors into the galleries through long sight-lines, so that a striking painting, for instance, might be seen at some distance from the foyer before the galleries are actually entered.

Space for a 'BLACK BOX'
(see notes on page 88)

The core of the building will be a gallery capable of presenting an innovative programme of contemporary art in new media, including video and digitally-based work. It should be possible to divide this space into as many as [8] semi-enclosed areas, each of which may vary in size from [15] m^2 to [50] m^2 and will have different shape, proportions and character. Gallery walls and ceilings will need to be able to sustain the weight of

projectors, screens or other equipment (which would usually be positioned by drilling and mounting). Ceiling height should allow for overhead projection and lighting systems. There should be a high level of security to protect expensive equipment. Installation of electric power cabling and points at ceiling and floor levels is also required to ensure maximum flexibility.

Space for a 'STRONG BOX'
(see notes on page 88)

A high level of security is necessary to protect valuable exhibits, and must be up to the general standards required for the Government Indemnity Scheme. Each space should be as large and open as possible, so that it can be supervised effectively by a single attendant. It should be conceived as a single space of [400] m^2, but some exhibitions will require it to be sub-divided, so a partition system should be devised which matches the walls in scale and appearance and which permits [6-8] basic configurations. All potential layouts should take into account the needs of security, lighting and environmental control and emergency egress. It should be possible to close each gallery and activate the intruder detection system as a separate zone whilst other parts of the building are open

and accessible to the public and/or staff. Each gallery space should be covered by sensors to detect if an unauthorised person has entered that area.

Museums & Galleries Commission, **Improving Museums Security,** MGC Guidelines for Good Practice, 1997. **ISBN 0 948630 54 X.**

Museums & Galleries Commission, **Guide to the use of closed circuit television in museums and galleries,** May 1998. This recommends recording of all cameras using a multiplex system, positioning of cameras at the entrance (to help to identify people who might have been recorded at a distance in the gallery), at emergency exits and in retail areas and to take account of blind or remote parts of exhibition areas or where valuable or vulnerable works are situated. Video recordings should be date- and time-stamped, so that they can be used as forensic evidence if necessary.

location:
Tate Gallery, Liverpool.

architect:
Michael Wilford and Partners.

description:
Recent refurbishment has enlarged
and made more visible and
accessible a bookshop that was
hidden away on a mezzanine.

photograph:
Richard Bryant/Arcaid, reproduced
courtesy of the Tate Gallery.

storage

When considering the spaces where works of art might be held, whether for a few hours or a few months, you should bear in mind the following considerations:

- works of art should be stored separately from other materials;

- security of handling and storage areas for works of art should be at least as good as that in the galleries;

- environmental conditions for handling and storage areas for works of art should be similar to those in the galleries;

- different aspects of the management of works of art in and out of the building have different requirements, which may justify dedicated spaces;

- storage requires active management.

For the movement of works of art, ◄◄ art route and loading bay, ►► vehicle access.

STORAGE IN GENERAL

In addition to works of art and their packing materials, a gallery may need to store some or all of the following:

- posters, leaflets and other promotional material;

- catalogues and other publications produced in-house;

- stock bought in for the shop;

- educational materials and equipment;

- chairs and tables;

- cleaning equipment and materials;

- electrical equipment and spare lamps;

- paints;

- access gantry, ladders, tools, lifting machinery, trolleys, etc.;

- screens;

- display cases, plinths, etc.;

- administration supplies, archives, etc.

All items which the gallery will need to store on-site should be listed, and the space required for each should be estimated, along with the shelving and other fittings needed, its location and how it should be accessed. For example, if the gallery holds an equipment bank of film and video equipment or runs digital workshops, the proposed arrangements for controlling users' access should be discussed. Where furniture and equipment are not specific to particular functions, their storage should be close to lifts and stairs for ease of movement throughout the building. Some of these general, non-art items are considered elsewhere (◄◄ artificial lighting, education, retail and screens).

The isolation of potentially dangerous materials in a separate chemicals or paint store is essential for the security of works of art as well as for meeting Health & Safety requirements.

HANDLING AND STORAGE CONDITIONS FOR WORKS OF ART

Handling and storage areas must not be given a lower priority because they are less visible. Each art-handling area between the loading bay and exhibition galleries should be subject to the same access and environmental parameters as the exhibition galleries, with the exception that daylight can be completely excluded. If fluorescent lamps are proposed, they must be shielded with UV filters. If incandescent lamps are used because of their low ultra-violet content, it is important that lights are switched off when no-one is in the store, to avoid increases in temperature. A computer-based Building Management System can monitor where lights are switched on, and can signal an alarm if lights in any area are on for longer than a set period. A level, heavy-duty floor will be required, for ease of movement of handling and carrying equipment which might include motorised pallet trucks or fork-lift machinery. Ideally, these areas should not be directly adjacent to heating and air-handling plant. If possible, pipe work should be excluded from all art-handling areas, but where this is unavoidable, any pipes should be at low level to minimise damage in the event of leakage.

Handling and storage areas require active management, and should be part of the job specification of a member of staff. A gallery will never have enough storage if screens, plinths, packing materials and almost anything left over from previous exhibitions are always stored for potential re-use, and if this clutter gradually takes over an area which is then urgently needed for an incoming exhibition. Handling and storage areas can be subject to heavy traffic in short, intensive periods, so overcrowding must be avoided.

The following describes different handling and storing functions. Each of these functions is distinguished as a distinct space, but the location, circumstances and needs of each gallery may require one or more functions to be combined.

HOLDING AREA

Where environmental control is critical, a holding area is necessary, immediately off the art route, preferably adjacent to the loading bay but within the environmentally-controlled area (unlike the loading bay itself) where the whole consignment can be placed immediately after it is unloaded from a vehicle. A holding area allows acclimatisation in secure and stable conditions for

unopened travelling crates. Crates are not normally opened immediately on arrival, but are left overnight (and sometimes for twenty-four hours if they arrive very cold or very warm) to allow them to adjust slowly to a venue's conditions. In a small building, it is possible to dispense with this holding area and move items directly to the exhibition area, but the consequence in a large building with long distances and several floors to negotiate would be a significant commitment of time, staff and equipment and a longer stay for the vehicle at the loading bay. All internal doors and access routes would also have to be capable of taking the crates and any truck or trolley used for moving them. The holding area needs to be large enough to allow a whole consignment to be off-loaded, which - depending on the size of the gallery and the vehicles it uses - might range from 15 m^3 for the smallest, 30-40 m^3 for the average carrier's vehicle, to 60 m^3 for the largest trailers. A wide, shallow space adjacent to the art route, but separated from it by retractable gates, would allow any case to be reached without disturbing the others.

REGISTRATION AREA

A registration area provides space for unpacking and re-packing, so should be large enough to remove the largest item from its travelling frame or crate and subsequently replace it. It also provides an area where couriers are able to check

the condition of works and where gallery staff can carry out their procedures for logging in or out. It should be equipped to allow uncrated work to be examined in strong and/or raking light and photographs to be taken.

ART STORE

Traditionally, exhibition galleries devote the maximum amount of space to display purposes, and few galleries have been designed with adequate storage. However, the nature of temporary exhibitions means that, at some time or other, a gallery will need space to store exhibits, empty crates and packing materials from the current exhibition, full cases for the last or next exhibition or for a touring exhibition, as well as screens, plinths and showcases from previous exhibitions. The type of programme envisaged will have storage consequences - in terms of gathering together loans from different sources at different times, safeguarding the crates in which loans arrive, accommodating touring exhibitions which leave later or arrive earlier than scheduled - which will determine the capacity required and how often the gallery will reach full capacity.

Storage on-site should aim to meet all needs but the extraordinary, in order to ensure that future programmes are not compromised. Inadequate storage can mean that exhibitions have to be stored in the exhibition galleries before and after a showing, so lengthening turnaround periods. Storage on-site ensures that revenue budgets are not compromised by the need to find storage elsewhere, involving time and effort and the cost of hiring transport and space. However, it would be expensive to provide and maintain storage capacity which is only used once a year for a few days, and in this case it may be more cost-effective to hire transport and storage off-site.

Exhibits have to be placed in storage because an exhibition space is not yet ready to receive them or because they are awaiting a carrier to return them to their lenders or to move a complete exhibition to the next venue.

For estimating storage needs, a collections-based gallery has a clear advantage over an exhibitions gallery in that the type and amount of storage can be quantified for the works already in the collection, and new acquisitions can take into account any storage implications. An exhibitions gallery cannot anticipate the nature of the individual items it may have to store, and it does not have total control over when and how much material arrives. Planning an art store must consequently be a deliberate exercise in anticipating worst-case scenarios.

The worst case for one gallery, for example, might be where one of its own exhibitions returns to base because a showing in a tour has fallen through, where the last exhibition has still not been collected and the next one has been delivered early.

As soon as exhibits are unpacked, checked and recorded, they will normally be moved into temporary storage. This is often the exhibition galleries themselves, if turnaround periods are sufficiently long. However, all construction (of screens, display cases, etc.) and re-painting (of walls, plinths, etc.) must be completed before the exhibits are placed in the display areas, because of the risk of damage from carpentry, electrical installations and any other work involving technicians using ladders, tools and other equipment. Paint must also be allowed to dry for at least two days under active air circulation, before works are moved into position. A separate art store allows such preparatory work to be completed without risk, and also allows exhibits to be removed immediately after the end of the exhibition, so that the galleries can be prepared for the next one.

A store with a single entrance ensures that it is not part of a through route and its consequent risks of damage, loss and environmental instability. Within the store, a stacking system should be provided to prevent exhibits from being leant one against the other. This might consist of stanchions which are anchored between floor and ceiling and against which two-dimensional work can be leant. It might be a sliding screen system, although this cannot be removed if, for example, several large sculptures need to be stored.
Any sliding mechanisms, whether for

vertical screens or for horizontal drawers should have cushioned bumpers, to avoid vibration and shock. Any shelving should not be too high or too deep to make access difficult or reaching hazardous.

CRATE STORE

Old master paintings, large modern canvases, architectural models, sculpture and new media will often travel in bulky crates with a volume considerably greater than the items they are designed to protect in transit. During the exhibition, these crates must be stored safely and securely so that they are ready for the next move. Where environmental control is critical, any environmental monitoring and control systems for the exhibition areas must also apply to the crate store, because exhibits will be subject to stress if they are replaced at the end of an exhibition in crates that have been stored at a different temperature and humidity. A store for empty crates avoids the need to bring them into the gallery to allow them to acclimatise, a process which might require as long as two weeks and which might impose longer turnaround times. The size of the crate store should relate to the carrying capacity of the vehicle that is likely to be used for the exhibitions the gallery shows (see above, 'Holding area'). Like the holding area, the crate store should be a wide, shallow space adjacent to the art route, but separated from it by retractable gates, in order to allow any case to be retrieved easily.

For the detection and control of fire, ◄◄ fire precautions.

Storage for an exhibition gallery
(see notes on page 88)

The following art-handling spaces are required:

- *holding area, off the service route between loading bay and exhibition galleries, to allow unopened travelling crates to acclimatise to gallery condition; floor area required [60] m^2;*

- *registration area, off the service route between holding area and exhibition galleries; floor area required [25] m^2; equipped with padded tables and adjustable lighting.*

- *art store, with a single entrance off the service route between loading bay and exhibition galleries; floor area required [80] m^2; equipped with a flexible stacking system which can be adapted for large- and small-scale work in two and three dimensions;*

- *crate store, situated by the holding area, off the service route*

between loading bay and exhibition galleries; floor area required [60] m^2.

Entrances to all art-handling areas should have openings measuring [3.5] m x [3.5] m and provided with a reinforced door, roller shutter or concertina shutter which can be securely locked and alarmed. Floors should be damp-proof and capable of taking an imposed load of [6] kN/m^2. They should be smooth, level and hard wearing. Ceilings should have [4] m of clear height, allowing for lighting and ducting. Daylight should be completely excluded. Illumination up to [500] lux is required, but the lights should switch off automatically when each area is closed and locked. Ultraviolet radiation should be removed, to less than [75] µW/ lumen. Ventilation should be mechanical, and any environmental monitoring and control systems for the exhibition areas must also apply. The ends of ventilation trunking should be covered by grilles or bars, with sensors to give warning of any attack. Within each space there should be intruder detector, flood sensor and heat or smoke detectors. Fire suppression should be by a sprinkler system.

---

location:
Harris Museum & Art Gallery, Preston.

architect:
Norman Jones Sons and Rigby.

description:
A sliding storage screen.

photograph:
Norwyn Photographics, reproduced courtesy of Harris Museum & Art Gallery.

Manufacturers of sliding picture racking and other storage systems for galleries include: **Stortech Ltd, Linney Lane, Shaw, Oldham, OL2 8HB.**
tel: 01706 840422
fax: 01706 882 340; and
Metalrax Ltd, Bordesley Green Road, Birmingham, B9 4TP.
tel: 0121 772 8151
fax: 0121 772 6135.

vehicle access

Issues of vehicle access are properly the concern of the feasibility study, when alternative locations are being considered, but decisions at this stage may affect the brief to the architect. You should bear in mind the following considerations, for vehicular access to the building which should:

- be reached by roads adequate for the likely size and weight of vehicle;
- have space for vehicles to manoeuvre and to park safely and securely;
- be separate from public access and other forms of service access;
- not compromise the internal layout of the building.

OPTIONS ANALYSIS

Given the importance to an exhibition gallery of the continuous movement of exhibits and exhibitions in and out of the building, any feasibility study looking at locations has to consider vehicle access to the site (◄◄ considering the options). Wherever possible, service access for exhibits should be separated from access for people (◄◄ loading bay). In part, this is for the safety and convenience of visitors and passers-by, but there may be parking restrictions

in front of public entrances that are often on main thoroughfares in towns and cities. Service access to a pedestrianised area may be limited to short periods in the early morning, which can restrict carriers' ability to deliver and collect exhibitions and will raise costs.

ACCESS ROADS

Any options analysis should ensure that the roads leading to the possible position of a loading bay should be evenly laid and should have no weight limits or low bridges which would be a problem for the largest vehicle that the gallery might expect. Such a study would ascertain how far vehicles will have to mount pavements to turn corners, and whether there is a risk that access or egress will be blocked by parked cars. As a rule, the better the service access, the cheaper will be the eventual transport bills and the less risk to the exhibits. Even though the gallery itself may be small, the vehicle delivering or collecting an exhibition may be a large one because it is carrying several part-loads. Conversely, a large exhibition delivered to a restricted site may require more trips and more handling if a delivery or collection has to be made with several small vehicles rather than one big one.

In extreme cases, road access can have a direct consequence on the maximum dimensions for exhibits.

VEHICLE DIMENSIONS, WEIGHTS AND TURNING CIRCLES

For very large vehicles, roads would have to be able to sustain axle loads up to 10 tons, and low bridges should have a clearance of at least 4.6m. Fine art carriers have a lot of experience of problems with access to galleries, and they should be consulted about the dimensions, weights and turning circle of the largest vehicle that the gallery is likely to encounter. If large and heavy sculpture are to be shown, it would be worth finding out about size and turning circle of the largest mobile crane that might be needed.

MANOEUVRING APRON

Service access should be designed as far as possible to get the vehicle off the public highway quickly and with the minimum of manoeuvring, preferably without reversing which usually blocks both lanes of traffic, and especially without a left-hand reverse which is a blind manoeuvre for British vehicles. The manoeuvring area outside the loading bay has to be planned for the maximum vehicle size, and also for the direction of traffic flow. If there is any possibility of deliveries or collections being made in more than one vehicle arriving at the same time, there should be a waiting area on the service road or apron outside the loading bay which does not interfere with vehicles manoeuvring into or away from the loading bay itself.

If a vehicle is unable to back directly to the bay, then the surface of the ground between vehicle and loading area should be as smooth, level and unobstructed as possible. Where a vehicle is not fully enclosed, the external apron may need to be provided with PIR (Passive Infra Red)-switched security lighting and/or CCTV coverage and secured with wall and lockable gate which deny the view and have to be scaled to make an attack.

Also ◄◄ art route, loading bay, storage.

Vehicle access
for a 'WHITE BOX'
(see notes on page 88)

The policy of the gallery is to show temporary exhibitions in a wide range of media, which will include paintings on canvas up to [3] metres high and sculptures

---

weighing up to [10] tons. Such works will normally be transported in wooden crates which can add up to [1] metre to each dimension or on pallets which substantially increase their weight. Because of these factors, the gallery must be capable of receiving vehicles of [50] tons deadweight, [10] metres long, [2.5] metres wide and [3.6] metres high. The roads leading to the building must be suitable for a vehicle of this size, and the loading bay should have sufficient manoeuvring room outside to enable such a vehicle to turn round and reverse up to the loading bay. As far as possible, the vehicle should not obstruct other traffic whilst manoeuvring or when stationary.

Vehicle access
for a 'BLACK BOX'
(see notes on page 88)

Gate and loading bay door should be provided with a bell or intercom, to ensure that a delivery can be made without the driver having to leave a vehicle full of electronic equipment in order to come round to the front door to gain attention.

Vehicle access
for a 'STRONG BOX'
(see notes on page 88)

A perimeter additional to the outer wall of the building should be provided at the rear, surrounded by a wall at least [2] metres high, with no horizontal ledges and bars to assist scaling. It should be possible to close and lock the gate. An artist may be commissioned to design a gate and fence in keeping with the purpose of the building. The courtyard between fence and building should be treated as a warning zone. It should be lit during the hours of darkness to act as a deterrent, with passive infra-red/movement detectors to give early warning of attack, and infra-red camera surveillance. Camera positions should take into account the possibilities of unauthorised access from adjacent buildings and the occasional need to provide secure overnight parking for carriers' vehicles.

➤

title:
Baltic Centre for Contemporary Art, Gateshead.

architect:
Ellis Williams Architects.

description:
Longitudinal section. The service areas, including the lorry-sized loading bay and the service lift, are shown in the deeper tint whilst the exhibition areas are shown in the lighter tint.

illustration:
Reproduced courtesy of Ellis Williams Architects.

Your local authority's Roads and Transport Department should be contacted about access routes, size and weight limitations and possibilities of directional signage.

Fine art carriers in the UK will be able to supply dimensions and weights. They include: **MOMART, 199-205 Richmond Road, London, E8 3NJ.**
tel: 0181 986 3624
fax: 0181 533 0122;

Oxford Exhibition Services, Station Road, Uffington, Oxfordshire, SN7 7QD.
tel: 01367 820713
fax: 01367 820504;

Trans Euro Fine Art Division, Drury Way, Brent Park, London, NW10 0JN.
tel: 0181 784 0100
fax 0181 459 3376; and

Wingate & Johnston Ltd, 134 Queens Road, London, SE15 2HR.
tel: 0171 732 8123
fax: 0171 732 2631.

Oxford Exhibition Services provides these details on the internet, in its 'Interactive Brochure' at:
www.oxex.demon.co.uk /brochure.htm

wall surfaces

This section is concerned only with the wall as a surface against which exhibits are displayed. It is not concerned with the structure of walls, with walls outside exhibition spaces, nor with the wall as a feature in its own right, e.g. when the whole or part of it is left revealed to show the original structure of an old building.

Like other surfaces (◄◄ ceilings, floor surfaces and screens) in exhibition spaces, the internal surface of the walls may need to be designed to accommodate several different and possibly conflicting functions. You should therefore consider the walls as surfaces that:

- are as large and uninterrupted as possible;
- include windows;
- can be screwed into;
- provide a suitable background for a wide variety of works of art;
- can be painted easily;
- are easily maintained;
- can support heavy loads safely.

For other aspects of exhibition galleries, ◄◄ doors and doorways and roof lights.

THE WALL AS THE PRIMARY DISPLAY SURFACE

The nature of wall surfaces has a significant influence on the character of the space and the quality of the experience of works of art displayed against them. Especially in the galleries of the Victorian and Edwardian periods, purpose-built with top-lighting, walls are the traditional display surfaces for conventional two-dimensional works of art, i.e. framed and unframed paintings, drawings and prints. They are not the only surfaces against which even conventional two-dimensional works of art are seen (◄◄ screens), and the variety of scale and media of works of art can make the composition and appearance of other surfaces equally important. Nonetheless, in the majority of exhibition galleries, the walls are the primary display surface; they define the character and nature of the space, and their colour, tone, texture, finish and acoustic properties will influence the quality of the visitor's experience.

MAXIMUM EXTENT IN BOTH DIMENSIONS

In the interests of maximum flexibility, these surfaces should be uninterrupted in both vertical and horizontal directions. A dado will mean that large paintings have to be hung high, and combined with a hanging rail will limit the size of work that can be displayed and where it can be placed. Windows, chimney breasts and alcoves give a room interest, but they also limit the size of work that can be displayed and where it can be placed. The aim should be the maximum height possible between floor and ceiling and the minimum interruption between the corners of each room, to allow for the display of large paintings and for maximum flexibility with the arrangement of smaller works.

Even where the service access (◄◄ art route) is unable to accommodate these dimensions, there may still be works of art (e.g. banners or constructions designed to be hung at high level) where the full height or width will still be needed. Under a pitched roof, the benefits of a high display surface may have to be balanced against the loss of floor area and hanging length, and you will need to decide whether maximum floor area and low walls are more important than a smaller gallery with higher display surfaces.

location:
Context Gallery, Derry.

architect:
Robert Toye.

description:
Exhibition installation, 'Hollow',
by Alice McCartney.

photograph:
Brendan McMenamin, reproduced
courtesy of the Context Gallery.

OBSTRUCTIONS AND INTRUSIONS

Standard hot-water central heating systems are usually ruled out from exhibition galleries because radiators need a large surface area and obtrude into potential display space (◄◄ **air-handling**). Where inlets or outlets for mechanical ventilation and air-conditioning systems have to be sited on the walls at low level, they must be as unobtrusive as possible, e.g. using a linear diffuser along the skirting rather than a rectangular grille. High-level grilles must be high enough to be outside the normal field of vision.

Precise briefing and careful checking are necessary during the design phase, to ensure that clocks, light switches, power sockets and punch-pads or swipe-card readers will not be installed in positions where they encroach unnecessarily on areas that might otherwise be useful for display. The position of these small items has to be thought out beforehand, so that they are placed where they cause the least inconvenience. The encroachments of electricians can be reversed after the event - though at a cost - but it is less easy to re-locate the devices required by the Fire Officer, and it is essential

that the latter is consulted early in the design process about the eventual locations of fire extinguishers, break-glass devices, alarm bells, emergency exit signs and door-release mechanisms. Ideally, recesses should be provided for fire extinguishers, not least so that they do not create an obstacle or a hazard for wheelchair users or those with impaired vision.

Monitoring devices constitute another category of clutter in exhibition galleries. CCTV cameras are becoming smaller and can be located discreetly at high level, along with volumetric sensors for the Intruder Detection System and loudspeakers for the public address system, music, sound-effects, etc., but there is then no excuse for obtrusive loops of cable. More problematic are sensors recording light and humidity levels, especially where they supply data to Building Management Systems. The solution is to understand how the internal environment behaves and to place sensors outside the visitor's field of vision but with settings that compensate for their positions and deliver the appropriate light and humidity at the level of the works of art.

HANGING METHODS

Framed works of art are normally held against a display surface using two basic hanging methods:

- track systems;
- direct fixing.

Hanging systems which support a framed work by two chains, wires or rods from a high-level rail or track are quick and convenient to use, and because they do not damage the wall surface, are often chosen for historic buildings. They can also have locking devices which prevent a rod from being removed, accidentally or otherwise, from the track and which prevent the exhibit also from being removed from the rod or wire. However, rods are obtrusive and are only satisfactory for easel-paintings: they can tip small paintings forwards and accentuate the shadows cast by frames; and they are unsuitable for irregular shapes and constructions. In addition, there are hanging systems with a track embedded in the display surface at eye-level, so that fittings in the frame are hooked directly in the track. This system is obtrusive, even when a cover is clipped into the slot showing between frames, and offers even less flexibility for placing exhibits in the vertical plane. Battens fixed to the surface of the wall - and projecting in front of it - are even more obtrusive, unattractive and insecure.

None of these track systems conforms to the general security conditions for the government indemnity scheme, which require paintings, drawings and similar objects to be secured directly to walls by mirror-plates and security screws. A mirror-plate (also known as an ear-plate) is a flat fitting, which has two holes in its rectangular part for fixing it with screws to the rear face of a wooden frame, and which has a third hole in its rounded part (the protruding 'ear') for fixing the plate, with the work of art attached, directly to a display surface. Normally, one mirror-plate is used on each side, but two may be used where security is important. Security screws which require a special tool to insert and remove are increasingly used to fix the plates to the surface. In special cases, paintings may even be mounted behind a glazed or polycarbonate shield bolted to the display surface. To support large and heavy works, a bracket is often screwed to the display surface to support the lower edge of the work of art. Direct fixing is crucial where installations, especially those including video monitors, slide projectors and other equipment, must be securely mounted within the exhibition area. In addition to security and safety considerations, direct fixing to the display surface has the advantages that it is unobtrusive, especially when the mirror-plates are painted over, that work can be fixed as high or as low as required, and that it can cope with irregular and projecting shapes. Its disadvantage is that it is labour intensive both to install an exhibition and to repair and re-touch the surface afterwards.

TEXTURE AND FINISH

Texture and surface finish are usually a reflection of personal taste and the fashion of the day. When the Tate Gallery was built, the considered opinion was that the best background for showing paintings was red silk. A generation ago held that the loose weave of hessian would close around screw holes, although paper-backed varieties worked less well and were soon painted over. Stretched fabrics attract dust, and lighter colours show dirt and need frequent replacement, and it is also expensive to change the colour for different exhibitions. More recently, wood-chip paper and plasterboard have been used as surfaces that are easy to repair. However, artists are increasingly working directly on the surface itself, whether in the form of installations, wall-drawings or projected images. Curators and designers also prefer surfaces that can be painted quickly and easily and that can have titles and headings sign-written onto them.

Matt white and off-white finishes are often used for the walls of exhibition galleries. The main disadvantage of very light tones is that glazed works reflect the white wall surfaces opposite them, unless they have a strong light on them - which may not always be possible or even permissible, for conservation reasons. The ability to repaint display surfaces, even if this is only done occasionally, is an important factor. If a colour scheme has to suffice for several exhibitions, retouching of filled screw-holes and other repairs will be easier if standard colours are used that are easily obtainable.

WALL-LINING MATERIALS

Direct fixing requires a solid backing, which generally means an internal lining of board attached by a supporting framework to the structural wall. At one time, this lining was tongue-and-groove board behind a fabric covering, but is

now increasingly a composition board - plywood, blockboard, medium density fibreboard (MDF) or a gypsum fibreboard such as 'Fermacell'. Before deciding on the material, it is important to test the performance of different types and thickness of boards, for ease of use and load-bearing characteristics. Using appropriate fixings is important for these tests, e.g. 'chipboard' screws should be used for MDF which resists the compression of normal wood-screws. Resistance to force is a consideration for high-value exhibitions: a small picture may itself be a small load, but a short lever can exert considerable pressure on a mirror-plate.

The tendency has been to use a thickness and type of board that can cope with most loads (e.g. 18 mm blockboard), but for fixing heavy or projecting pieces to screw through into wooden studding which is set at known intervals (e.g. every 0.6 m). An alternative would be to use a thicker board bolted to a proprietary metal studding. The present need is for a plain smooth surface, and 25 mm MDF painted with emulsion is probably the closest to today's requirements. Jointing is an inherent problem with any timber-based cladding material, as joints open up and become more visible, because

the boards expand as they absorb moisture (e.g. when they are painted) and contract as they dry.

OTHER CONSIDERATIONS

Because boards are porous and absorb and desorb moisture, they can be an aid to maintaining humidity levels in exhibition galleries, provided the wall behind is adequately insulated (◄◄ air-handling). A vapour barrier is critical for ensuring that board materials are not actively transferring moisture from the outside to the inside.

An advantage of cladding the walls is that the boarding material allows dimmers and switches for lighting, as well as sockets for power and data, to be hidden in recesses off the plane of the display surface. Sockets in particular need to be provided at frequent intervals if they are to cope with the diversity of wired services - power, data, telephone, alarm system, etc. The space behind cladding can be used for the trunking which enables new wiring to be laid to keep up with new technology (►► wired services).

Wall cladding materials need to satisfy the Fire Officer in terms of any inherent fire retarding characteristics or the use of appropriate fire retarding solutions (◄◄ fire precautions).

| Wall surfaces for a 'WHITE BOX' (see notes on page 88) | Wall surfaces for a 'BLACK BOX' (see notes on page 88) | Wall surfaces for a 'STRONG BOX' (see notes on page 88) |

Walls should provide smooth and uninterrupted surfaces for the support and display of works of art, which may range in size from [0.30] m square to [5] m in length and [3] m in height, which may project from the surface as much as [0.30] m and which may weigh as much as [50] kg. It should possible to place exhibits at any position on the display surface, e.g. large hangings would require fixings at high levels, whilst some equipment would require brackets close to the floor. It should be possible to screw directly into the surface, and to be able to fill the screw-holes and repair the surface subsequently.

Walls should provide smooth and uninterrupted surfaces both for framed work and for projected images which may range in size from [0.1] m square to [5] m in length and [3] m in height. The surface material should be sound-absorbent, but it must be possible to fix shelves for projectors, TV monitors and other equipment weighing as much as [50] kg at any position. Equipment should be supplied with power and data may be fed from remote amplifiers, video-players, computers, etc., and sockets and wiring should be as unobtrusive as possible

It must be possible to drill directly into the surface and provide a secure purchase for security screws, holding mirror-plates that are normally fixed to towards the corners of frame uprights.
It should be possible to change the colour of the surface easily and inexpensively. Wall finishes should be as dust free as possible and easily cleaned without the use of solvents.

The Tate Gallery has tested various board materials singly and in combinations, by loading a test rig with weights until the material failed. 25mm MDF proved to offer the best combination of strength, cost and ease of repair. The results of these tests will probably be published in a book about the Bankside project.

windows

Lateral windows in galleries will be a consideration especially in conversions of buildings which were not designed as galleries and which do not have top-lighting (◄◄ roof lights). Windows can have several functions, and their provision and design will be a balance between the different requirements of exhibits and people. You should bear in mind the following considerations, and might even define the order of priority to be given to requirements for windows to be designed so that:

- exhibitions benefit from the quality of natural light;

- visitors enjoy the views out of a building;

- ventilation can be provided;

- the attention of passers-by is attracted by displays that are visible from outside;

- service access can be provided for large work;

- the amount of display space is maximised,

- any security hazard is minimised;

- the internal environment is not upset by solar gain or heat loss;

- light does not fall on sensitive materials.

AESTHETIC REASONS FOR USING DAYLIGHT

More than any other requirement in the design of a gallery, light is the essential medium for the visual arts. For most people, it is the primary medium through which works are experienced and enjoyed, and the management of light to give optimum viewing conditions is arguably the single most important consideration in the design of galleries and the one which causes most soul-searching. Most visitors would prefer daylight to artificial light, and would like to experience works of art in traditional media in natural light rather than under artificial conditions. Daylight also allows visitors to retain some contact with outside, even if that awareness extends only to the weather and time of day.

REDUCING OR ELIMINATING LIGHT FOR PARTICULAR EXHIBITIONS

There may be exhibitions where natural light needs to be reduced or eliminated completely. Digital and multi-media technologies use TV monitors or computer screens, but even older film and video media also have their own built-in light sources. Especially where images are projected onto gallery walls and other surfaces, the ability to control

light levels is crucial to the viewer's experience. A gallery used only for these media may not require any natural lighting at all, but a brief that emphasises flexibility will help to ensure that photographic and other work which rely instead on reflected light can be exhibited in natural lighting if so wished. Simple systems, such as shuttering, are suitable for small windows that can be easily reached, but opaque fabric blinds are preferable over larger and less-accessible surfaces (◄◄ roof lights).

COLOUR RENDERING

Daylight gives the best rendering of colour, whilst the commonly-used artificial sources are incomplete in the full spectrum. The colour rendering of natural light can be maintained by ensuring that any light control system alters as little possible the spectral characteristics of light entering the gallery spaces. In order to be as clear as possible, glass has to have a low iron content (which gives a green tint), and the colour rendering index (Ra) of the glazing system should not be less than 98. Areas which are likely to reflect light also need to be neutral. This includes not only the components and surrounds of the glazing system but also floors,

since a large area of wooden floor, especially one that has been carefully polished, can reflect a yellow light (◄◄ floor surfaces).

ECONOMIC REASONS FOR USING DAYLIGHT

There are economic as much as aesthetic reasons for using daylight. Almost three-quarters of the time that a gallery is normally open in a year has a high enough level of illumination to make natural lighting of exhibition galleries a possibility. Daylight gives a quality of light over large areas for long periods at low cost even when there are relatively few people visiting the exhibition. In contrast, the European tradition for evening performances is based on the dramatic use of artificial light for an audience that has been gathered together for a short period of time.

CONTACT WITH THE OUTSIDE

Views from the inside allow visitors to look out, vary their experience and orientate themselves, and viewing windows are often deliberately designed into non-sensitive areas to give visitors some relief from conditions which are otherwise for the benefit of the objects. A glass box allows passers-by outside to see what is on show inside and, if left illuminated at night,

can make a dramatic statement and advertisement. Display windows can be even more useful for new media, if back-projection screens can be rolled down at night and are used to show projected work.

SERVICE ACCESS

On a site that is too restricted to allow service access from the rear or through the building, or where large objects may be too infrequent to justify the space and expense of a large lift, a large sliding window and a hoist might be the preferred way of moving exhibits into and out of a gallery on an upper floor (◄◄ art route).

DISPLAY SURFACES

Windows help to enliven wall surfaces and provide variation and interest to a space, and like doors or other openings, they will determine how exhibitions are hung. However, a gallery with a large expanse of window may have limited hanging space in proportion to its floor area, so some or all windows are often blocked up to create longer lengths of display surface when existing buildings are converted for exhibition purposes. Such action often brings other benefits in terms of stabilising the internal environment by reducing heat loss and solar gain (◄◄ roof lights) and in terms of control for conservation purposes

(◄◄ light). Hinged or detachable panels can be used to close windows (and other openings) on a temporary basis.

HEAT LOSS

Windows are a significant cause of heat loss from buildings and contribute to high energy costs. A single sheet of glass provides relatively poor thermal insulation: its U-value - the rate of transfer of heat - is 5.7 W/m²K, but double-glazing will usually halve this figure, depending on the width of the cavity between the two sheets of glass. Double-glazed units with low-emissivity (low-E) glass - which reflects long-wave (infra-red) radiation back towards the interior of the building - can bring the U-value down to 1.9 W/m²K, lowering energy costs and stabilising the internal environment even further. Sealed and draught-proofed windows also inhibit the penetration of dust and pollutants from outside (◄◄ air-handling).

SOLAR GAIN

Low-E glass and light-reflecting films and - where the type of building permits and where the resources are available - measures such as brises soleil and deep window reveals outside the glazing can be used in preference to internal shutters and blinds for controlling solar gain, since they reduce the need for ventilation or other control systems to extract any heat building up inside the glazing.

SECURITY CONSIDERATIONS

Like any other opening, windows are weaknesses in a strong perimeter, and will require defences in proportion to the risk to the exhibitions, to deter and delay unauthorised entry and to enable the police or security company to arrive in time to prevent any loss. Unused windows should be bricked up and keyed in, to the same structural strength as the wall. Otherwise the aim should be to strengthen windows to resist a determined physical attack for as long as the time needed for the police or security personnel to respond to an alarm, and to provide an alarm system which will give notice of an attack (◄◄ exterior). Even very high windows must be protected, especially when they can be reached from adjacent roofs and ledges.

The nature of physical defences will depend on the risk and the location. For example, the possibility of driving a vehicle close to a plate-glass window carries the risk of a ram-raid, but steel roller shutters or fixed grilles may not be acceptable on a listed building. Horizontal metal rolling shutters are easy to accommodate within the cavity of a double brick cavity wall, and have also been successfully used in historic buildings. Reinforcing existing folding shutters with steel plate on their internal faces is an option for historic properties, but hinges, bars and locking devices will all need to be upgraded at the same time, to take the extra weight as well as the anticipated force of an attack. Wrought-iron grilles designed by an artist or craftsperson are a more attractive alternative to industry-standard shutters.

Iron or steel bars should be no more than 0.18 m apart. Pivoting aluminium louvers to control light and heat can be mounted on full-height metal bars to provide a good level of defence as well. Other options include retractable gates and secondary glazing using anti-bandit glass or a lamination of glass, polycarbonate and glass. Current UK standards for anti-bandit glazing are designed to resist only a blunt instrument, so DIN 52290 Part 3 is a better specification. New glazing with steel frames should include a thermal break to avoid condensation, and panes no larger than 0.23m x 0.18m would be an advantage. In all cases, the strength of the security screen across the window will depend on its surrounding frame and on its fixing to the rest of the building, whether it be metal bars that are permanently embedded in masonry or brickwork, or whether it be a security gate that is closed and locked.

Windows for a 'WHITE BOX' ☐
(see notes on page 88)

Windows should be exploited to give good viewing conditions for visitors to the exhibitions and to give people outside views into the galleries. The colour rendering of natural light should be preserved as much as possible. It should be possible to open windows to provide natural ventilation when required, but the windows should also be insulated and draught-sealed to minimise heat loss and reduce energy costs. Glazing systems should give a maximum U-value of [1.9] W/m²K, and solar gain should be reduced by external shading and/or by providing appropriate glazing

Windows for a 'BLACK BOX' ■
(see notes on page 88)

Windows should be fitted with retractable back-projection screens that are easy to operate and maintain. Taking into account Health and Safety considerations, it should be possible to use for service access a sliding window which should be the full height of the room and be provided with a retractable jib and electric hoist.

Windows for a 'STRONG BOX' ▩
(see notes on page 88)

Unused windows should be bricked up to the same structural strength

as the surrounding wall. Remaining windows should be strengthened to resist a determined physical attack, and should be provided with detectors. When the gallery is open to visitors, daylight should be controlled in such a way that a level between [50] lux and [200] lux can be set for each exhibition and will not be exceeded. The amount of ultraviolet radiation on any display surface should be less than [200] μW/m². Daylight should be totally excluded when the gallery is closed and when required for particular exhibitions. Physical protection and alarm coverage of windows must satisfy the security conditions of the Government Indemnity Scheme.

BS 5357, Code of Practice for Installation of Security Glazing covers such matters as frame strength.

Chartered Institution of Building Services Engineers, Window Design, CIBSE Applications Manual 2, 1987, provides guidance on resolving problems of glare, noise intrusion, solar gain and excessive use of energy. Part A examines the interaction between daylighting requirements and other design considerations, whilst Part B provides design information required for window design.

Museums & Galleries Commission, Improving Museums Security, MGC Guidelines for Good Practice, 1997. **ISBN 0 948630 54 X**

Suppliers of glass for conservation purposes include: **Rankin (Glass) Company Ltd, The London Glass Centre, 24-34 Pearson Street, London, E2 8JD. tel:**0171 729 4200 **fax:** 0171 729 7135/9197 **web:** www.yell.co.uk/sites/rankin-glass

The "teachins" that are part of the Saint-Gobain website at: **web:** www.solaglas.co.uk

are useful updates on the current state of glass technology, especially in relation to resistance to intruders and control of solar gain and heat loss.

Reducing both solar gain and heat loss are the aims of **Libbey-Owens-Ford's Sun Management Glass System,** see **web:** www.pilkington.co.uk

ⓘ

wired services

Galleries are increasingly using a wide range of electrical equipment for a variety of purposes, ranging from monitoring and controlling devices, to interpretative and educational equipment, as well as equipment which is part of the exhibitions. This section is concerned not with anticipating what new technologies will be introduced and what equipment will be required, but with ensuring that there is the capacity and the infrastructure (space, cabling, power, etc.) to add new equipment as and when required.

When briefing for the installation of wired services, you should bear in mind the following considerations:

- what priority should be given to supplying electrical power to any point within the volume of the exhibition space;
- what priority should be given to the supply of data to any point in the exhibition space;
- how the exhibition space will cope with the present variety of wired services and how the infrastructure can provide for the future;
- how to minimise the obtrusiveness of sockets and outlets;
- where to locate outside the exhibition space any equipment that is supplying data to monitors and projectors within an exhibition.

THE PROBLEM: THE EXAMPLE OF POWER SUPPLIES

Part of the services engineer's job will be to ensure that the electrical system is adequate for lighting, heating and the other needs of the gallery. In an exhibition space, power sockets are often installed at such wide intervals that they are clearly intended for use when the gallery is closed, for cleaning equipment and powered tools. However, exhibits increasingly require a power supply, and the brief must indicate where an electrical supply is needed, whether it be for lighting for display cases for small objects and/or as power for mechanised or computer-driven exhibits.

The brief will sometimes specify power sockets at certain intervals: for the walls, this might be every metre, whilst for the floors it might be a 2-metre grid which gives a socket at every intersection. For the walls, the main requirement then is to ensure that sockets are located close to the floor, so that they obtrude as little as possible into the display surface. For the floors, the equivalent requirement is for sockets that are recessed and provided with a hinged flap for access. The latter is intended to minimise the trip hazard, although the detailing will sometimes compromise this purpose if the fittings are more suitable for a carpeted office

location:
Lux Gallery, London.

architect:
McCreanor Lavington.

description:
View over Hoxton Square:
The windows open to allow large work to be hoisted into and out of this first-floor gallery. The window reveals have tracks for two retractable blinds - one opaque for when the gallery needs a complete black-out, the other a translucent back-projection screen to allow projected artworks to be seen from outside when the Gallery is closed. Each of the square floor tiles can be lifted to gain access to power and other cabled services running within the suspended 'computer floor'.

photograph:
Hélène Binet, reproduced courtesy of London Electronic Arts.

environment (e.g. with prominent hinges or without a slot for the emerging cable). Curiously, the same attention to recessing sockets is not given to the walls, although this would be one solution to obtrusiveness on display surfaces.

The number and frequency of power sockets may be determined by aesthetic and/or economic factors: a grid of floor sockets will be expensive to install and may be unacceptable visually. However, a new gallery devoted to contemporary work should not have to route cables across floors, where they can cause a hazard, especially in the lower light levels required for much new media, even for people without impaired vision or mobility. In a low-ceilinged gallery lit largely by the light from display cases, it may be acceptable to run power for display cases from the overhead lighting track, but this option will be less acceptable for higher and better-lit spaces.

These problems with obtrusive cables and sockets are then multiplied if power is supplied not only at the UK single-phase standard, but also at three-phase and North American voltage standards to support exhibits from overseas.

THE PROBLEM: OTHER WIRED SERVICES

Comparable problems arise with other wired services. As often as not, a project to refurbish a space provides an opportunity not only to rationalise and make safe power circuits and other wiring systems which have been added over the years, but also to disguise something that has been attached to the surfaces of wall and ceiling. These circuits include systems which can be at best concealed within the ceiling zone or which might be at least less conspicuous simply because they are at high-level, beyond the visitor's normal field of vision:

- public announcement system;
- movement detectors and sensors, and the wiring linking them to the IDS;
- smoke/fire detectors and the wiring linking them to the FDS;
- CCTV cameras, and the wiring linking them to monitors and recorder;
- emergency lighting system.

More conspicuous because they are at a lower level and - unless a deliberate effort is made to hide or designed to be plumbed-in - obtruding into the display surface, are:

- alarm bells and lights, emergency signs, break-glass fittings and the wiring linking them;
- sensors monitoring light, temperature and humidity, and the wiring linking them (unless more expensive radio transmitting devices are used);

- telephone points at standard invigilators' positions (unless again radio transmitting devices are used);
- sockets for CCTV monitors at standard invigilators' positions;
- static loop system to wire exhibitions for sound for people with hearing impairments;
- controls and switches for lights and blinds.

CONDUITS

Some video and digital works will require only power because all the necessary equipment is included in the exhibition as an integral part of the installation. However, the equipment supplying the data - computers, video players, amplifiers, etc. - is increasingly being located outside the exhibition area, for increased security, safety and control. In addition, the use of internet and web sites require telephone connections or ISDN lines. Each type of equipment requires its own distribution cable because of different hardware and frequency standards. Although convergence is promised, the diversity of technologies used by artists is likely to increase before there is any significant improvement. Different cables can, however, share the same distribution conduits or trunking. With a refurbishment or a new building, the issue is therefore not how to anticipate changing technologies and avoid premature obsolescence, but whether a network of distribution conduits can be installed to enable future needs to be met.

Conduits can accommodate the circuits needed immediately, e.g. for the alarm systems, and make it easier to upgrade them subsequently. With appropriate access panels, the conduits can then allow new cables to be laid as and when required at a later stage, whether it be for the gallery in general (e.g. if it is decided to introduce CCTV) or for a particular exhibition. Galleries can do this because of use of wall linings, suspended ceilings and - very recently - raised floors (◄◄ ceilings, floor surfaces and wall surfaces), which allows conduit to be set behind these surfaces.

EQUIPMENT BOOTH

Where satellite receivers, computers, video players and other equipment supplying data are separate from the projectors and monitors in an exhibition or education space, provision must be made for installing the former in a convenient position, so that it can be switched on and off and otherwise checked and controlled by gallery staff. This might be in the gallery office or - if the position can be made sufficiently secure - in the foyer or reception area. It might be a separate control room, which might also double as a lockable store with equipment accessible on waist-high shelving.

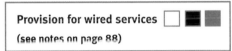

Provision for wired services (see notes on page 88)

Many exhibits will require an electrical supply, to provide lighting for a display case for small objects or to provide power for mechanical or computer-driven exhibits or for interpretation using video or CD-ROM. It must be possible to supply power to any position in the volume of the exhibition area with the minimum

of trailing or obtrusive cables. In some cases, video projectors and computer monitors will be supplied with data from outside the exhibition area via co-axial, computer cabling or ISDN lines, and it must be possible to supply data as well as power unobtrusively to any position in the exhibition space. Above all, cables should not be routed across floors where they will be a trip hazard, especially in low light levels. All sockets and any switches, for power as much as for data, should be recessed behind wall, floor and/or wall surfaces and be accessed by flush-mounted covers. Provision should be made in the reception area for a ventilated cupboard with adjustable shelving, power supply and lockable doors, for locating up to [10] items of equipment (computer processing units, video players, etc.) supplying data to the exhibition.

Chartered Institution of Building Services Engineers, Information technology and buildings, CIBSE Applications Manual 7, 1992, covers architectural and structural requirements, environmental systems, fire detection and protection, electricity supply, earthing and distribution, power and heat load characteristics, electromagnetic compatibility, cabling distribution, public communications, regulations and standards.

workshops

When considering technical facilities for the fabrication of exhibitions, you should bear in mind the following considerations:

- whether the gallery's technical staff have provided detailed advice and a 'wish-list';
- what type of workshop provision is needed to cope with the full range of the gallery's activities.

TECHNICAL ADVICE

As in the design of spaces for exhibitions, education or retailing, the persons using the workshops should have a direct input into the brief and should vet the design proposals. If technicians are not yet in post, then a consultant should be commissioned to advise on the technical operation and on the brief for the design of the workshops. It is crucial that people with technical experience contribute to decisions on location, layout and lighting design.

TYPES OF WORKSHOP

Workshop facilities will depend on the envisaged operation. Exhibition galleries normally need a 'clean workshop' for delicate operations - often around works of art themselves - in a dust-free environment. This enclosed space might also be used to examine loans in safety, for condition checking, registration and photography (◄◄ storage). To ensure that the clean workshop does stay dust-

free, there should be a separate enclosed space, for work usually with powered equipment and power tools, on making frames, plinths, showcases, travelling crates, etc. Adequate provision should be made for the storage of materials, so that they are available to hand without compromising health and safety.

'Clean' workshop   □ ■ ■

An enclosed 'clean' workshop should be situated close to the art store, off the art route between loading bay and exhibition galleries. It would be used by [1] technician, for mounting works on paper and other precise work. It should be equipped with work tables and chairs, and storage for sheet materials (e.g. plan chests). There should be a high level ([500] lux) of ambient light, provided by natural light supplemented by artificial lighting, with additional task lighting at worktables.

'Dirty' workshop   □ ■ ■

The 'dirty' workshop should be situated off the art route, towards the exhibition galleries. It will be used for up to [3] technicians to pre-fabricate exhibition installations (frames, plinths, screens, cases, etc.) and making

location:
Photofusion, London.

architect:
Krys Brooks.

description:
Black-and-white darkrooms, designed by Nick Jones.

photograph:
Reproduced courtesy of Photofusion.

travelling crates and other packaging. Fixed workshop equipment may include panel saw, band saw, drill press, grinder, universal wood worker. Power service should be high. There should be a bench with sinks, work-bench and shelving and racking for storage of materials. There should be a high level ([500] lux) of ambient light, provided by natural light supplemented by artificial lighting, with additional task lighting at work-benches. If fluorescent lamps are used, they should have high-frequency ballasts to avoid stroboscopic effects when machinery is being operated. Natural ventilation should be supplemented by mechanical dust extraction around the machinery.

index